FORBIDDEN JOURNEY

FROM PEKING TO KASHMIR

ELLA K. MAILLART

TRANSLATED FROM THE FRENCH BY THOMAS McGREEVY
WITH AN INTRODUCTION BY DERVLA MURPHY

THE MARLBORO PRESS/NORTHWESTERN
NORTHWESTERN UNIVERSITY PRESS
EVANSTON, ILLINOIS

THE MARLBORO PRESS/NORTHWESTERN
NORTHWESTERN UNIVERSITY PRESS
WWW.NUPRESS.NORTHWESTERN.EDU

THE MARLBORO PRESS/NORTHWESTERN EDITION PUBLISHED
2003. COPYRIGHT © 1937 BY ELLA MAILLART. INTRODUC-
TION COPYRIGHT © 1983 BY DERVLA MURPHY; REPRINTED
BY PERMISSION OF JOHN MURRAY (PUBLISHERS). FIRST PUB-
LISHED IN GREAT BRITAIN IN 1937 BY WILLIAM HEINEMANN
LTD. ALL RIGHTS RESERVED.

PRINTED IN THE UNITED STATES OF AMERICA

10 9 8 7 6 5 4 3 2

ISBN-13: 978-0-8101-1985-7
ISBN-10: 0-8101-1985-4

LIBRARY OF CONGRESS CATALOGING-IN-PUBLICATION DATA
ARE AVAILABLE FROM THE LIBRARY OF CONGRESS.

∞ THE PAPER USED IN THIS PUBLICATION MEETS THE MINI-
MUM REQUIREMENTS OF THE AMERICAN NATIONAL STAN-
DARD FOR INFORMATION SCIENCES—PERMANENCE OF PAPER
FOR PRINTED LIBRARY MATERIALS, ANSI Z39.48-1992.

To
My Father's Memory

The translator's thanks are due to Sir E. Denison Ross and Mr. Owen Lattimore for help with some problems in spelling, and to Sir E. Denison Ross and Miss Murray Browne for suggesting and giving him free access to necessary works of reference at the Library of the School of Oriental Studies.

CONTENTS

PART I

ix

CONTENTS

PART II—THE UNFORESEEN

CONTENTS

xi

INTRODUCTION

Consider some of the place-names in this book: Pingliang, Lanchow, Koko Nor, Tsaidam, Bash Malghun, Khotan, Yarkand, Kashgar ... Each syllable rings out a summons to adventure; for centuries—millennia—European minds have associated The Silk Road with peril, mystery and endeavour. Yet Ella Maillart and Peter Fleming would both deplore any attempt to give their journey from Peking to Kashgar a "romantic" gloss. Although part-time journalists themselves, they abhorred the average journalistic approach to travel in far-flung places. Resolutely and disarmingly, they refused to stick the label "Adventure" on their own extraordinary experiences. To some, this may seem almost an affectation, when they had completed—with no fuss and the minimum of equipment—a peculiarly hazardous trek from Peking to Srinagar through some of the most anti-human territory in the world. Yet it is a fact that the sort of people who do this sort of thing for fun (rather than to make money or get into the headlines) rarely think of it as "Adventure". And they find it incomprehensible and rather tiresome that their idea of innocent enjoyment should seem to others like heroism or masochism—or a mixture of both. This does not necessarily mean that they are particularly modest or self-effacing. They just have different standards of comfort, hygiene and diet from the average person's—and perhaps more physical stamina and mental adaptability.

Ella Maillart belongs to the Mungo Park school of travel writer. She echoes, probably unconsciously, that famous Scotsman's comment on his classic *Journal of a Mission to the Interior of Africa*: "It has nothing to recommend it but the *truth*. It is a plain, unvarnished tale without pretension of any kind except that it claims to enlarge the circle of African geography." Like Park, and unlike Peter Fleming who was very much a sahib in a hurry to get home, Ella Maillart was at ease with the people among whom she found herself. Superficially there might be much to bewilder, alarm or even irritate her, yet all the time she was receptive, tolerant, interested—aware that there was a lot to be received, but also anxious to give what she could.

They could not know it, but the great travellers of the 1930s, of whom a remarkable number were women, represented the last generation of a special breed. The degree of fearlessness demanded for such a journey as Ella Maillart describes in this book is simply not required any more. Technology has intervened. If Ella Maillart had become seriously ill in 1935 between Lanchow and Kashgar, that would have been that: end of Ella Maillart. If the same fate befell a latter-day Ella Maillart, she could radio for help and her newspaper could subsidise an air rescue—and would certainly do so, for circulation if not for humanitarian reasons. Sophisticated communications have thus taken the challenge out of travel in remote places and reduced even the most adventurous would-be travellers to the status of Super-Tourists. Unbeaten tracks still exist but are increasingly hard to find and are rarely genuinely inaccessible. The modern traveller therefore has to face a decision unknown to previous generations: whether or not deliberately to cut him/herself off from civilisation. This at once introduces an element of artificiality into the whole enterprise. A journey no longer *has to be* hazardous. Danger is chosen, not merely accepted as inevitable. In the 1980s it will usually be the traveller's own fault, rather than an Act of God or sheer bad luck, if he/she doesn't survive. And this in turn introduces an element of something not far removed from irresponsibility. Most travellers have families and friends who want them to get home alive and whose grief, if they never reappeared, would be made more bitter by the realisation that they need not have died if they took "the proper precautions". So most travellers *do* take "the proper precautions". And books like *Forbidden Journey* are not—cannot be—written any more. Ella Maillart was born in 1904 into the hyper-conventional world of middle-class Geneva society. Yet by the age of thirty she had taught French in a school in Wales, sailed for Switzerland in the Olympic Games, acted on the Parisian stage, captained Switzerland's Ladies' Hockey team, helped on a dig in Crete, taught French in Berlin, studied film production in Moscow, published a book about a north–south walk through the Caucasus and ridden a camel across the Kizil Kum Desert in mid-winter. Like so many women travellers of the 19th and early 20th century, she was Liberated with a capital L—and without benefit of any Feminist Movement back-up. Which raises the question: Why, since 1945, has travel been dominated by men? In *The Challengers*, Ingrid Cranfield suggests one plausible answer—"A few adventurers—particularly women—take up a life of adventure as the result of an unsatisfactory relationship or a tedious occupation." In our day, it is almost impossible to imagine the asphyxiating boredom and infuriating constrictions of the average middle-class woman's life before the Second World War. When the freedom and self-assertion taken for granted by men in everyday life were denied to women, they could experience normality only by seeming to be abnormal and heading off into the swamps of West Africa, or the ravines of the Caucasus, or the deserts of Arabia. Now, they can express themselves as forcefully at home as abroad; and all the available evidence indicates that this new freedom has destroyed one of the women travellers' traditional mainsprings.

INTRODUCTION

Younger readers may be most impressed by the physical hardships and perils so light-heartedly described in these pages. But to Ella Maillart herself, the only obstacles of any significance were political/bureaucratic. Of course these were also, potentially, physical dangers; at any point between Langchow and Kashgar, she and her companion might have been murdered on suspicions of spying. Sinkiang was then— as it had been for centuries, and still is—a stage on which Great Powers manoeuvered ruthlessly to gain advantages over the enemy of the moment. Since the days of Peter the Great, Russia had had one eye—and sometimes two—on Sinkiang. Eventually Mao Tse-tung was to outwit Stalin in the area; but in 1935 the political waters were very muddy indeed. During the previous two years, a series of bloody civil wars had rendered the province ungovernable. In January 1934 there was a self-appointed provincial government in Urumchi; and this the Russians chose to protect from the ferociously efficient Tungan rebels by furtively sending their army and air-force into Chinese territory. By the spring of 1935, it seemed to the outside world that hostilities were in abeyance. But nobody quite knew the score and Peking seethed with rumours. Characteristically, Ella Maillart plays down the dangers inherent in this situation. Yet these were considerable, and the reader's awareness of them heightens the suspense of *Forbidden Journey*.

This is, on the surface, a simple traveller's tale; it can be romped through for fun as "a light read". But below the surface, almost diffidently concealed, is a great deal of solid matter. The political and military tangles of the period give *Forbidden Journey* real value as an historical document. At that time few people penetrated to the areas described and not all who did emerged to tell the tale. Ella Maillart did not set out to be any sort of political commentator; she simply recorded the mood of the locals as she found it. But

INTRODUCTION

her observations, read in the 1980s, are most moving. Sub-
sequent developments have wrecked the way of life described here; there is more in common between the *Travels of
Marco Polo* and *Forbidden Journey* than there is between *Forbidden Journey* and Jan Myrdal's *The Silk Road*—published in
1979. This "so near and yet so far" (in time) flavour gives
Ella Maillart's book a special piquancy. It is not a fabulous
tale of times past and unimaginable; it is a record of the
watershed period—that brief era when life in Western Europe
was (almost) as it is today, while life in the remoter bits of
Asia remained as it had been for 2,000 years. So in this book
Ella Maillart enables us to look at the past through the eyes
of the present. Here we can see the immemorial pattern of
Central Asian life as it was before the brash uniformity of
the Technological Age reduced the squalor and nobility of
old, distinctive traditions to something predictable, anony-
mous, controlled—neither squalid nor noble . . .

An incidental interest of *Forbidden Journey* is the relationship between the author and her companion, a relationship
that by now has taken its place in the mythology of travel. It
is often referred to by people who have never read a word
either writer wrote, and so it has acquired bizarre accretions
which are unfair to both Ella Maillart and Peter Fleming.
Clearly, Ella Maillart found travelling for six months with a
companion (*any* companion) more trying than the most
gruelling of the physical hardships she endured; and every
traveller who is by nature solitary will appreciate her feel-
ings. But both she and Peter Fleming came through their
shared ordeal with the banner of civilized intercourse un-
besmirched. And Ella Maillart's brief references to the con-
straints imposed by having a travelling companion tell us a
great deal about her own extraordinary and complex
personality—at once straightforward and subtle, tough and
sensitive, thoughtful and impulsive.

INTRODUCTION

This reissue of a modern travel classic inevitably stimulates all sorts of comparisons. In the 1930s, to travel through obscurest Asia for fun (as distinct from propping up an Empire) was to be eccentric. Fifty years later, half the world travels to Asia: to Bali, Sikkim, Malaya, India, Japan, China—even Tibet. And yet, reading *Forbidden Journey*, one is reminded that they *don't* travel. Wherever she went, Ella Maillart experienced life *as it was on the spot*. She did not, as modern travellers do, bring her own life with her: air conditioning, good cosmopolitan food, comfortable beds, clean clothes, daily baths, effortless transport from A to B—to Z. Having read *Forbidden Journey*, we know what life was like for everybody between Pekin and Srinagar in the 1930s. Ella Maillart is the most unpretentious of writers. And yet, like all intelligent travellers of her own and earlier generations, she is spontaneously an anthropologist of the best (jargonless) sort. She went, she felt, as reported. And she did feel; she never merely *saw*. If there were fleas or lice, they bit her; if a pony or camel collapsed, she walked; if there was no food, she went hungry; if the sun was too hot, she sweated; if blizzards blew, she froze; if the water-holes were dry, she thirsted. This is what travel—and travel writing—is all about. Make the best of *Forbidden Journey*. We shall not read its like again.

DERVLA MURPHY

FOREWORD

IN 1932, having gone east from Moscow, I climbed a mountain nearly 17,000 feet high on foot, and succeeded in reaching the eastern frontier of Russian Turkestan. There, at last, from the heights of the Celestial Mountains I could descry, on a plain far away and further still to the east, the yellow dust of the Takla Makan desert. It was China, the fabulous country of which, since my childhood, I had dreamed. There the caravan trails that were as old as the world, still wound. Long ago Marco Polo followed them as far as Peking. But I had found it impossible to secure the visa necessary to enter Chinese Turkestan, a practically independent province which, like Outer Mongolia, was isolated from the rest of the world owing to political troubles. If I went on I should be arrested at the first Chinese village. Sadly I retraced my steps, turning my back on the limitless unknown that beckoned. . . .

Still, perseverance, even in nothing more than a desire, has magical virtue. Two years later, as a result of unforeseen circumstances, I was trying to persuade the editor-in-chief of a great Parisian daily that his readers were impatiently waiting to learn the true facts about Manchukuo from me. And my interlocutor agreed! It was decided that I should go.

That stay in Manchukuo served me as an introduction to Chinese life. In October I landed at the great port of Dairen and laid eyes for the first time on Japanese women wearing the kimono. Their wooden sandals clattered on the concrete platform of the harbour station.

I spoke Russian, which is known all, over the northern

part of the country, and I penetrated into the most varied circles. For nearly three months I went, wherever my curiosity led me, about this new state—in area the seventh in the world, equal to France and Germany together, and with a population of thirty million Chinese.

I put as many miles as possible between myself and the world of luxury hotels and stream-lined expresses. I explored railway lines in course of construction, one of them running through a region infested with bandits near the Soviet frontier. In Korea, on the shores of the Pacific I saw the Japanese actually creating from the beginning, the immense port of Rashin on the fastest and surest line of communication between Japan and Hsinking, the capital of Manchukuo.

Far to the north of Harbin I visited lost villages where Russian *émigrés* live like animals. There, little Japanese men, tireless pioneers of the Nippon Far West, were building mushroom towns and surveying limitless plains, trying to forget that they are islanders on a continent which is so large that it makes them feel giddy. Everywhere I came on those stubborn workers, devoted whole-heartedly to their native land. Settled at the very heart of the country, regardless of the Siberian winter, with their wives, their offices, their food, their lorries, their·sandals and their kimonos, it is they who, in reality, control the yards, control industry, control public administration. I stayed in Chinese inns lost in the depths of the everlasting Manchurian plain. I ate in native cookhouses, I slept on the *k'ang* of dried earth and, at the time of year when watch-dogs are no more than balls of hoar-frost crystallized round a warm sleep, I spent nights in felt tents with natives. That was in the Barga country where the theoretically self-governing Mongols are petted by the Japanese in the hope that they will prove useful against the influence of Soviet Mongolia which is quite close.

FOREWORD

At Tsitsihar, with the thermometer at twenty degrees below freezing-point, I questioned the Fathers of the Swiss Mission while we played volley-ball, and I realized what a scourge banditry is. In another place, sitting at a round table, eating a vegetarian supper with fair-bearded Canadian Fathers, I learned something of the misery of the natives. Later when I was staying with a Chinese postmaster, who, with his family and a young concubine, lived in one room, my host's conversation made me realize the utter impossibility of an understanding being come to with the Japanese—there is an incompatibility of temper which will decide the future of the Far East.

Once again I saw the military supreme, not only over civilians from their own country, who often have different ideas from theirs, but also over the natives, who are full of hatred of their brutal masters.

But above all I was struck at every step by the hatred of the Japanese for us. They detest us all, us whites, whether we be *émigré* Russians or Red Russians, Americans or Europeans, Catholic missionaries or Protestant missionaries, and they miss no opportunity of maltreating us. This racial hatred is a primordial fact. It is a fiercer antagonism than any other—and if war were to break out we might well see Bolshevik Russians and *émigré* Russians on the same side of the barricade. It is fair to say that I only realized the full ferocity of that hatred when, for no apparent reason, I had been brutally kicked and beaten by Japanese soldiers whose compartment I had to go through to reach the restaurant car of the Vladivostok–Harbin express.

On leaving Manchuria I went south and on to Peking. I spent a week crossing the mountainous and little-known province of Jehol, Japan's last official annexation. And day by day, the strange character of the Chinese, with its underlying sense of humour—a quality lacking in the

Japanese—stirred me to curiosity and sympathy, and added to my desire to understand their part in the affairs of Asia. It was in this state of mind that I arrived—by lorry, at night —before the monumental North Gate of Peking.

My heart was beating fast, and I wondered by what gate, towards what destiny, I should set out from the city when the time came. Might it not be possible for me to cross Asia and regain Europe from the point where my eastward track had stopped short three years before? And finding myself on the eastern side of the Celestial Mountains, a huge unmodernized stretch of territory, try to discover how the situation of the natives compared with that of their brethren in Russian Turkestan?

PART I

CHAPTER I

PEKING

JANUARY, 1935. Peking. It was a day when a strong west wind was driving a thick wall of yellow sand before it. I was abroad in quest of information. The results were not, to begin with, encouraging. At the Geological Institute of China, Père Teilhard de Chardin, who, in 1931, had crossed Asia with the Citroën Expedition, could only confirm me in my fears. Szechwan was ravaged by civil war and inaccessible. Chinese Turkestan was more "taboo" than ever. It was impossible to obtain a visa to enter it, and if I were to try to slip in unofficially by the caravan route I should inevitably be sent back, as so many others had been, to the coast.

Also, the few Europeans who were still at Urumchi, the capital of the province, could not, in spite of every effort made by their legations, get out. The governing authorities there took a malicious pleasure in keeping the few Germans and Swedes who had gone in for business purposes, under lock and key. The Citroën Expedition could count itself lucky that, thanks to the magnificent gifts it made to the Governor, Chin Shu-jen, it had been detained only five months.

A prince of Central Asiatic archæology, Sir Aurel Stein, had been forced to leave Turkestan in 1931 and was not allowed to return. Even that famous and clever Swede, Sven Hedin, had just been having trouble with the provincial authorities. He had gone on behalf of the Chinese Government, which was anxious to create motor routes, and it was only on that plea that he was able to continue his work in

3

Central Asia. Then, there was the case of Orlandini, the Italian, who, after spending a year in China, had just been expelled from Sinkiang (the Chinese name for Turkestan). He had covered enormous distances on a bicycle (the ideal means of getting about Central Asia), and retailed a curious story of an attempt having been made to poison him in Inner Mongolia on suspicion of being a spy.

A young German road-builder had also arrived recently at Peking. After several attempts he had, by means of forced marches and following a roundabout way, escaped from Urumchi, but as two of his compatriots were still detained there he did not want to talk.

And it was a long time now since there had been any news of young Hanneken. Probably he was killed in the course of his expedition south of Hami in Sinkiang.

Why was there such a "Chinese Wall" all round the province? I gathered that it was, once again, a question of prestige. The Nanking Government people claimed to be rulers of Sinkiang—the word means "new dominion"—and did not want anyone to have first-hand evidence that they wielded no authority whatever there. On the other hand, they were anxious to avoid being held responsible for the kidnappings and assassinations which are always possibilities in those remote regions, so preferred not to allow foreigners to undertake any journey into the provinces of the interior. And the governor of Sinkiang, on his side, had no wish to disclose the methods by which he ruled a Chinese province while taking no notice of orders from the capital. Far more than the inherent difficulties of the journey, it is the politics of men that make these regions inaccessible.

The result of my enquiries amounted to the fact that nobody knew what had been happening in Sinkiang for four years past. Yet it is an immense province, which touches Tibet, India, Afghanistan and the U.S.S.R., a province in

4

which the interests of these countries are engaged in secret and unending combat.

The desire to undertake the journey to Turkestan took a firmer and firmer hold on me, and I began to perceive the means by which it might be realized.

I must, above all, avoid the known routes. Following them, one was bound to be sent back. The thing was to chance entering Sinkiang at some point where there were not as yet any orders relating to foreigners; then, as quickly as possible, make for Kashgar on the north of the Pamirs, and there put oneself under the protection of the British consul, so as to avoid being taken for a spy, as every foreigner was, and arrested.

Might not the great desert stretches of the Tsaidam to the north of Tibet be able to provide a roundabout way of access?

News from the Tsaidam.

It was at this point that I made the acquaintance of a young geologist who was studying at the Institute. Working for Sven Hedin, Erik Norin had for several years gone up and down in the Tarim Basin.

He had been in the southern oases of Sinkiang when a group of Moslem fanatics rose, spreading holy war and hatred of the foreigner in their wake, and obliging everyone to embrace the faith of Islam. Norin was forced to fly and, avoiding the known routes, he had reached the immense Tsaidam plateau, nearly 10,000 feet above sea-level. A month later he got to the town of Sining near Koko Nor, a great salt lake without any outlet, and thence on to the route to China. In the Tsaidam, he said, there were watering points within a day's journey of each other. Up there, camels might be hired for a few dollars. The guides were paid with lengths of cloth or bricks of tea.

Allowing myself a wide margin, I needed six months to

5

reach Kashgar. The Himalayan heights are not closed by the newly fallen snows until October. It was now January. Soon I was telling myself that I must be off in a month if I was to avoid spending the winter in Kashgar. . . .

But I had only had eight lessons in Chinese and should find it awkward travelling. Erik Norin then told me of the existence of a Russian couple who had had to fly from the Tsaidam at the same time as he. The Smigunovs wanted to go back to the Mongols amongst whom they had lived. They would serve me as guides and as interpreters in Chinese, Mongolian, Tibetan and Turki. . . . He would write to them at once and ask them to get in touch with me.

It seemed that fate had arranged for everything. From that moment, at one blow as it were, Peking and all that had interested me until then, took a secondary place in my mind. The decaying capital, the incomparable city, might tremble before, or might make terms with the ever more threatening Japanese menace. My friends might discover marvels of art, relics of the great dynasties of the past. . . . The legations might move to Nanking. . . . It mattered nothing to me. Everything in me was set towards Central Asia.

Mystery about Turkestan.

Peking is three months' caravan trek from Urumchi and it used to be to Peking that all Turkestan news came. Now everything was changed. The routes were closed, and I could gather only vague and contradictory information. Who was fighting with whom? Who was on top? Who fomented the trouble? Was it the Chinese? Or was it the Soviets, trying to establish a protectorate over the immense area which China was unable to govern? Or was it the fanatical Turkis, perhaps bribed by the British? Or those Tungans* who had revolted under the terrible young Ma

* Chinese Moslems.

6

Chung-ying? And he, where had he disappeared to after laying the country waste? And was one really to believe that these men were maintained by a Pan-Islam-Japanese league? There was no answer to these questions. One thing only was certain. The governor who received the Citroën Expedition had been overthrown and put in prison . . . and Urumchi itself had very nearly fallen into the hands of the rebels.

In the little bar at the Hôtel du Nord I was ruminating on my plans when I was introduced to a young Swede dressed in leather and wearing a fur cap. He spoke Chinese and German. He and his friends were swallowing pints of beer before setting off for the interior, where no beer is to be had. After Sian, the railway terminus, Tannberg would be in charge of five lorries. Once again, a modern Jason, he boasted proudly that he was the one man who could bring back (it meant weeks of questing), not the Golden Fleece, but a rich cargo of sheep casings for sausages which had been bought by an American company and which, as a result of the war, was held up somewhere.

Tannberg talked of the oases of Kansu as if they were in the suburbs of Peking.

"It's a pity I never take women," he said as he left; "but you'll find other lorries that will carry you as far as Lanchow. And if you don't want your hair to turn grey, go from Sian with Popzoff. Have nothing to do with Chinese chauffeurs. . . . Oh, and above all, don't let Nanking know what you are up to or they'll put a spoke in your wheel!"

So my plan grew clear. I would go to Sian like Tannberg, then to the Tsaidam. There, with the help of the Smigunovs, I would work out the best means of getting to Kashgar.

I told my news to Peter Fleming, a young writer whose services *The Times* had been fortunate enough to secure for the carrying out of an investigation into conditions in Manchukuo. Fleming was a great traveller. He had already crossed Brazil in the most singular circumstances and, two years before, he had been up and down Southern China in pursuit of Communists. He had planned to return from Peking to Europe by Mongolia and Urumchi. The idea was partly suggested by Owen Lattimore's admirable book, *The Desert Road to Turkestan*, Lattimore having been the last foreigner (it was in 1927) to succeed in getting across China to India. Arrived in Peking, after visiting Shanghai and Tokio, Fleming had just begun to realize that his proposed itinerary was impracticable. Hearing me speak of the Tsaidam and the Smigunovs, he had said coldly: "As a matter of fact, I'm going back to Europe by that route. You can come with me if you like . . ."

"I beg your pardon," I had answered. "It's my route and it's I who'll take you, if I can think of some way in which you might be useful to me."

The controversy still rages.

I had met Peter Fleming in London six months before when I was looking for information about China. He had advised me to take hundreds of visiting cards and also note-paper with showy lettering—it would prove very useful when I had occasion to write to the authorities of small villages!

Then we met at Harbin. Fleming, who had come from Vladivostok, arrived in the most devastating ill humour because he had not succeeded in killing a Siberian tiger. *Intourist* had promised him he should, but it was in vain they took him hunting. In village after village nobody had been able to put him on the track of the sport he sought.

In Manchukuo, where we were both acting as special correspondents, the same questions interested us. The Japanese had given us similar letters of introduction, so we joined forces in an attempt to study, amongst other questions, the position of the Mongols in the Barga. I appreciated Peter's brilliant intelligence, his faculty of being able to eat anything and sleep anywhere, and also his sure grasp of the kernel of any situation, of the essential point in any argument. I appreciated still more his horror of any distortion of facts and the native objectivity with which he recounted them. Further, I knew that Fleming would tolerate neither my tuneless singing nor my primitive cooking. And finally I knew that I myself would not be intractable about any of the three questions that were liable to ruffle his calm. They were his pipe, his hunting and his opinions on dramatic art.

But would our understanding last? I remembered that after travelling in Manchuria with him I had rejoiced at the idea of starting off on my own again to discover the world. And Peter warned me that his affected manner and languid Oxford accent had driven his last travelling companion nearly crazy. Then I put him on his guard against my grumbling, which had exasperated the friends who travelled with me on board different sailing ships. . . .

We had to get over these qualms. There was a graver cause for hesitation about our plans. Peter wished to travel as quickly as possible. For many reasons he felt obliged to get back to England. Whereas I wanted to dawdle in my usual fashion, as if I had the whole of eternity before me.

We could only leave the problem to be decided by events.

So our departure was agreed upon. We would share the travelling expenses of the Smigunovs and, ultimately, the hardships of prison. My knowledge of Russian, which was greater than Peter's, would help in our relations with our guides who knew no western language. On the other hand, if we got as far as Kashgar it would be all to my advantage to have an Englishman as fellow-traveller when it came to entering India over the Himalayas.

Finally, and what put the seal on my decision, Peter, from what I knew of his life, had been born under a lucky star.

9

Preparations.

The Smigs (as we came to call them) soon arrived from Tientsin. Round of figure and with large grey eyes, Nina was charming. She was the daughter of a Russian doctor of Urumchi, a true child of the steppe, had always lived in Central Asia, could make bread, look after horses, even make a tent—for she had spent many months amongst the Kirghiz and spoke the language well.

He, Stepan, a former Cossack, had taken refuge in Turkestan after Annenkov's retreat. Having lived over five years in the Tsaidam, he had covered hundreds of miles collecting wool and furs for export. He rejoiced at the thought of going back to the life he loved. To convince me that he would be the best of guides he made a great display of all he knew. And my imagination took fire. Stepan's yellow eyes shone as he conjured up the unknown valleys of Tibet where he had hunted the wild yak. He knew rivers rich with gold, flowing at the foot of towering mountain chains crowned with snow and ice. He even talked of making skis if we wanted to do some climbing. He was friendly with the Mongols and knew all the lore they recounted over their argol fires. Scarcely turning a hair, he suggested that he could lead us to the gates of Lhasa if we found that the civil war barred our route to the west.

But the exciting talk had to be interrupted, for we must make out a list of provisions and objects which we should not be able to obtain in the provinces of the interior. There was coffee and cocoa, jam, chocolate, curry, macaroni, Quaker Oats, mustard and, not least, half a dozen bottles of good brandy for very cold days and hours when morale fell low. Also, four enormous boxes of tobacco for the pipes of our smoking gentry.

As for camping materials and clothing, we already had sleeping-bags, fur caps, thick woollen garments and big winter overcoats. In addition I bought a leather jacket, a very useful protection against the furious winds of Central Asia, and stout knee-boots for splashing through the Tsaidam marshes.

In the middle of my preparations Smig calmly offered a word of advice that left me open-mouthed.

"You'll want strong glasses to protect your eyes against the pebbles blown up by the wind!"

And again, when we were talking of exploring the real Tibet, he added:

"You ought to carry a revolver on you, because the bears are so inquisitive that often in the morning you can't get out of your tent for them!"

Every day at the French Legation I armed myself with a Colt and, in the compound, tried to decapitate a dozen empty bottles.

As for medicaments, when we had arranged for valerian, which steadies the nerves, Amara tincture to help against mountain sickness, and digitalis to sustain the heart, Stepan observed:

"Don't forget menthol to help the horses' breathing when they get exhausted climbing heights!"

I dared not show any surprise because, to soothe his apprehensions, I had told him I knew Central Asia well from having lived amongst the Kirghiz of the Celestial Mountains.

We had also to think of presents for the tribal chiefs on whom our fate would often depend. Binoculars and telescopes suggested themselves. We bought some in the street markets in Peking, as also electric torches, pocket knives, fountain pens (for literate lamas), necklaces, playing cards and sweets.

Precautions against Lice.

I agreed to be responsible for the care of our health. In the course of my vagabondings in Manchuria I had found that vermin rather "fancied" me. Typhus is transmitted by lice and I was determined not to fall a victim to any parasite in China. After all, I might have to stay in the country much longer than I thought.

For two years back, missionaries had been rendered immune from typhus by means of a new vaccine which was produced only at Peking.

As I had to have some four or five thousand million germs, collected from about two hundred lice, administered in three injections by Dr. Chang, I had leisure to visit the laboratory at Fujen University. Peter maintained that no louse would dare attack his "iron" skin, and I had great difficulty in persuading him to go. But I pointed out that if he were taken ill it was on me it would fall to nurse him and that he must therefore obey orders.

The Weigl vaccine is produced in such a curious way that I shall say a few words about it. A guinea-pig has some blood of a person suffering from typhus injected. A fortnight later, the guinea-pig, being very ill, is anæsthetized. The cranium is opened and the cerebral matter, virulent in the highest degree, removed.

But to produce a vaccine efficacious for human beings, the disease has to be transmitted to lice, and this is why the Peking laboratory has a nursery of these insects. It is the only one of its kind in the world.

Chinese who have recovered from typhus and are therefore immune, come twice a day to serve as grazing grounds for the lice. For half an hour the little beasts suck the blood which is a necessity to them. On his legs each man nourishes two hundred, distributed in little boxes which have netting at one side. This side is held against the skin. Eggs are laid on a rag in each box and are collected so as to have broods of the same age.

"The men who nourish the lice," Father Rutten writes,

"are often ragged beggars. Nowadays they are agreeably surprised to find themselves paid for nourishing parasites which they used to carry on them for nothing all day and all night."

When the lice are ten days old it is time to infect them. A little of the cerebral matter of the typhus-stricken guinea-pig is injected into their intestines. Within a few days the microbes are swarming. Then the lice are dissected with a scalpel. The intestines are placed in a mixture of carbolic and water. The whole is well pounded, purified, kept for half an hour at a temperature of 160 degrees—and the vaccine is ready!

But to return to our journey—we still had to arrange about arms, money and passports.

Peter managed to have a small rifle, a .22 B.S.A., sent from Shanghai by a friend. Owing to a railway accident there was a delay and it only arrived the day of our departure. But my companion did not consider this a reason for not taking out the necessary hunting licence, and secured one in record time. To ensure supplies for our victualling department he also brought a Winchester .44 rifle.

So as not to have to carry a heavy cargo of Mexican dollars (the money that circulates in China), in trains and lorries, Fleming obtained a cheque on the office at Sining, the last town before the uninhabited regions of the Koko Nor, from the Peking Postmaster-General. What we should do after that we had no idea. According to Owen Lattimore, the Indian merchants of Khotan could not export their capital and would gladly accept cheques payable in India. Still, at the very last moment, I thought of the Himalayas and bought ten English pounds so as not to arrive in India with nothing in my pocket.

In theory, only passports countersigned by Nanking were valid, but in view of the clandestine character of our journey and our desire to pass through unperceived, we made no attempt to obtain Nanking visas. We expected to be interrogated, but we could always produce the permits given by the legations to persons setting out from them.

When I was asked at the French Legation what provinces they were to mark on mine, I merely suggested, with a detached air, that they should put down as many as possible. What was my astonishment to find that they had included Sinkiang, the Chinese name of the forbidden Turkestan province! After all, it might some day justify me in a very Chinese controversy.

As for Fleming, I do not know whether his legation was better informed on the subject of forbidden areas, but the name of Sinkiang was not entered on his paper.

"My dear Peter," I said mischievously, "I foresee a very melancholy day when I shall find myself obliged, since your passport is not in order, to abandon you on the road."

As for the Smigunovs, we thought they were completely in order, not only because they had already lived on the Tsaidam but also because some years previously their applications for naturalization had been approved at Urumchi. They were Chinese subjects.

And then suddenly it was the evening of our departure.

In the afternoon I had gone to say good-bye to the Imperial Palace and the marvels of the Forbidden City, good-bye, not *au revoir*, for a return to Peking could only mean a set-back, the thought of which was not to be entertained. I was about to turn my face away from civilization and from all the term implies: art treasures, refinement, comfort—beds, baths, newspapers with their day-by-day history of the entire world, arm-chairs, letters, fruit, surgeons, clean linen and fine

14

stockings. I was setting out for the Middle Ages, even for the Bronze Age.

The taxi, with all our baggage piled on it, stuck—a bad omen—and the four of us had to push with all our might. I was half dead with a cold and a touch of fever—perhaps the results of my inoculation—but I had to keep a brave face and say my thanks to the friends who came, at eleven o'clock at night and with a wind whistling about the horned roofs of the city, to the station.

Norin came, bringing me his liquid compass, which I accepted with gratitude. He had tried in vain to make us take a hypsometer, a theodolite and heaven knows what besides. He was sad because we were not equipped for the carrying out of scientific investigations and would have given a great deal to be going with us.

Our friends had only come away for a few minutes from a fancy-dress ball and their motley brightened the dreary platform. The jokes were flying. Somebody observed that Peter's last book had been called *One's Company*, and the English edition of my last book, *Turkestan Solo*. Now here we were, contrary to all our principles, going off together!

The activities of Bosshard, a compatriot of mine, suggested other considerations. He was a reporter for the illustrated papers and went on taking flashlight photographs of us. It was perhaps the last time we should be seen. Adventurous strangers had sometimes disappeared after leaving the larger towns on the coast. . . .

Ostensibly we were going away to hunt and take photographs about Koko Nor . . . The train began to move . . . We were off. . . .

A new life began.

CHAPTER II

INNER CHINA

WE were all counting up the pros and cons of our journey as we started. Peter said to me that we should have reason to feel proud if ever we set foot on Indian soil. But that goal seemed so impossible of attainment that we kept it out of our talk until we had reached the Turkestan frontier. What we had to do now was make our way, first to Chengchow and then to Sian, by train; then to Lanchow by lorry; after that to Sining by mule; and from there, by chance caravan, to the Smigunovs' *yurt* at the heart of the Tsaidam. Beyond that everything was vague. One must count on nothing rational happening in China where the proverb runs: "Mr. Perhaps has married Mrs. Quietly, and their child's name is 'Twill Do!"

During the night we crossed the Yellow River. If all went well, we should meet it again, higher up. It is some 3,000 miles long and what with floods and changes of its bed it brings ruin on millions of human beings.

And then we were at Chengchow. Out on the platform we told the coolies to put our luggage on the Sian express. We had only a couple of minutes in which to take a few turns, but the rascals chose not to understand, and led us to the exit. From the footbridge we saw our train pull out.

Our coolies, who must have been in league with the innkeepers, were enchanted and proceeded to recommend a hotel close by. But Peter detests waiting about and we decided not to fall in with the coolies' game. There was a slow train leaving at night and we decided to take it.

16

Smigunov was grousing. Up to then Peter had given in to him. Now he reasoned—we were sitting on our luggage with the night about us and the wind blowing through us. Peter thought we ought to be drinking tea with the station-master, having all the honours due to noble foreigners paid us. I thought of Russia. For here we were, sitting, Russian fashion, on our boxes, as though we were the most negligible of Soviet travellers at the other end of the continent. To Smig it might seem quite natural . . .

Since chaos arose, since the war broke up the solidarity of Europe, people of the white race in China have "lost face," and they are losing it more and more every day. We are not feared. We are mocked. What was there for us to do in a country where the people would rather die than "lose face"?

Third Class in China.
A train went through. We had still to wait . . . The next one, which looked like a goods train, was ours. The waggons seemed to be packed, but leaping up, Peter spied a corner, managed to make the people he disturbed smile—was it conceivable that with his three or four words of Chinese he could make himself understood?—and we handed him up our luggage.

That third-class waggon had four benches running length-wise, two against the sides and two, back to back, in the middle. Worn out, I slept, curled up, until morning. There was a little window like a ticket-office aperture above my head. Kneeling on the bench I looked out at the country. It was a land of fields, chocolate colour, but, in intense con-trast, the deepest blue-green shoots were already showing above ground.

There was a stop at Loyang, an ancient capital of China. A beautiful name, and lovely ruins, but they were not for us.

Those who have far to go may not dally. On the platform the China that is changeless was very much alive. With hair drawn back on her neck and full-moon face brown from exposure, a woman in trousers walked with little stiff steps on her tiny triangular feet. Behind her, the wind was blowing out the flowing robes of a man who wore a little round cap of black satin on his head.

We were in the province of Honan, very far, even already, from the immensity of the Manchurian plain. The ground rose in terraces. At the base of each ledge, the miserable habitations of the peasants opened out of the face of the cliff, which, above the door, was blackened by the smoke escaping from within.

Now and then my musings on the changing scene gave way to a feeling of uneasiness. For, at every station, we saw trains full of soldiers in their uniforms of padded grey cloth and with the Kuomintang sun on their caps. They were the Nanking government's men. Sitting in their waggons, they ate their rice. One of them was actually washing his feet in a basin. The masculine population looked on, passive, from the platforms. Some of these onlookers wore ear-covers of satin lined with fur to protect themselves against chilblains. . . .

No matter where one went war seemed to be imminent. Even in the heart of pacific China where, until now, the soldier's trade had been esteemed the lowest of all! Modern war, the necessity of arming oneself, of militarizing a country if it was to maintain its independence—that was the West's gift to the Far East. To unify four hundred millions of peaceable Chinese so as to militarize them effectively, hatred of a neighbouring nation—the only lever powerful enough to succeed—had to be cultivated. Progress indeed!

We asked ourselves anxiously whether we were going towards war. Was the road before us barred? Could the

Chinese Communists who were masters of Szechwan away to the south, have got as far as this?

But how were we to find out anything whatever? From whom? Were we not going to ask ourselves those questions every day for months?

We were nearly seventy in our waggon, including two soldiers with their basins and their hats of oiled straw.

"We are going to fight the *tu-fei*," they told us.

But we were no wiser than before. *Tu-fei* means bandit and might apply to anybody.

At last there was a diversion. The ticket-collector had opened the door and discovered two young rascals hanging on to the waggon, with the train going at full speed. Hirsute, with clothes in rags, their hands black, their bright eyes twinkling in their filthy faces—it was the second time they had been caught that day. The younger, looking like a whipped cur, nibbled the stalk of a sugar-cane and everyone regarded him with sympathetic eyes. The ticket-collector administered a kindly paternal rebuke, making the entire waggon laugh, and I thought the incident was closed. But no! The lesson continued. They ought to live according to the precepts of the New Life Movement, keep themselves clean, keep to the rules . . . The lads finished by paying the semblance of a fine.

These two youngsters were like twin brothers to the *bezprizorni* of Russia. As a matter of fact, all these Chinese heaped together in the waggon suggested Russia. Above them, on the racks, they had their bundles tied with string, and their bedding rolled up. At every stop they wrapped their knitted mufflers about them, and getting out, strode off along the platform in search of food, steaming *pao-tze,* a kind of boiled ravioli not unlike the *pelmenie* of the Russian peasants.

Our Chinese companions, a mass of synthetic humanity in

which I distinguished no one person, took us for missionaries. The missionaries are, in fact, the only foreigners who travel in the interior nowadays.

At Tungkuan we were held up. To our astonishment the stationmaster spoke French.

"*Le prochain train direct pour Sian ne part que demain après-midi.*"* The Lunghai line had been constructed by French engineers.

Our rickshaws carried us through the crowd towards the old city, enclosed within a rectangular wall above the Yellow River. The monumental curtain-walled gate was surmounted by a five-storey keep with the sky showing through rows of empty window spaces.

Tungkuan.

At the "China Inland Travel" Inn, European in style, a porter, in a hat worthy of Messrs. Thomas Cook & Son, could not even settle the inevitable dispute about the fare with our coolies. The wire mattresses on the little iron beds were slack and the metal stove gave out only the feeblest suggestion of warmth.

To gain time, Peter took the first train, a slow one, to Sian. He would see the doctor at the Baptist Mission and arrange about lodgings before we arrived.

I went out walking. The wide Yellow River was filled with drifting ice, but by the steep bank the junks raised a forest of masts to a colourless sky. My seaman's instinct was stirred. I wanted to see how a river junk was constructed and decided to go out and look. I had to cross a very wide strand to get to them and decided to follow some marks of bare feet, but at the first step I sank to above the ankle in soft, bluish mud. It was with considerable difficulty and with a beating heart that I extricated myself. My boots were

* "The next through train for Sian does not leave till to-morrow afternoon."

heavy with slime. No doubt the thaw was the cause of this ridiculous misadventure.

In the main street people were working at their trades in open-air booths, and I could almost imagine myself in some old-world French town, only that the tiled roofs turned up at the corners and here and there a stone lion, the god of the hearth, flanked a wretched doorway. And then there were the carriers with their yokes that swung at every step and that had the points of the shoulder-piece curved upwards.

The women had beautiful, regular faces, and round their heads, like a narrow turban, wore a black veil. They were all going in the same direction and I followed them.

Their mutilated feet, looking like pointed stumps and hitting the ground with a dull clatter, made my heart sick. When they walk their knees seem to be devoid of flexibility. The effect was of a caricature of a ballerina dancing on her toes.

It must have been a religious festival, for they were all carrying little bundles of incense sticks in their hands. In spite of the rounded paving stones with which the steep street bristled, they went quickly up towards two little temples that dominated the town.

When I got up there I felt myself very far away indeed from my own world. A toothless little priest, dressed in a voluminous but dirty kimono, was standing on the terrace, admiring the view of the mountains and the battlemented wall that gave an air of gaiety to the hillside. His pigtail was hidden beneath a flat sloping hat which he wore over a cap. He invited me into a little room opening out of a chapel which had numerous gilded statues of the Buddha. The whole furniture of the room consisted of a k'ang (the raised platform which serves as a bed), a table and two chairs. There was no door, only a curtain. Red paper ends, souvenirs of gifts received, were stuck on the wall, as were also quantities of fly-blown visiting cards.

We drank tea, a melancholy soldier, who took no notice of me, making a third. Unlike the soldier, the little old man asked me questions, and I found myself enjoying the feeling of mutual sympathy that, for a moment, joined our lives. Not being able to understand what he said, I could only smile and in my few words of Chinese tell him who I was.

"French . . . Yes, I have come from Peking . . . A beautiful city . . . No more tea, thanks."

Then I went through the form of polite greeting, joining my two hands, and presented my visiting card. It was in both our languages, my name being adapted into Chinese under the form of Ma Ya Ngan.* Finally, retreating backwards, I took my leave.

In the courtyard the women were putting burning incense sticks in the bronze urn, prostrating themselves and praying. Numerous gods with various attributes occupied sheltered positions all round. The god of fecundity had a chaplet of pink babies under his arm. There were swarms of real children and little behinds showed through the openings of divided breeches. The face of one baby was tattooed, no doubt to prevent evil spirits from seeing how beautiful he was. He looked as though confetti had been scattered over him. A cockade of pompons in his hat created a most dashing effect.

Almost asleep from the sweet-smelling fumes of the incense, I forgot that time was passing and had to run on my long, un-Chinese feet, to find the Smigs and catch the train.

* The name Ma Ya Ngan has amongst a thousand other meanings that of "International Peace Horse!"

CHAPTER III

S I A N

THE railway line came to an end in fields outside the town gate. Peter was waiting for us in the twilight. Coolies and rickshaw men fought each other to carry our luggage.

In accordance with custom, Peter presented his card to a soldier who then half-opened the huge gate, and we entered Sian. But what a surprise! Inside the gate it was again fields and waste ground.

We were soon at the Mission, which consists of a considerable group of houses, hospital, etc., surrounded by a newly built wall. I was to be the guest of a charming English nurse . . .

The military situation was critical. Only a few days before, the town had almost fallen into the hands of the Communists. There was no news of two missionary couples who lived in the war zone. And nothing could be done for them. The strain of events weighed all the more heavily on everybody owing to the fact that the town had suffered terribly in the great famine of a few years before. In the field at the back of our house the corpses had been piled up till the place became uninhabitable. The siege lasted six months and the famished population had eaten hundreds of dead every day. The mayor had no alternative but to distribute the money from the city treasury amongst the people. However, I had one good laugh that evening. I was chatting with my hostess and it came out that the Mr. Fleming with whom I had arrived was the author of *One's Company*. She was outraged.

"He has a cheek," said she, "to claim hospitality from us after making a mock of missionaries the way he did."

The next day was very full. We had to get a lorry to take us to Lanchow, four hundred miles away, before the thaw came and made the clayey roads impracticable.

Some owners were waiting for a sufficient number of passengers to book places before arranging to send a lorry. We went, the Smigs accompanying, to several garages and examined many wheels and many engines. Popzoff, the only European driver, was away, and we had to be satisfied with a Sian driver. Peter insisted, therefore, on a contract guaranteeing transport to Lanchow in six days and the right to take another vehicle in case of a breakdown. The fare demanded was twenty-five Mexican dollars per person.

The Governor.

After that we called on the governor of the province with a view to obtaining passports which, seeing that those we had were not exactly in order, might prove useful.

Shao Li-tze proved to be an affable little man, dressed in Chinese clothes. He had made a stay of several days in Paris in 1916 and could recall a few French words. We were received in a room furnished with Spartan simplicity. Shao Li-tze's wife was young and lively. Having made a prolonged stay in Moscow, she spoke excellent Russian and it was in that language we exchanged the usual polite greetings.

"We heard, even as far away as Peking, how perfectly His Excellency governs this part of the country."

The governor in turn said he had read in the newspapers about my arrival in China . . .

If words meant anything, Shao Li-tze and his wife were on the side of the Nanking government and the New Life Movement. I gathered later in the town that everybody distrusted the all-powerful military commander who allowed no one to approach him and who, it was said, had been on the point of going over to the enemy with his men a few days before. In this connection, Shao Li-tze congratulated himself on a recent visit paid to his area by Chiang Kai-shek the Nanking Commander-in-Chief. As a result, the 100,000 men stationed in the province were now confirmed in their loyalty to the government.

General Chiang had even considered the possibility of making Sian, a town of 150,000 inhabitants, the capital of China, for the laws of extra-territoriality which gave all foreigners the right to sail up the Yangtze, exposed Nanking rather too much to the potential danger of bombardment.

As for the bandits about whom we had heard so much, yes, they did exist, but a punitive expedition had just set out, so we should strike a quiet interlude.

In spite of all expectations to the contrary, Chiang's efforts had not proved fruitless. Order had been restored. New roads were helping to reduce the cost of living. The number of children attending school was steadily increasing. . . . Everywhere it was becoming clear that the best propaganda against Communism was to raise the standard of living.

As the governor talked, I was studying his young wife. With her slim fingers she was peeling pears for us. I wondered whether she had not come back from Russia holding Communist beliefs and whether she did not secretly wish to see Shensi in the hands of the Reds. It would be a great step towards the junction of the Soviet forces, which were still scattered through Outer Mongolia, with Sinkiang and with the rebels in Szechwan. Such a junction would probably cut us off from our objective. The sooner we got to the mountains the better!*

* According to a Reuter's message, Madam Shao Li-tze was executed during a rebellion amongst the government troops at Sian in December, 1936. The rebels, in alliance with the Chinese Communists, wished to force Generalissimo Chiang Kai-shek to declare war on Japan. It was denied later that Madam Shao Li-tze had been executed.

As we were leaving, the governor gave us a huge passport filled in in Chinese characters. We accepted it gratefully though we knew that if we got into difficulties a military permit alone would be of any use. To show the high esteem in which he held *The Times* and Fu Lei-ming—the Chinese transcription of Fleming's name—the governor escorted us through the three courts of his *yamen*, though at the portico of each we, retreating backwards before him—did that custom arise out of courtesy or out of prudence?—begged him not to trouble.

On the construction of the railway, Sian had immediately proceeded to modernize itself. American manners came in via the cinema and now the young women went through tortures in the attempt to wave their straight hair. The police patrolling the streets were zealous supporters of the New Life Movement and twice stopped Peter to tell him he must not smoke his eternal pipe when walking abroad. It could not be denied that in his long, full, beige great-coat, bought at Samarkand in Russian Turkestan, and striding somewhat erratically on his way, Peter might well arouse suspicion. From every point of view he suggested the Soviet officer. All over Manchuria he had, as a matter of fact, been followed by suspicious little Japanese, he himself being much amused by the curiosity he excited.

Religious Cross-roads.

It was the old town that interested me most and I decided to go to the huge deserted temple of Confucius which stood sleepily amidst enormous cypress trees with swarms of screaming magpies flying round and round it. Close by, I opened a closed door and marched boldly into a museum that is in its way unique, consisting as it does of a regular forest of antique steles . . . Placed on symbolical turtles, they are carved with decrees by the hundred, with genealogies and praises of the dead, some of them dating back twenty centuries. One of them, bearing the date 781 and the Cross of Jesus Christ, had the inscription in both Syrian and Chinese. This was the celebrated Nestorian Tablet which bears witness to the antiquity of Christian missionary endeavour at the very heart of China.

It was in that astonishing town of Sian, the capital during the Han and Tang periods, and a cross-roads where all religions meet, that I also visited China's oldest mosque. The floor of the great praying hall is blackened where the foreheads of generations have touched the earth. After five-o'clock prayer had finished I passed Chinese Moslems with white turbans on their heads. Their very closely united communities are numerous, not merely throughout north-west China, but all over the country, even to far-away Yunnan. In Asia generally the Chinese Moslems are referred to as Tungans. But in Kansu they are called *Hui-hui.** They are feared because of their warlike character and their recurrent rebellions. I was astonished at meeting their type in China. With eyes scarcely aslant at all, with thick eyebrows below a square forehead, a straight nose with fine, arched nostrils, delicately cut lips and a beard worn like a collar below the jaws, it is in pronounced contrast to the unbearded oval Chinese type. The proud faces reminded me of the bazaars at Samarkand three thousand miles away. Could it be that the Tungans' ancestors came from the West?

Amongst the foreigners who live in Sian—Swedes, Germans, English—I frequently heard the word "uncertainty." In that Chinese land European precision and European logic are alien and nothing is ever known for certain. You are

---

* *Tungan* is not a Chinese word. It was in 1850 that it was first used to indicate a racial distinction, which *Hui-hui* does not. But *Hui-hui* may be synonymous with *Uighur*. In Chinese literature of the fourteenth century both terms are used to indicate either Turkish colonies in China or Chinese Moslems.

always on the watch. Day after day you wait—for bandits for war, for the resumption of business. . . .

Talking of forbidden Sinkiang, Herr Rehder, a sympathetic man who was engaged on engineering work for a Tientsin firm, recalled the sad case of his young colleague, Dorn, who, for no reason, had been, these months past, lying in prison at Urumchi. Another compatriot, Georg Wasel, also . . .

Sven Hedin accompanied by Joe Söderbom had passed through Sian on the way back from Sinkiang some days before. But he was very reticent. He and his lorries had encountered numerous difficulties owing to the civil war.

At eight o'clock the next morning our lorry stood ready, with us perched on top of our luggage. But hours passed and nothing happened. We never set off. At last, reduced to a state of complete exasperation, we flourished our contract in the face of the garage proprietor and threatened him with unutterable things. That was the first time I saw a Chinaman throwing a fit. His fury abated after a time, sufficiently at least to let him stop stamping the ground, and we made out that one of the passengers owed money in the town, so the authorities had decided that none of us could start.

Peter was furious. I was enchanted. The delay gave us an opportunity of lunching at the Chinese inn where the Smigs had stayed, and making the acquaintance of our friend Norin's old cook who had arrived from the north with Bökkenkamp, the ethnographer.

We learned from him that Smig's old partner was still on the Tsaidam. That meant that the country was quiet and that our Russian was going to find his *yurt** once more.

Bökkenkamp had been imprisoned at Hami, but effected his escape by a clever ruse. His gaoler had sore eyes. Bökkenkamp poured some drops inside the eyelids for him,

* A round felt tent.

and then blindfolding him, told him he would lose his sight unless he remained in the darkness for three days!

Late in the afternoon, in spite of the protests of the chauffeurs, who wanted to spend another night in Sian, we persuaded everyone to start. It was not only because Peter had to live up to his nickname of "Galloper," but also because we were afraid lest, between then and the morrow, Mr. Perhaps and Mrs. Quietly might play another of their jokes on us. We won our case for departure on the argument:

"We should 'lose face' if we had to ask our Western brothers for hospitality again after saying good-bye to them this morning."

CHAPTER IV

By Lorry

THE week it took us to reach Lanchow, the capital of the province of Kansu, was one of the most wearing that I can remember. During the first three days I was lucky enough to have the place beside the driver. The stink of the ill-burning gases from the engine was a trial, but I escaped the cold which cramped my companions at the back.

Our misadventures were numerous and exasperating. We got ourselves covered with mire; we got caught in a river when the ice broke down under our weight; ordinary punctures kept us standing about for hours. The chauffeur would throw his sheepskin on the radiator and get busy. The passengers on the three lorries, united in misfortune, would speechify, stamp up and down and untiringly give advice. Stifled "Ei-yahs" came through their knitted mufflers. But they took good care not to handle the shovel or to assist in pulling the cars out of the mud.

Another privileged passenger sat with the driver beside me. Wearing European clothes and smoking a small, pretty pipe, he had shining teeth and smiling eyes. He was a Cantonese, the son of a rich merchant, and he was going to see the world, just to amuse himself.

"I am going to Urumchi," he said as though it were quite a simple matter. "A friend who is a general has invited me. I'll take an aeroplane from Lanchow."

"But," I protested, laughing, "the air service has stopped. You'll never get there."

30

I was certain of my facts, but I did not disclose the secret of my own itinerary.

"Haven't you heard," I enquired, "about the mortifying experience of Lo Wen-kan himself?"

Lo Wen-kan was one of the Nanking ministers. Following an ill-advised order to make a landing at Urumchi, he had only been able to get back to China by going round through Siberia.

My fellow-traveller began to ask questions and I told him we were going to visit the famous lamasery at Kumbum. But suddenly a terrifying idea crossed my mind—unjustified, as it proved, in the event. Perhaps he had been sent to spy on us? The other passengers were all plain people. He alone travelled in comfort. At the inns every evening, he produced a camp bed and tins of food. We only had sleeping-bags, which we unrolled on the k'ang. The k'ang is a raised platform of hard earth which may be warmed from underneath. It is the only "fixture" in Chinese houses.

We went on, slowly.

Beneath the pale-blue sky, a few green shoots were already showing in the fields. Sometimes wooden coffins lay out in the fields, as though abandoned to the elements. It is the immemorial usage of China, where the peasant merely leaves his dead laid on the ancestral ground. Here and there a mud-spattered stele, or an alley of archaic animals in stone which formerly marked the way to the tomb of some rich person, seemed now to be waiting patiently for the misty horizon to bear down on them.

The first night, our three lorries stopped not far out from Sian, at a village which was muddy and black as pitch. After swallowing some watery mess, for which we paid a few pence at an eating-house on a corner, we slept between partly collapsed mud walls. A lamp, consisting of a piece of cotton floating in oil in a broken bowl, gave practically no light.

On the second evening, at a town where the inns were full to overflowing, we decided to pay a visit to an Italian priest and found him eating his supper surrounded by his flock. He was very sad at not being able to put us up and made us a present of some butter properly packed. That was luxury. It had been made by the Franciscan sisters of Hopei. For years his own life of devoted service had been spent here. When there was famine or when banditry was rife, he took special care of the Christians. I shall long remember the great smiling *Madonna* in a gilt frame that was the full height of one of the refectory walls.

Towards evening on the third day I was amazed to see a church like one of our European churches looming up out of a continent where nothing higher than a ground floor is ever built. The Chinese do not look with a favourable eye on these spires that transpierce the good spirits and prevent them from descending to earth. This one was at Chingchow. In the high street the inhabitants, smoking long tiny-bowled pipes, were passing the time of day with each other. The ground was so slippery that the women, because of their stunted feet, had to carry long sticks to support themselves.

The Chingchow missionary and his wife gave us a delicious supper. Unlike the priests, the parsons return to Europe regularly, and our hosts of that evening were on the point of setting out for Norway. The man, who was sturdy and cheerful, had himself built the soaring church. It was the pride of his life. Mrs. Gjelseth, his wife, told how when, some short time before, the locality was pillaged, they and their girls' school were spared because she had once nursed and saved the life of the robber-chief. She confessed that in four years she had never rested properly at night. But amongst the compensations for all the uneasiness there was one that I found touching. She had helped to abolish the torturing of the women's feet out of shape.

The new road (the one we were taking the loan of) was slowly transforming one of the most backward regions in China.

Troglodytes.

As in Honan, so in Shensi, the wretched peasants live in caves scooped out of the porous yellow earthen cliffs. Their fields are poor. Every fall of rain carries off land which goes to heap up the bed of the Yellow River, far from there, and, bit by bit, to provoke the terrible shiftings of its course. To make up for the losses caused by rain, the men work tirelessly, like ants, bringing new earth in baskets hanging from yokes. There are no forests left to temper the climate or provide a brake in the case of landslides. For centuries the sons of Han used wood for fires, cutting down trees and cutting down trees, until to-day there is not a tree left.

This earth that is, as it were, impalpable, gives its most marked characteristic to the Chinese landscape. It slips away under a shower of rain, slips away even through the chinks of the baskets in which the peasants are carrying it. Here, the very notion of a rock, of a pebble even, seems to belong to another planet.

The fluidity seems to have affected the speech itself of the Chinese, with its modulated, muted, singing vowels through which the ear has to wait for the occasional passage of a solid consonant to hold on to.

Even Chinese food seems allied to the quality of the land. It includes no bones, is prepared so as to be eaten with chopsticks, triturated, cooked for hours and hours in delicious sauces, and appears at last, looking like a variety of dumplings, served in little heaps in which nothing is whole and entire. *Tou-fu,* the sole diet of millions of peasants, is a kind of flabby, yellowish custard made with bean-flour.

Do not the daily round of work in such a soil, the daily consumption of such a diet, and the daily use of such speech, go far to explain the Chinese character?

Pingliang.

When we arrived at Pingliang on the fourth evening, the driver informed us that we should have to wait there until a broken spare part could be replaced.

We refused to do anything of the kind. We had had enough of his fifty-five-miles-a-day efforts, and being guaranteed by our contract in case of such a contretemps, we set off in search of a better vehicle for the morning. It was fortunate that we did. For, of his three lorries, one took ten days to reach Lanchow, another twelve and the third finished up in a ravine on the Liu Pan Shan, a mountain pass 10,000 feet high which had to be negotiated on the way.

The inn at Pingliang had some pretensions to comfort. There was a rug on the k'ang, there was a candle instead of the archaic earthen lamp, and numerous servants—only they never brought the water we called for.

"We shall be free soon and have all the water we want," said Nina, dreaming longingly of her yurt. Her face was good to look at. It had lost its Tientsin pallor. After the few days in the open air she was already beautifully tanned.

The Spanish priests who had an establishment in the village were bright young men of an infectious gaiety. It was Sunday. Vespers were over and they were just sitting down to their cocoa when we arrived. They were so surprised as to be almost upset at seeing us. Everyone of them offered his place. They loaded our plates with pastries and seemed genuinely glad to see us. Full of the spirit of youth, they laughed delightedly at our Latin-*cum*-Spanish verbal inventions and at my remark that I had the misfortune not to be a Catholic. They talked of the number of people they had under instruction, of the beautiful souls they had found amongst them. They certainly had no fear of the Communists.

We also went to see General Yang Pu-fei. Dry, small, nervous, dressed in plain grey clothes, he was in command of the Sixty-first Division, formerly a unit of the Nineteenth Army, which had made itself famous during the events at Shanghai. Thanks to the Nanking government his soldiers were paid, shod and armed—as soldiers are not always in China.

He asked us pleasantly if we would drink tea with him in his bedroom at the barracks. The room was clean and very plainly furnished. In answer to our questions he said he felt he was in a very strong position as against the Communists and that we need have no fears about continuing our journey to Lanchow.

Lanchow at Last.

Our new lorry went well, but for human muscles what a journey! We were twenty, clinging on, on top of our luggage, holding on, against the pushing of our fellow-travellers, with our hands and with our heels, while they, tortured and cramped, saved themselves from slipping off as best they could.

The place beside the driver was not free and, the more easily to climb up at the back and hold on there, I had put on men's clothes. It was cold. Snow had just fallen and we had chains on the wheels. Climbing the Liu Pan Shan from one steep bend to another, a Chinaman next to Peter got sick; and there Peter had to sit, his elbow raised in self-protection! But a little thing like that could not stop Smig, unweariedly the cicerone, from discoursing to him about everything we saw, the little forts set up against brigands, a surveyor and his assistants measuring the road, naked children playing in the frost and snow outside a hovel, dead donkeys lying on the roadside. . . . Poor Smig was to be pitied, for his suède overcoat, bought as a bargain, tore under the slightest strain, and the buttons were falling out. His hat had ear-flaps and was lined with fur, but when it snowed the dye from it streamed down his face and we teased him, promising to buy him an umbrella at Lanchow.

On the following day the journey was agony. Some new passengers succeeded in clambering on to the lorry—a soldier who was abused by everybody, and a fat slut wearing a grey felt hat like a mushroom. Everyone was cross.

Smig had, as usual vainly, tried to make us get up two hours before we were due to start with a view to securing good places. Now we sat at the back, choked with the dust raised by the lorry. But a brand-new iron stove was fixed close to where we were, so that we could hang our kettle-teapot (the most precious and indispensable of all the objects we carried) on it.

Nina was feverish. Smig, though he had lost his voice, was fulminating against a Chinaman who, without realizing it, was pushing him. Peter was simply "fed up" with the dust, with his cramped position which made it impossible for him to sleep. Then a catastrophe occurred. He broke the stem of his pipe. But worse still was to follow. Suddenly, rounding a turn, we lurched, and Peter, caught unawares, was thrown into the air. I just managed to catch him in his flight and plant him down beside us. I had saved his life. But he complained that I had hurt him. . . .

The scene in the middle of the lorry was, however, still funnier. Two of our fellow-travellers had got into a state of complete exasperation with each other and come to blows. Now they were at it with their fists, hammering each other's faces till blood flowed. And I who had believed that in China there was always a third party ready to prevent fighting as an activity unworthy of civilized people!

CHAPTER V

First Difficulties with the Authorities

JOYFULLY, at last, we came down towards the Yellow
River. There was the aerodrome of the Eurasia Company! There were the fields of tombs! There the walls of
Lanchow! We were very much alive during those last
minutes on our lorry, our last modern vehicle.

For a very modest payment we were all four to be put up
by Mr. and Mrs. Keeble of the China Inland Mission. We
had cause to be grateful to them. Like all the missionaries
I met in the Interior, they were both dressed in the crossed-
over Chinese dress lined with lamb's wool. In their house
we were at last warm. We ate till we were satisfied. We slept
between sheets. . . . But, on the other hand, there was bad
news. The road to the west was closed to foreigners. The
police came and asked about our destination. We had to fill
up forms. Our Peking passports were taken away.

Smig was of opinion that this new way of treating foreigners
boded ill for our journey, and Mr. Keeble, in his reticent
way, gave us to understand that he thought travelling had
become impossible.

Actually what we had to do was not let ourselves grow
uneasy, but wait for our papers to be returned to us, and
remind ourselves that in China one must never be in a
hurry.

We were twelve days' journey from the coast. The general
opinion at Shanghai is that the inhabitants of Kansu are
barbarians. But the men were tall and robust with long
and often remarkably beautiful faces. And was it likely that

a city of half a million inhabitants would be barbarous? Electric light had just been introduced. It is true that it was still rather anæmic. The schools and university were packed with students and there were fond hopes of obtaining a grant of 500,000 dollars from the Boxer Fund for the foundation of a library and a laboratory at the university.

My informant was Mr. C. C. Shui, the head of the Education Office, a most sympathetic man whose son I had met in Peking.

The streets of Lanchow are wide and lined with stalls that have counters, with the stall-holders busy behind them. Some of the porcelain and cloth businesses could almost be called shops, for they had glass windows giving on to the street instead of the classical wooden lattice with white paper.

In the square in front of the residence of the governor—he refused the interview we had requested—a policeman was insisting on loaded mules, cyclists (still a little wobbly on their machines), rickshaws and vehicles of all kinds observing the one-way traffic regulations.

Every day some readers in black satin jackets over a long blue robe might be seen perusing the newspaper which was pasted on the walls round the square. It was called *The North-West Daily* and gave the latest information about the Communist advance.

Lanchow even had its cinema—in a shaky-looking hut. I have a strong suspicion that it was worked by hand. The projection of some very scratched views of Shanghai was of the palest. But to tell the truth, I was paying more attention to the task of trying to follow our neighbour, a certain Mr. Wang, who talked to us in very bad English, hinting all the time at something not stated. Whether he was or was not a police agent, he seemed to know that enquiries were being made about us at Peking and that it would be five or six days before we were told what was to happen to us.

My favourite walk during the days of enforced leisure that followed was at the heels of the water-carriers. In the full pails swinging from the ends of the yoke a piece of wood always floated to prevent the water from splashing and over-flowing. Street hawkers went up and down, each giving his own peculiar cry. There were barbers as well as menders of broken bowls, and vendors of frozen pears or of thick bean soup with almonds floating about in it. Street urchins ran here and there in their comfortable divided trousers, each little pigtail sticking out at a right angle to the owner's head.

Whenever I stopped to recharge the mysterious little box that was my Leica camera, the brats would surround me like a cloud of mosquitoes to pounce on the strips of film I threw away, and the apathetic policeman would, for a moment, look terrible and disperse them.

All the men wore full trousers gathered in with little bands about the ankle, which made them look like skiers. Working-men do not wear the long robe but a short jacket lined with sheep's wool. Following the water-carriers, I went out by the North Gate which pierces the high *enceinte* like a tunnel and which is dominated by a pavilion of three decreasingly wide tiers. Beyond, I found myself in complete quiet, on the banks of the great river and facing a wide, restful landscape. On the shore, a raft of twelve goatskins was propped up against its oar, drying in the sun. Later it would be carried back on the shoulders of one man to the village from which it had come, situated many days' journey up the river. Farther away the marvellous frame-work of an irrigation wheel, motionless against the pale yellow sky, caught the eye. The river was very low, and as the wheel was at a distance from the bank, its buckets must remain long unfilled.

Further up, the river was crossed by an iron bridge. Opposite me, on the face of the cliff, like a *Way of the Cross* at home, a series of little temples led up to a pagoda several storeys high, faced with glazed tiles.

Should We be Able to Continue?

The same news met us each evening when we returned to the Mission:

"Your passports have not been sent back."

Smig had come across wool and leather merchants of his acquaintance and enquired about the state of the markets. But he had also learned that fifteen Russian *émigrés*, arriving to do some work at Lanchow a month before, had been sent back to the coast in accordance with the terms of a recent Nanking decree which forbade all persons of Russian origin to remain in the North-West. The anti-Communist war was of course the explanation of this measure. Were we going to lose our interpreters with our journey scarcely begun? Even the bare rumours emanating from police headquarters suggested that we were. Obviously the fact of being Chinese subjects told, not for, but against, the Smigunovs. Their naturalization papers were made out at Urumchi, a town that had fallen into Soviet hands, therefore they were suspect. And the anxious Smig would complain: "You aren't doing all you might do to help us, Mr. Fleming."

But even the most princely gifts would have made no impression on the governor. He was the "modern" man. An attempt to continue on our way without authorization was, on the other hand, liable to spoil everything. Why had we not avoided Lanchow and cut across country?

However, we made one last visit to the police. Peter had already done everything he could, going over and over all the arguments we had prepared until they were worn threadbare. Did they really want us to "lose face"? If the Smigunovs, who were working for us, were sent away, we *must* "lose face"! And how would the governor feel when our two newspapers, the most important in Europe, spoke of Lanchow as a town that still employed the methods of the Middle Ages? We got only the most casual answers. How was one to know who was trustworthy? who was influential? In the street where he had to go to smoke his pipe (for the pernicious practice was prohibited at the Mission), Peter mocked me for beginning all my opinings with the remark: "We must, at all costs, try to understand . . ." When everything was incomprehensible!

The impossibility of directing events, or even of forming an opinion about them, the uncertainty, and perhaps the unfeasibility, of a journey without interpreters, the rapid dwindling of the small capital we had brought with us—all these questions would plunge us at times into an abyss of discouragement, which doubtless was as unjustified as the hopes we let ourselves entertain a few minutes later. Sitting together at a table with our *shao-djiu*—a warm alcoholic drink served in China—before us, we recalled the ardour with which we had sworn to make our way west, no matter what it cost, and, as if to put that decision into at least the beginnings of execution, we rose on the spot, marched into a goldsmith's, and, for a thousand Mexican dollars, bought a bar of gold as big as a small bar of chocolate for our needs on the journey.

* * * * *

"The Ma Ya Ngans* may proceed, the Russians must return whence they came."

Thus ran the definite police order. Nina, sitting on her suit-case, was crying quietly. Smig was very discouraged, but said he would try not to go back. He could not give up the dream of reaching his paradise.

* The first part of my Chinese name, "Ma", is similar to that of most Chinese Moslem names in the area and is in consequence easily remembered by everybody. *Ma* is supposed to be an abbreviation of *Mahomet*.

It was hard for them. What was to become of them? Would they be able to find some modest employment in Tientsin once more? And as for us, how were we to get beyond Sining without them? Smig gave us introductions to two of his friends who might be in a position to help us—if we were able to find them!

We hurried on our preparations, anxious to get away before we were detained in accordance with the terms of possible new decrees.

After breakfast, we for the last time took our turns at reading the Bible. Then, kneeling in front of our high-backed chairs, we listened to the prayer for all those who were in great need, for the missionaries captured by the Communists, that they might be sustained in their courage; for the "Bible Women" and "Tent Work" activities, that they might receive aid; for the Mission, that the gifts on which, alone, it was maintained, might not fail to be forthcoming. And then Mr. Keeble was kind enough to ask for Heaven's blessing on "two young travellers, setting out on an uncertain expedition, and now at our side for the last time."

In front of the round door of the courtyard our three mules were loaded. We had hired them at a local hotel which ran an agency for one of the great travelling companies that, for centuries, have divided the country between them.

Accompanied by our friends, we crossed the busy town with its hanging signs and their vertical Chinese writing. Just as we arrived at the great Western Gate I noticed a European coming along under an escort of Chinese soldiers. Peter said that as he passed him the poor fellow said: "*Caput!*" Was it an omen? The Smigunovs had heard that an order to return awaited us at the Kansu frontier. . . .

It was time to say good-bye. I tried to console Nina.

CHAPTER VI

FREEDOM

THE two of us set off with nobody except Wang the
muleteer.

It was true we were going to miss the services of the
Smigs, even to miss them cruelly, but carrying it out alone
added some suggestion of bravura to our exploit. Our
conquest of Tartary would seem all the more fascinating if it
were due entirely to our own efforts.

It was a joy to be going forward, to be on the road again,
to have left those poisonous bureaucrats behind us; a joy to
be one's own master, to forget the lorries and being shaken up
in them, packed in amongst twenty-five Chinese; a joy to feel
the gentle wind on one's face; the warm colour of the mule
was joy, and joy the rhythmic sound of his hooves on the road.
Between Lanchow and Sining, the capital of the province of
Koko Nor, where, doubtless, our difficulties would begin all
over again, there were six days of respite in which to re-
discover the world.

Jumping off my mule, or rather off my perch on the boxes,
I walked along the clean road. There is no highway cleaner
than the Chinese highway, for animal droppings are ceaselessly being gathered up, to be dried and used as fuel. I
could have shouted for joy and the echoes rang with my
Alpine songs. The puffs of smoke from Wang's black cigar
reminded me of our own short Swiss *Grandsons*, and as if
by magic, transported me to a third-class smoking compartment between Lausanne and Berne.

Wang sang now and again also, at the same time slipping

43

the handle of his whip down the nape of his neck and scratching his back with it. As the heat increased with the light, he took off one jacket after another and finally transformed the black material which served him as a sash into a turban. On top of a mud-built wall, a variegated cock crowed at the blue sky. A shabby cart passed, laden with a gay lacquered coffin, no doubt the only luxury some poor man had allowed himself. The peasants, blue spots against the soil of the fields, were extracting virgin earth from deep pits, dark earth that would regenerate the glebe exhausted by fifty centuries of cultivation.

Life in Kansu is really wretched. Squatting in front of their mud hovels the women were stitching at thick cloth slippers for their husbands. With vacant faces and dressed in dusty jackets and trousers, they seemed to have no sense of feminine coquetry except in the matter of their stunted feet. These they had shod with embroidered materials attached to little curved wooden heels. Many times I saw mothers on the side of the road tying up the feet of tiny girls—poor resigned little things!—with dirty bandages. Miserable children, prematurely serious, are put to work in Kansu as soon as their limbs are strong enough. Here were four of them directing a primitive plough under the supervision of a man who, as he ambled up and down, was spinning a handful of brilliant white cotton. Sitting in the dust near him, a mother and a bitch, equally human, equally animal, were suckling their young.

Each evening as night came down, we would stop at some village we had decided on as marking a stage. Wang would open a side of a swing door and we entered a long courtyard with eight or ten rooms opening off it. The largest, facing the entrance, is reserved for distinguished travellers. But we always refused it, as its size, its badly jointed roof and its broken windows inevitably meant that it was icy cold. The

44

pack-saddles would be unloaded by the light of an oiled wick while we scoured the village in search of food.

Sometimes we could not get even *mien** and had to send an appeal to the headman of the village to be allowed to have some flour. There was little to be seen in the shops except *Hatamen* cigarettes, onions, an occasional length of cotton, and oil. Eggs were rare, an unhoped-for quantity, but when we found any we took them to an eating-house. There the children would gather to watch our awkward efforts to negotiate the chopsticks. The one way of putting them to flight was to make the gesture of folding back one's two middle fingers under the thumb and pointing the index and little fingers at them.

Then, even with a torch, we would have to spend quite a while making out which, amongst so many exactly similar doors, was ours. The cold was piercing and we slept in all our clothes, having soon made up our minds that we preferred not to be asphyxiated by the herbs with which the k'ang was usually heated. Outside, we could hear the mules munching their hay. Peter found a cloth bag into which he could slip his laced knee-boots and thus he would get into his sleeping-bag without taking his boots off. He was proud of his ingenuity, but I was openly contemptuous of such laziness.

Wang wakened us before dawn, bringing boiling water to make tea. Then, in the cold of the early morning, we would set off at a steady pace for Central Asia, in advance of our convoy. Half-awake, I would hear Peter recounting the odd dreams he had had. He had landed on the coast of England in a mail-coach launched from the top of a skyscraper! Or he had seen himself on the stage, obliged to play Hamlet

---

* Mien is the daily food of the northern Chinese. It consists of wheaten flour boiled for a few minutes in water, looks like noodles or vermicelli, and is prepared as needed. Those who can afford it add little squares of meat to the soup, which is flavoured with red pepper.

with his wig awry and half strangled by a purple scarf!

At Oxford, where he had won a first in English literature (to his own great astonishment, he said), he was president of the O.U.D.S. and produced and acted in several plays.

Sitting on the steps of some little rustic sanctuary, our feet tortured with blisters, we would discuss, say, Bernard Shaw, till the mules overtook us; or perhaps the talent of some actress, or the apparent decline of the theatre. Or I would tease.

"You realize what the Lanchow authorities said? 'The Ma Ya Ngans may proceed . . .' They saw at once that I was the head of the expedition—you were the interpreter! It is I who must decide everything. We shall therefore go and have some of that mien that is simmering on the side of the road, there, by that eating-house."

And he: "If you knew Asia as I know it you would wait until the end of the march and had an appetite."

"You're a humbug," I would answer. "If you knew Asia so well, you wouldn't have blisters on your feet, like a child just out of the nursery."

Though I liked the companionship and it had considerably ameliorated the anxiety of our wait at Lanchow, it nevertheless deprived me of the greatest thrill the sense of discovery had given me on previous journeys. I had lost the intense joy, the intoxication, of blazing my own trail and the proud sense of being able to get through alone, to which I had become accustomed. Above all, a piece of Europe inevitably accompanied us through the mere fact of our association. That isolated us. I was no longer thousands of miles from my own world. I was not submerged by, or integrated into, Asia. Travelling in company, one does not learn the language so quickly. The natives do not make their own of you. You penetrate less deeply into the life about you.

Our last passage across the Yellow River, on a ferry filled

with men and horses, was easy enough. Then we began the ascent of the valley of the turbulent Sining Ho, which was to bring us to the capital.

We were approaching the mountains. The air grew lighter. Fields, where nothing was as yet showing its head, were covered with blue-tinged pebbles. Suddenly I realized that I had left my revolver behind me at Lanchow. The lady explorer having come without the principal item of her equipment, was going to be at the mercy of the Tibetan bears! But, as a matter of fact, she was rather pleased. Circumstances which seem desperate are bound to arise, but now I was, all at once, secure against the consequences of any ill-considered gesture I might have been tempted to make.

On the evening of the fourth day we arrived below the walls of Nienpai and found ourselves in the thick of a crowd of dusty soldiers and camels. But, fearing that the gates would not open early enough for us next morning, we camped in the yard of a farm out amongst the fields. For Peter, always the "Galloper," wanted to do the two stages from there to Sining in one day.

The docile Wang fed the animals at midnight but called me at one o'clock, thinking it was three. I was furious and rounded on Peter for a bad interpreter. He admitted his fault and added without a smile:

"I don't understand anything whatever. Why can't those people talk the way I do?"

In reality the dialect of the north-west is very different from the mandarin Chinese of Peking. To get water to wash in, we had now to ask for *fi*, the local variation of the word *shui*.

It was icy cold as we set out. A cutting wind swept through the bare valley. The sun came up and produced a series of magical horizontal effects, but that phase was of brief duration. Before midday I was to suffer from its vertical

47

rays. I got up on my mule to avoid ceding to the temptation to go to sleep on the side of the road, and rode on somnolently. Wang walked like a drunken man and slept clinging to his mule's tail, but, as if in training for some Tibetan marathon, Peter lengthened his stride through the impalpable dust. I faintly remember canals of clear water, built like those at Samarkand; a white temple hollowed out, half-way up an immense red cliff, like a gleaming eye in the night; a litter hung between two mules wearing red pompons with a pale old man squatting inside. . . .

The deafening river became sombre in colour, like thick cocoa. On their crests, its waves were tossing some great goatskin rafts with the stiff, shortened legs of the skins pointing towards the sky. These rafts were bound for Lanchow, perhaps even for Paotow, with cargoes of wool and coal. The sailors, leaning on their enormous steering oars, had a powerful cry, like the cry of conquering men. I answered it with the cry of our mountaineers, giving a piercing yodel that made them turn their heads towards the path we were following. Who knows but they may now be calling out in the style of Ober-Haslital!

At the edges of little creeks of calm water, gold-washers were shaking their double baskets. A company of badly-equipped soldiers came towards us. They were on their way to join the anti-Communist forces. The civil war must not interfere with the caravan traffic, which is the chief source of wealth to the *Ma* dynasty who govern the province.*

These Tungan soldiers—Chinese Moslems—are afraid of nothing and are said to terrorize the sons of Han. The troop we met were trying to persuade a tired camel, loaded with great cauldrons, to get up. To help them, Peter lighted a few sheets of *La Croisière Jaune* under the hindquarters of the indifferent beast.

* It was to facilitate that traffic that General Ma had roads constructed, and—a great innovation—important bridges built.

48

FREEDOM

The province of Koko Nor was created in 1929, from parts
of Tibet and Kansu, to appease the incessant claims of the
Tungans to be masters in their own house. At the same time
orders were issued for all Mahometan troops to withdraw
from the Amdo region of Tibet, where they were detested.*
But how are these disciples of Allah going to deal with
Occidental methods of waging "modern" war which are
utterly contrary to their traditions? A Tungan Army Corps
which, under the command of Ma Chung-Ying, had conquered
Chinese Turkestan, was recently put to flight by a few gas
bombs dropped from the air.†

One could not help wondering about the Tibetans away to
the south, whose attitude is quite different. They shut
themselves up in their mystical Buddhism and only allow the
twentieth century to penetrate drop by drop, so as to be
assimilated gradually. On the other hand, Siberia in the
north, under the lash of the second Five Years Plan, is being
mechanized. What, exposed between the two influences, and
still Moslem, is Central Asia going to do? Will it revolt
against the priests or against the agents of Russian manu-
factured goods through whom its own artisan class is
disappearing? Serving alternately as a Chinese frontier
against the hordes of the Occident and as a buffer for Russia
against the growing imperialism of Japan, is it possible for it
to become independent and remain true to itself? Will some
Ma emerge as the Ibn Saud of the Koko Nor? And where is
Ma Chung-Ying hiding? And what are his plans? Nobody
knows.

*   *   *   *   *

The valley opened out, the fields became continuous, and,
behind a curtain of young poplars, Sining stood, smiling;

* See note, p. 301.
† A moral defeat resembling that of the Abyssinians, who are as brave
as the Tungans.

49

Sining, the objective of caravans, Sining from which we were to set out on the Tsaidam trail, provided the authorities did not take it into their heads to bar the road to us. . . .

A boy on a bicycle came up against a fat woman on a donkey. A novice in the art of bicycling, he zigzagged, sounded his bell dementedly and brushed against the donkey, which bounded in terror to one side. The matron, clutching on wildly, screamed. Her lord ran up. Then giving chase to the delinquent, he had no difficulty in over-taking him in the marshy ground and proceeded to give him a good hiding.

Scenes from modern life. . . .

CHAPTER VII

IMPATIENCE AT SINING — THE LAST TOWN

IN the Moslem town, which is separated from the Chinese town by a great wall pierced by a single gate, I received an entirely new impression. It certainly did not come from the principal street with its artisans working in the open air but under pent-roofs; or from the ornamented porticos framing vistas of streets in perspective; or from the lace-paper signs hanging outside the restaurants. No, it was that in this Chinese scene one felt for the first time the atmosphere of Islam. Old men, dressed in silk, like mandarins, but wearing white or yellow turbans, mixed with the crowd. These Tungans resembled the Kirghiz who affected a *barbiche*. I recalled with surprise that amongst the Kirghiz of the Celestial Mountains I had, contrariwise, thought the Tungans Chinese-looking. Women rode astride on shaggy, wide-browed ponies and though they wore Chinese dress their faces were hidden behind horsehair veils like the *chedra* of Bokhara over two thousand miles away.

And then caravan camels, as thickly-coated as sheep, crouched, ruminating, in great courtyards, their nosebags over their heads while they waited the hour for packing up. With which of those great beasts were we going to reach the immensities of the west?

The principal street of the Chinese town was decked with Kuomintang flags—a white sun on a blue ground in a corner of the red flag. Surprising-looking barbarians went along with heavy steps. They were from the Tsaidam and Tibet, from the regions into which we were trying to penetrate, and where our traces would be lost. I stared at them in wonder. Perhaps they were as astonished at the sight of me as I at the sight of them, but by a kind of dignity natural to them they were able to hide their surprise. The straight-nosed Tibetans looked elegant, their heads encircled by dark red turbans or the skins of wild foxes. Their red woollen cloaks were barred with a single wide strip of sheep's wool. The wealthiest of them had an edging of panther at the neck.

But the Tsaidam Mongols were stranger. With one arm encased in a sleeve of a sheepskin garment, worn hide outwards, they leave half the chest exposed. Hanging from the neck they wear a little silver box containing an amulet or a clay Buddha. The garment itself is tied in at the waist and hangs, like a skirt with innumerable pleats, to the knees. In the voluminous pocket formed by the sash the wearer carries all his belongings. A great sabre hangs at the side. The copper bowl of a long pipe shows out of the top of one of the massive boots which have turned-up toes. Sometimes they wear a brown cap braided with gold, but most of them have "fallen for" the latest fashion and adopted the dull European soft-brimmed felt hat.

Our Friends Lu and Ku.

At the other end of the town, Lu Hwa-pu, to whom we had an introduction from Smig, was in residence. That was unhoped-for luck. Surrounded by a crowd of clerks and apprentices, Lu ran a shoe-and-stocking business as well as a photographer's studio. He was a charming, roguish man and had the good taste to know Russian—he had lived a long time in Urumchi.

Drinking tea in a room at the back of the shop we lost no time in explaining what we wanted: passports for the interior of the province, a caravan setting out for the west, camping materials, and a servant-interpreter who would be *persona grata* amongst the Mongols.

Lu, in turn, lost no time in leading us to the governor's yamen where he was known. We handed our passports over to Feng, the secretary, for the governor, Ma Lin, uncle of General Ma Bu-fang, was unable to read. We waited in a warm guard-room, drinking tea under the inquiring gaze of the subalterns who passed in and out. I had to laugh at a very amusing fresco painted on a wall in the courtyard. It represented a ventriloquist with his doll on his knee—Japan and Manchukuo, of course! But we waited in vain. It was impossible to guess at our chances of success. Once more we had only to be patient. So we left.

Peter had the bright idea of at once looking up C. C. Ku, to whom we had an introduction from his brother, a student in Peking. Ku spoke fluent English, having studied at Cornell University. He had been sent from Nanking to Sining with the rank of lieutenant-general, and succeeded in making a good impression on "The Young General," Ma Bu-fang. His opinion was that it would be advisable for us to have military permits from the latter. Our new friend approved our avowed purpose of living the lives of hunters in the steppes—we did not dare speak of Kashgar—for shooting was his own great passion. He was leaving the next day for Tangar, the last village before one comes to the solitudes, at a day's journey from Sining. But he then and there took the trouble to write to Feng, who was a school friend of his, and also to "The Young General," saying that we were his friends and that we might safely be helped on our way.

Everything seemed to be working out for the best in the best of all possible worlds, and Peter with triumphant audacity proclaimed:

"I hope you realize now why I wanted to do the last two

stages here in a day. One day more and we should have missed that providential meeting with Ku!"

Then we met some missionaries, the Plymires and the Woods, who preached the gospel of the "Pentacost" sect at Tangar. They said they had received orders from their consul to return to the coast before the Communist advance cut them off. Mr. Plymire had been a long time in the country. At the time of the last official evacuation of foreigners in 1927, he had had to fly and went across Tibet in the direction of India. At Lhasa, however, he had been turned back and forced to make for Kashmir. That meant that he knew the country well, but his advice left us in some perplexity. From under his threadbare cap, from out his untidy beard, came disturbing hints about the spies of "The Young General." He maintained that they were everywhere, in all sorts of disguises.

"No," he told me, "you'll get nothing from the General by making him a present. . . . But you must hurry if you want to join a caravan. Most of them have already left with cargoes of tea and flour. Incidentally you'd do better at Kumbum than here."

Father Hesser of the Austrian Mission was of the same opinion. We could not get even a permit to leave the town. I hoped the good father would have only to strike the ground like a conjurer to produce an interpreter-guide-treasure ready to set off for the ends of the earth with us. But no more than Lu could he think of anyone he would recommend. It was an important question, for there might come a day when everything would depend on whom we had with us. As we were going to be at the mercy of Mongols and those pillaging Tanguts I had no intention of putting myself in the hands of a Chinese servant, for the nomads hate all men of Chinese race. We could only wait.

54

IMPATIENCE AT SINING

"Patience" Games.

The police used to come at any and every hour of the day and night, to examine our arms, to examine our luggage, or simply to see how our typewriter worked. We were lodged in a mud-built inn in the Moslem town. The doors would not shut and the neighbours walked in and out as they chose, or with inquisitive fingers made cracks in the paper of the windows to spy on us. In the morning we were wakened by the loud scraping noise with which the Chinese unfailingly clear their throats.

Before we left I knew the town backwards and forwards, the hammerings of blacksmiths and coppersmiths, and the sliding noise of the bellows worked by scullions under kitchen hearths. There was the eternal beating of the flour sifters (a kind of hanging shakers), and there was the cry of the soup-vendors. Near the river, in the bare fields surrounded by low dykes, a seed-sowing apparatus that looked like a variation on a plough "theme" was stuck in the earth.

Back at the inn I would warm myself over a tray of live coals and read. Peter buried himself in *The Weekly Times* crossword puzzle. The missionaries had lent him the paper, but apart from that one gesture the gentlemen of the China Inland Mission at Sining showed no great cordiality. They had probably heard that we were in difficulties with the authorities and as a matter of principle they avoided everything even remotely touching on politics. They refused even to agree to act as interpreters in the event of our obtaining an interview with the General. Perhaps also they thought we ought to have a chaperon. Unhappily the Smigs were no longer available.

Peter also killed time playing "Patience." He only knew one variety, but it lent itself to all kinds of tricks. If it came out—which was almost impossible—it meant that India was ours. So, to all intents and purposes, was the

55

moon! If there were ten cards left over, it meant a prison in Turkestan—but it would be a triumph if we got so far. Twenty cards over, with black predominating, meant a complete set-back.

I would listen to these discouraging oracles with an inattentive ear. Peter suffered more than I from our compulsory inaction.

"If you knew Asia as well as I do," I would say, "you'd know that this sort of thing must happen."

He could, however, remain outwardly impassive and smiling. That was our greatest asset in dealing with the innkeeper, with the inquisitive police, with the scratchers at our paper windows. Never did a gesture of Peter's betray the hastiness that often characterizes Occidentals.

Before we left we were known everywhere. Salesmen no longer ran out from the backs of their stalls to stare at us as we passed along the street. One day when we were buying two enamel mugs at a little shop, a Moslem standing by defended our interests by making the Chinese shopman give us the proper change.

Meantime Lu and I went over the list of things we should need for what we modestly called our "Tsaidam tour." His employees would put down their ball frames and go off to do messages for us, returning with samples of raisins, a copper saucepan, tent-cloth, sheepskins, etc.

Lu helped in every way, and even decided to put us in touch with certain Mongol lords then staying at Sining.

In a room giving on to a carpenter's yard the Princess of Barun received us, sitting over a brass teapot that was placed on the k'ang, and a plate of flaky Chinese pastry with rose jam. She wore a sheepskin pelisse which hung almost to the ground, and she studied us out of a beautiful face with regular features, pale under the rim of a pointed hat. Her plaited hair escaped from underneath the hat, the plaits, bound in rolls of embroidery, being gathered on both shoulders. Her old mother was similarly dressed but untidy and shiny with dirt. She had a face that was tanned, and wrinkled like a bulldog's. Ultra-modern, wearing that is to say a European man's soft hat, a girl who had her hair in about a hundred plaits kept her eyes closed. She reminded me of a dazed cat. All three wore enormous necklaces, ear-rings and amulet cases inset with turquoises and coral.

They had left their far-away steppe and yurt to be with the young Prince of Barun* at Sining, where he was attending school before taking up the reins of government. This boy wore dreary clothes of some grey material and was said to be sixteen years old. He had his mother's beautiful features and his cap hid a long black plait of hair twined round his head in the fashion at one time affected by schoolgirls at home. With great dignity and deliberation he was binding voluminous puttees round his thin legs.

The beautiful Princess and the members of her family allowed themselves to be photographed from every angle. I made the most of my chance. If we were sent back to Lanchow we might not meet any more Mongols.

Close by was a school founded to educate the sons of Mongol and Tibetan chieftains. The pupils were all dressed similarly. And if some had the air of sprigs of nobility, most of them looked disguised and unhappy. Their socks were falling down and their shoes did not always match. The teacher had a noble brow which cleared as he regarded his ill-fledged brood.

Our friend Lu was holding court when a police officer came and augmented the attendance.

"The Governor must have wired to Nanking about you," he said to us.

* The Tsaidam consists of five principalities.

57

Alas, if the Central Government began busying itself on our account we must expect the worst. . . . But, an idea! What we ought to do was change our tactics and instead of letting it be seen that we were afraid of Nanking, make use of every possible piece of influence we had there. To find out officially whether the Waichiaopu* would visé our passports, Peter telegraphed to a colleague, one Chao, who was Reuter's correspondent at Nanking and very well informed. Everything now seemed to us to depend on him, and the longer we waited the more I became convinced that he had power to smooth the way before us. . . .

"Visas doubtfullest."

That was the reply that came in the end, with the advice to apply again to the local authorities.

Had we lost our time and our money to get only as far as this? In theory we were in order, for Koko Nor was mentioned on our passports. I took a chance and wired the French Legation at Peking begging for a word in my favour to be sent to Nanking. It still might prove useful to have it made known from several quarters that we were esteemed honourable persons.

Was it a change of luck? At any rate, our captivity was made less irksome. One of the town magistrates sent delightful gifts to our lodging, a sheep, two boxes of tea and two packets of sugar wrapped in red paper (as gifts are in China), and with them the permit, for which we had applied, to visit Kumbum. A light covered cart was placed at our disposition, with a decrepit old soldier on horseback to act as escort. We might set out at once!

* Ministry of Foreign Affairs.

CHAPTER VIII

KUMBUM

IT was half a day's journey to Kumbum, the biggest monastery of the Amdo country. There are three thousand monks, Tibetan, Mongol and Chinese. Pilgrims visit it in great numbers every year, bearing rich gifts which assure them of places in heaven after they die. There is so much gold at Kumbum that the great copper roofs of the pagodas have been covered with it. The chief pilgrimage takes place in winter at the "Feast of Flowers." In preparation for this, the lamas spend weeks sculpturing flowers in coloured butter kept hard by the cold.

The monastery was built over the spot where the reformer Tsong-K'apa was born in 1358. He founded the Tibetan Yellow Sect. Tsong K'a, the Valley of Onions, was the original name of the place. Legend has it that drops of blood fell from the umbilical cord of the predestinate child. From them rose an umbrella-shaped tree which had a hundred thousand leaves like parrots' wings, and these leaves gave forth a perfume which could be scented nearly five miles away. The leaves are also said to bear a representation of the Buddha's face.* The trunk of the legendary tree was still, the lamas said, preserved for veneration in a tower-shaped reliquary, called a chorten,† beneath the great pagoda of the monastery.

We climbed a little hill and Kumbum appeared suddenly, an amphitheatre of buildings in a little bare valley. The

* The word Kumbum means "a hundred thousand images."
† The structure called in Sanskrit "stupa."

59

gold-roofed pagodas glittered like jewels amidst dull rows of dwellings. These cluster round long, whitewashed walls. The charm of Kumbum is its colour: white walls and pastel tints making harmonies under the pale-blue sky; fawn-coloured earth, gleaming walls, the soft gold of the pagodas, grey leafless trees and the brown-red dots which are lamas wrapped round in togas that leave only one arm free. From a distance, the holy men, thus enveloped in draperies with innumerable pleats belling out as they fall, look like so many perambulating tulips.

We went along a dried-up ravine, passed an imposing range of eight chorten like spiked helmets; and then, by a paved way dominated by two hayricks about forty feet high, we at last entered a courtyard surrounded by a double ring of stables and other outhouses. Here was the residence of Kumbum's lay secretary.

In a dark room, Chinese in style, a brazier was glowing. A tall, toothless man, wearing a toga, invited us to be seated on the k'ang, and left his abacus and his writing-table to do the honours of tea. But there should have been some conversation and we could not engage in any, even with the help of our old soldier escort whose knees were shaking and whose eyes had gone dead. No doubt he was weak for want of opium since we left Sining.

Beside me was a bowl full of grey powder which looked like fine salt and on which rested two slabs of butter. With a dignified gesture the secretary indicated that we were to help ourselves. Perhaps it was a matter of form? I refused, but ate a little of the unknown and most unsavoury powder off the tip of my finger. Could it be the ashes used in some religious rite? But when it came to his turn, our old man helped himself and with nimble fingers mixed the powder and butter in his tea, and kneaded them into a ball. Then I understood. This was the famous *tsamba*, a Tibetan food made from

toasted barley flour—*tsamba*, which we were to come to regard
as the most precious of the products of the earth!
A lama servant led us to a clean room on the first floor.
The k'ang had a rug on it. A tea-kettle sang on the edge of a
big tray of live coals. In a corner, on the ground, was a basin
to wash in.

In the middle of the night I was wakened by the sound of
cymbals clashing, a heavy gong being struck, and the
lugubrious notes drawn from shells. Were the religious being
called to prayer? Or were the demons of the darkness being
driven off? I lay till daylight waiting to get out of my
sleeping-bag.

Breakfast in the sculptured wooden gallery on to which our
room opened was an unforgettable experience. The gallery
ran round three sides of a courtyard. Opposite us rose a little
disused temple. Under the portico of this, hundreds of
fritters, that gave off a strong smell of frying, were being
dried. All the colours with which the wooden façade of the
little temple and its super-imposed geometrical designs were
ornamented, sang in the sun. Red, gold and brown pre-
dominated. Rose designs, arrows, Tibetan and Nepalese
characters, all blended in a counterfeit of lace work. A great
flagstaff, flying an oriflamme covered with prayers, rose in
the centre of the yard. Near-by, a camel tethered to our
cart was grinding his teeth. And dominating the whole scene
were the many-storeyed roofs of two pagodas built on the
slope of the hill.

The outer façades of the office buildings where we stayed
were painted dark red and had fantastically shaped windows
surrounded by light frames widening towards the base. The
terraces consisted of small beams resting on a thick surface of
fascines neatly cut flush with the façade. Our first steps
inside the maze of buildings brought us to the enormous
kitchen used for feast days. Three gigantic cauldrons, each

on its own hearth, were for use only when there was a great pilgrimage or when some devout person offered to treat the entire monastery to a bowl of tea. On the wall hung rows of wooden buckets bound with tin. They were used to carry round the tea.

In a chapel near-by was an enormous cylinder over-charged with ornament. With what looked like an air of pride, a fat peasant man effortlessly set it in motion. It was a prayer-wheel. Inside these prayer-wheels endless litanies are inscribed on rolls of paper. Similar machines were to be found in every corner of the monastery. In some places there were whole batteries of them, revolving tirelessly, sending the supplications of the faithful up to the gods.

And then suddenly, without any preparation, without passing through any monumental entrance, we found our-selves in a narrow forecourt, facing the holiest of all the pagodas. And growing there was a slip from the miraculous tree of the Buddhist images.* But it was winter and the tree was bare. The pagoda is in the Chinese style, low, with roofs turned up at the corners. A gallery, with pillars hung with yellow embroidery, and with a floor of polished wood, runs along the entire façade. When we arrived, some ten of the faithful—skirted lamas and simple pilgrims—were there, throwing themselves down on their stomachs, rising to their knees, standing up, kneeling and throwing themselves on their stomachs again. This ritual, during the performance of which the hands are covered with felt pads so that the palms may slide easily along the wood, has been observed for so many centuries that the polished floor is hollowed with deep grooves. I passed amongst the worshippers and pushed open the door of the sanctuary. A ray of light struck the gilded face of a great Buddha in wood, enthroned on top of the

* It is said that the mysterious image is also visible on the trunk of the tree, produced perhaps by an injection made in the bark.

chorten containing the trunk of the holy tree over the very spot where Tsong K'apa was born. The Buddha's arms were hung with votive sashes and before it was a long table for offerings with butter burning, as it burns perpetually, in a multitude of cups. Some lamas squatting on their heels were muttering prayers. With kindly smiles they gave me to understand that I should not be disturbing them by taking photographs.

Near-by, a spacious and beautiful courtyard with wide paving gave access to the second pagoda, which consisted of a vast prayer-hall. Here also one entered by a colonnade hung with embroideries. The interior was very dark and crowded with silken banners, many of them painted with religious themes. Whole walls were covered with bookstands on which the sacred writings rest. At the foot of a pillar, a priest, in a skull-cap surmounted with a high yellow crest, was squatting. On his knees rested a sacred book out of which he murmured prayers, passing the leaves as he finished with them to the nearest lamas, novices and postulants in the parallel ranks that squatted in front of him. The long, printed leaves were passed from hand to hand and finally returned to him. I was stiff with the cold, but none of the lamas appeared to feel it in the slightest degree, though their heads were shaven; they included old and young, elegant and frowzy; Tibetan literates with fine features, and full-faced Mongols; and their clothing, apart from the claret-coloured toga and dark skirt, consisted only of a sleeveless jacket, the rich brocade of which was not, in every case, hidden by dirt. At the ends of the ranks were the little *chabis*, ten or twelve years old, dirty, sniffling, finding it difficult to remain motionless, and playing surreptitiously amongst themselves. A server passed from one row to another with a great copper pot. The faithful took their wooden bowls from inside their vests and without quitting their hieratic posture, greedily sampled their tea—tea with milk.

Temples of lesser importance are scattered throughout the lamasery. One was decorated with paintings of men being skinned alive, and of gods who for saddle covers had human skins and for ornament collars of human eyes and human bones. In other temples there were stone dragons and stuffed animals, terrifying yaks, bears, monkeys and tigers. All that world becomes propitious if these are kept anointed with butter!

CHAPTER IX

THE CHINESE FAR WEST

A Lusar Merchant.

THE whole place fascinated me, but it did not get us any further on our way. I wanted to make a munificent gift to the Grand Lama and ask in return for some badge, or a letter of recommendation to all his coreligionists. It was possibly the one way of taking flight without having to worry about the Sining authorities. But we did not know how to speak or to whom to speak.

We still, however, had one resource, in the person of Ma Shin-teh, a rich Moslem merchant living at Lusar, a little village half an hour's walk from Kumbum. Caravans used it as a halting place. We went to Lusar. Its mud houses with their terraced roofs suggested a Moroccan village. Preparations were already under way for the reception of the Panchen Lama, who was due some months later on his way through to Tibet. We were told that camels had already been requisitioned for his caravan, which would be a big one. But it was added that he would never get across the frontier with 8,000 contraband rifles stowed in his baggage!

However, it was Ma Shin-teh who interested us. We arrived at his house, bringing modest presents—the tea and sugar we had been offered at Sining. The master was out for five-o'clock prayers and, surrounded by a dozen clocks, none of which agreed with the others, we waited. Tea and Chinese rolls—steamed flour-balls—were offered us by servants who came and went just to have a look at us.

After a time Ma returned, a sympathetic figure with a

bulging forehead and sly expression. Peter tried to make himself understood and I did not know which to admire more, Ma's patience or my companion's ingenuity. Peter made himself charming, apologized for his travelling clothes, smiled and protested his unworthiness of the compliments which he guessed were being paid him. Taking advantage of a respite to light his pipe, he remarked to me that he could make nothing whatever of the conversation.

We presented Smig's visiting card (his name amongst the Mongols was Oross Baï*) and giving Ma to understand that we were Smig's greatest friends, explained that we wished to join some big caravan going to the Tsaidam. The position was, I think, that Ma owed money to Smig and so had every reason to make himself agreeable. He controlled the greater part of the business done in the Tsaidam, so it would be most useful to us to have him at our back. And he had given his daughter in marriage to "The Young General," so was not without influence at Sining. He brought in a timid sharp-eyed lad, half-Mongol, half-Chinese, whose name was Li. Li was setting out with a big caravan in five days' time and could look after us till we got to Teijinar, where we should, perhaps, find Smig's old partner. At Peter's suggestion Ma also agreed to write to Feng, the Governor's secretary, saying that there was no need to be uneasy about us, as we should be with one of his men.

When we returned to Sining we sent a beautiful letter to the Governor exonerating him from all responsibility in the event of anything happening to us. For in the past the explorer Dutreuil de Rhins had been killed in the region and, more recently, in 1927, two Frenchmen, Louis Marteau and his companion Louis Dupont, had disappeared with all their belongings somewhere in the southern part of Koko

* By stretching the European, "Mr. Russian."

Nor.* And in the end all the efforts we had made bore fruit, for the next day Peter returned from the yamen with the much coveted passport. His face was shining and he looked like a schoolboy setting out on a holiday. His usual phlegmatic expression had given way to an expansive smile. We had, of course, to have an escort, one man, but only as far as Tangar. We could not get over the surprise at our unhoped-for triumph.

When I went to say good-bye to the Austrian sisters I had the luck to be able to get one of them to stop a tooth for me. It might be the last time. . . . Toothache and appendicitis are the two things I am afraid of when I have left the last town behind. The compassionate sisters then let me shut myself up in their dispensary with a pail of hot water and there I waged, as I could not at the inn, a royal war on the parasites which had been disturbing my sleep.

We invited Lu, whom we could never sufficiently thank for his help, to a last meal at the Chinese restaurant. In an adjoining room some Chinamen were raising a terrific row, gambling for money with dominoes, and drinking heavily.

"*Kaan pei!*" cried the robust Lu, inviting us to empty our little cups of warm shao-djin. Our spirits were raised and we confessed to him that we were going to do our best not to return to Sining. But Lu was not frightened at the thought of our plan. He had travelled a great deal and lived a long time at Urumchi.

Our last civilized evening! Soon there would be no more delicious pork, no table, no roof. . . .

---

* It is thought that they may have insisted on having pack animals for a sum paid down. But this does not give any right to have *oulas*—relays, which are reserved for the use of the Dalai Lama—and so they may have exasperated the native Goloks. Dimitri Guerki, the third member of the expedition, seems to have succeeded in escaping across Tibet and it was perhaps he who wrote the pencilled note received by Paul Pelliot asking for money to be telegraphed to Leh in Ladak.

The Last Europeans.

Our two conveyances were not long getting over the twenty-five-mile journey to Tangar. We went up a rocky valley which stirred Peter to thoughts of the Scotland that was very far away now. We overtook a caravan in which several she-camels had just given birth to young ones. The woolly babies, tied on their mothers' backs in baskets, cried unceasingly. They were famished, or perhaps frightened by the clouds of dust. A mother stretched out her head and twisted it round in answer to the moaning from her back.

Situated near the Tibetan frontier, at an altitude of nearly 9,000 feet, Tangar is said to harbour the worst half-castes in Asia. It is considered wise to believe nothing anybody in Tangar says and to keep everything under lock and key. There was hard frost and the river-bed was filled with ice as opaque as a candle. At the inn, the k'ang was, for once, warm—probably there were trees in the neighbourhood—so warm that I could not sleep in spite of the bags and felt rugs piled under me. It is not surprising if Chinese babies sometimes do get roasted . . . .!

The town is built on the spur of a mountain, and the climbing narrow streets reminded me of certain Alpine villages. It is the seat of a representative of the Dalai Lama* and its open-air fair attracts many Tanguts—northern Tibetans, magnificently hirsute creatures, who wear a gold ring in the right ear.

Hoping for some news from the west we went to see Mr. Marcel Urech of the China Inland Mission. At his house we were received with open arms. The Urechs carried us off from our squalid inn and established us in tiny rooms with beds that had cretonne coverlets.

I thought I ought to address Mr. Urech in German. He answered in French that he did not know German. He was a

* See note, p. 301.

THE CHINESE FAR WEST

Swiss from Neuchâtel! In reality, however, my compatriot's
French had grown somewhat rusty and it was in English that
we continued our talk. He knew nothing about Sinkiang.
It was three months' journey away, and for two years nobody
had crossed the immense Tsaidam. But, on the other hand,
one could get to Jye-kun-do on the south. There was a postal
service once a month. Situated near the source of the
Yangtze, beyond the Amnje-ma-tschin, which is 26,000 feet
high, it was one of the places in the world to which I felt
drawn.

Mrs. Urech was a witty Scotswoman who found it hard to
take us seriously. How could we expect to cross Asia with so
little luggage? It must be admitted that, having no scientific
instruments, no cinematographic apparatus and no boxes of
tinned food, we made a poor show. Still, Peter and I, having
learned from our earlier travels, were in complete agreement
on the point.

Mrs. Urech really has a heart of gold. She anticipated my
needs. She sensed that I detested sewing and she herself
made new bags to carry our supplies of toasted barley flour
(tsamba), of sugar and dried fruits. . . . She went so far as to
patch the seat of a pair of trousers Peter had passed on to me
when he himself took to suède plus-fours.

The truth of the matter is that when you arrive amongst
missionaries who live miles from everywhere and often see
nobody but natives for a year and more at a time, they are so
glad to see you that they are more than likely to endow you
with a thousand imaginary virtues.

Visitors were so rare at Tangar that young Malcolm, aged
three, had never seen any. He called us "the Mongols," the
term being for him synonymous with "foreigners." He also
had a great success when he called Peter "the *old* Maillart."
Only Peter was not flattered.

Mrs. Urech was quite proud when she found that Fleming,

69

the brilliant author by whom she had just read an article in
The Reader's Digest, and the young man whose coming she had
been warned of, turned out to be one and the same person.
"Malcolm!" she said. "Take a good look at the famous
man we have the honour to entertain in our house."
"Then he isn't a Mongol?" asked the puzzled little boy.
"But he isn't a Chinaman either. He doesn't know Chinese."
"No," I said. "He is what is called in Europe a 'special
correspondent.' He writes in the newspapers about what he
has seen. Only he has a curious way of doing things. For
instance, he says my linen takes up too much room, though
actually it consists of three sweaters and three pairs of
woollen pants. And all the time it is he who has my cases
bursting with his enormous boxes of tobacco . . ."
Then Peter: "If you don't stop grouching I'll wire to *La
Vie Parisienne* to recall you!"
And I: "Mrs. Urech, I've told him a hundred times that
Le Petit Parisien and *La Vie Parisienne* are two entirely different
periodicals. And, just imagine, *he* thinks I ought to be
satisfied with a camel crossing Asia! Of course that won't
stop me from having a horse. I don't see why he should be
the only one to play the lord."
"Well," he protested, "you'd be a lot better off on a camel,
since you are accustomed to it from your other journeys."
"No," Mrs. Urech intervened, "she ought to be able to get
on ahead and prepare supper for the lord."
"I know," I said, "I am to be cook to my interpreter. . . .
Peter, I've been given dried apricots, onions . . ."
" 'Been given!' You've been robbing Mrs. Urech, that's
what you've been doing. I know the old sea-dog, Mrs.
Urech. Give her back those apricots, you! We don't want
them."
"Listen to him, Mrs. Urech! He who wants to cross Tibet
and doesn't even know what scurvy is . . ."

Just then I noticed something the Chinese servant had brought in and involuntarily I cried:

"Oh, two kinds of jam to-day."

Peter was scandalized.

"Really, Maillart," he protested. "You are a disgrace to the expedition."

*   *   *   *   *

Black with dust, Peter arrived back one morning from Lusar, where he had returned for information with Ngan, the Mission's man of affairs. Having left the inn where we were to meet Li, we were afraid we might miss him. Besides, we were not very clear about the arrangement with Ma Shin-teh. As a result of Peter's expedition we learned that the Prince of Dzun, at the head of two hundred and fifty camels, had set out on his way home to his property in the Tsaidam. We were to overtake and join him. Four hired camels were to transport our luggage for seventeen days and the cost would be eight dollars per camel. Li would be paid ten dollars a month. He was to come for us the next day.

Peter told me one delicious thing that revealed the degree of intelligibility of the conversation on our first visit to Ma. The latter, looking at me, had asked:

"How old is she?"

"No, only friends," Peter had answered.

Our Real Departure.

On the 29th of March, 1935, six weeks after leaving Peking, we set out.

We had been to the post office—only Heaven knew when we should see another—and stamped our letters for Europe.

"If all goes well," I wrote home, "my next letter will be dated from India in six months from now. It will be time enough to begin to feel uneasy if you have no news of us within a year."

71

Which is a comment on this century of aeroplanes and radio messages.

We should find no more markets and had made all our purchases and packed them in bags and cases. There were bricks of tea with a drill to cut them when bargaining with natives. There was barley for the horses, and saddles, nose-bags, whips, fetters, axes, ropes, etc. I had spent part of my evenings trying to remember all the things I had found necessary on previous expeditions. I had appealed to Peter and he remembered that we should need fishing-hooks to catch river fish with. As a matter of fact, water-courses, which were marked on our map with dots, were rare and capricious in the Tsaidam. Fortunately we might expect to find sheep and make them the basis of our diet.

Now, in the courtyard of the Urechs' Chinese house, the kneeling camels were slowly being laden. A Mongol with his sheepskin loosed, leaving him naked to the waist, lifted a case against his chest, matched it with another and tied them together with a horsehair rope. Then, with the help of an assistant, he balanced the double load across the padded pack-saddle. The camel, when he felt his humps were getting unnecessarily rough handling, would give a whine that sounded like the creaking of a door. Amongst the lively Chinese surrounding us, Li, with his little eyes half-closed, looked as if he were asleep, and for the moment he was unable to make out a single word Peter said to him.

We crossed Tangar for the last time and left by the South Gate. On the other side of the bridge we took leave of the Urechs. They had proved such charming and helpful friends. To trick the evil genii, who might be tempted to punish our presumption, we said jokingly:

"It isn't good-bye. What with the war in Sinkiang and the authorities at Lhasa, we're bound to be back in a few months."

Then we marched towards the great solitudes of Asia. I sat enthroned on a wooden saddle with raised bows and padded with my sleeping-bag. My good horse, crazy at getting out of the stable, was rearing in every direction. Thinking of the skis I was not to use that winter I christened him Slalom. We turned aside from the view of the town with its many-roofed minaret and set our faces towards the west. . . . We had but to continue in that direction to reach Sinkiang. But where and how we should reach it, and in how many months, those were things we did not even try to guess. I was devoured with curiosity as to what the immediate and uncertain future was going to be like. And very sensible of a feeling of relief at being free of man-made obstacles! Overjoyed to think that every day would be a new day, that no day would be the same as the one before! And determined on observing only one solitary rule—to go straight ahead!

CHAPTER X

CARAVAN MARCHING WEST

AFTER four days' riding I saw, beyond the gilded grasses of the steppe, a great light below the leaden sky transforming itself bit by bit into an immense stretch of whiteness—the frozen waters of Koko Nor!

When we left Tangar we went up the course of a torrent in a rocky valley. That was the last time we saw water flowing to the sea. For months thereafter we were to march in the closed basins of Central Asia.

The first evening we found asylum in a comfortable Chinese house where the women, following the Tibetan mode, wore their hair in long plaits sheathed in embroidery. On the walls were pictures of the Russo-Japanese war, like Epinal prints but with the inscriptions in Russian. Probably they were a present from some Siberian traveller, on his way, perhaps, to Lhasa. I had believed that we were on the outer edges of the world, and behold, we were crossing a great international highway!

Newly-falling snow was whitening the earth on the second day, and we had to put on our heavy winter clothes. By a shut-in valley we had reached an altitude of nearly 10,000 feet. But now the landscape opened out over rolling country. There were telegraph poles along the road. It led to a customs post which we wished to avoid, so we broke away from it in a westerly direction. In the bare grass-lands cattle were grazing. One beast had a curiously curved horn which was slowly penetrating in through its forehead, but the animal did not seem to be in any way affected. Some miles away a

74

pine forest made a dark blur and I rejoiced at the thought of camping in an Alpine scene. But our trail did not go that way, and the pine-trees, perhaps the last trees on our road, disappeared behind us.

Then, at the foot of a mountain, we came to the long flat buildings of the Tung ku-ssu lamasery. Its walls were painted in shades of blue, white and pink. Two series of chorten—enormous white reliquaries shaped like wide-swelling bottles—stood on platforms near a stream.

In a room from which air was carefully excluded a lama suffering from a bad cold did the honours. He must have been a practised jobber, for, using Li as intermediary, he offered to exchange his own little Tangut pony for Peter's horse *and* twenty-five dollars. The negotiations that took place over the pot of tea (tea mixed with milk and butter) were long. Our host had claims to distinction. Not only had he photographs of himself in hunting costume, taken at Lhasa, he also did not blow his nose with his fingers but used a piece of dark blue linen which he kept under the rug of the k'ang. At last the bargaining was finished and Peter was the proud possessor of the pony, which was as black as the devil and much prettier than my good Slalom. But it was often to make Peter see red. He christened it Greys.

The hours seemed long. The warmth indoors made one lazy. The cold outside was sharp and the mountains were white with newly-fallen snow. I had not the courage to visit the little courtyards and pagoda and decided that they were probably much like those I had already seen. I made our little lama laugh by taking a pinch of the green powder to which he helped himself out of a pretty polished horn. After an uncontrollable outburst of very loud sneezes I decided to stick to my pipe. It had been company through long hours at the tillers of sailing boats and slow hours in mountain huts. Now, as on those expeditions, my face was burned from marching against a west wind heavy with snow. Here my pipe surprised nobody, for in China the women smoke as much as the men.

At last it was supper-time. A pot full of strips of dough was brought in. The lama heaped our bowls generously. We ate with bamboo chopsticks given us by Mrs. Urech. To show our gratitude for the lama's great hospitality I could not do less than offer him a photograph of the Panchen Lama. According to Smig, we should be able to get anything from a Mongol in return for a representation of that great spiritual chief and I had ordered six copies of the photograph from Lu. The inscription read: "Homage to the Shining Sun of True Doctrine, the Omniscient Depository of Royal Teaching."

The next day, branching off towards the south, we came by a low mountain to an immense tract of bare steppe which seemed scarcely broken by the hills in the distance. We picked up another trail here. Hares, grey in colour, scampered off at our approach and leaving his horse to Li, Peter set off after them. It would be a stroke of luck if we could have game simmering in the pot our first night in camp. The mutton diet to which we imagined ourselves—wrongly, as it turned out—condemned for months would be postponed for another day. I rode in amongst the high tufts of stiff yellow grass—it was like the twigs of brushes—and acted as beater, trying to drive the hares towards Peter. Slalom was interested in the game and turned his head round to watch me as I peered about. He would plunge suddenly into the depths of the grass after a bounding ball of fur. The lively little beasts were terrified and would appear as though they had been catapulted out of the sandy dunes. One, two, three—away! Each short gallop ended in an incredible jump. Standing in my stirrups and twirling my whip, with the wind whistling in my ears, I excited Slalom with wild cries. I had

76

reached the steppe. . . . It was mine. I felt myself invincible. That was a moment of rare joy.

In spite of my efforts Peter killed nothing. He put the blame on my horse, said he was a frightful animal, only fit for a tilt-yard. . . . My incomparable Slalom! How could Peter say such a thing? Slalom had realized exactly what I wanted him to do! His ambling trot, too, was so comfortable. Of course I defended him warmly.

That evening we set up our little tent for the first time. We had it made for us at Sining at a cost of ten Mexican dollars. In case of sandstorms I had had it streamlined and low at one end. We felt that, as little rain was to be expected, a single thickness of white cotton would suffice.

After its first night under the Asiatic sky it was covered with frozen gold-dust. We realized that we must be near a Tangut camp, for yaks appeared, looking, in the distance, like black cubes in a sea of straw. Inquisitive but timid natives, in cloaks shiny with dirt, came to look at us, accompanied by their watch-dogs, enormous masses of black hair with short muzzles, very fierce with strangers. Smig had advised me to carry stones in my pocket always and to practise taking aim in case I had to keep any of the dogs at a distance while waiting to see its master. But what was one to do in the steppes, where there are neither stones nor sticks?

Two Tangut girls, with their hair in innumerable plaits and with stiff sleeves that hung to the ground, were shy and would not be reassured by my smiles. At Tangar I had read about the odd customs of the T'u-jen ("men of the earth"). They are an aboriginal Koko Nor tribe. According to their code of hospitality, a host lends his daughter to his guest for the night. On leaving, the guest is expected to make a present and with it to hand over his belt. If the young woman should become pregnant, a "belt marriage" takes place and when he grows up the child of the chance union has the right to go and claim his father, provided he takes with him the belt given long ago as a pledge to his mother. But should a woman not wish to divulge the father's name, a "mast marriage" is all that takes place. The mast is a holy mast on which an oriflamme, inscribed with prayers, is hoisted. This means that the gods have willed the birth and that the child shall belong to its mother.

Perhaps the two girls before me were of the T'u-jen tribe and attracted by the rich white traveller. . . . But Peter was not interested in tribal customs.

When I dreamed of discovering and studying unknown ways of living Peter would talk of his desire to find some rare bird for the Zoo. It would make his fortune and he would see his name immortalized as "(Something) Flemingium" on the label attached to the specimen killed in the Tsaidam. A born hunter, he described the cry and the plumage of the various birds he hoped to bag and was very contemptuous about my ignorance of the feathered tribes. . . .

CHAPTER XI

WITH THE PRINCE OF DZUN BY THE KOKO NOR

The Prince of Dzun.

WE approached the Koko Nor, where we were to join the Mongol Prince's great caravan as promised by Li.

It was about half-past eleven in the morning, with a wind blowing from a sandy hill, when we saw a group of white, pointed tents with camels browsing about them. Galloping behind Li, we rode across the frozen mud of a tiny watercourse and dismounted close to the Prince's tent, which was decorated—the only one decorated—with a geometrical design. By the time our camels came up we had unsaddled and fettered our horses and sent them hobbling away.

As soon as we had our tent up we asked Li whether it would be in order to offer the Prince our telescope when we were paying our compliments. Li approved the idea. Li was a gentle lad, but seemed more wide awake since he took to the Tibetan fashion of big boots and a red serge *pulu*. As he came to know us better he grew less timid. I do not know what reputation white people enjoy at Lusar, but the first thing Li said to Marcel Urech was: "Everything will be all right if the gentleman does not lose his temper when anything goes wrong."

He was familiar with Mongol ways and carried the telescope laid on a *katag*,* a presentation scarf I had brought from Sining, spread over his open palms. We reminded each

* In Mongolia and Tibet, this is of bluish voile. It is a symbol of peace exchanged with greetings.

other that one did not enter the Prince's tent carrying a whip! Or, inside, knock the ashes out of one's pipe against the fender rail! And so we set off. The tent was set up on the caravan packs, arranged like a little wall, oval in form. It was wide open, to let the smoke escape, and the furniture was of the simplest.

Dzun No-yeh was seated, Turkish fashion, on an old sheepskin. A brown felt cap, braided with gold and lined with fur, sat anyhow on his head. His sheepskin robe was faced with red satin. He was about twenty-six and quite goodlooking, had a round face, eyes only slightly slanted, high cheek-bones, a little nose and a small mouth. He wore a turquoise ring on one finger, and in one ear a great ear-ring. And, like all his countrymen, he had a metal amulet box hanging from his neck.

He listened impassively to the shy compliments that Li uttered for us in the Mongol tongue. The tea was singing in a copper pot over the fire of argols* in front of him. Butter was offered in a wooden box. We brought out our bowls and I sipped my tea rapturously. It was buttered and steaming, and warmed my hands, which had been frozen. The dull silver lining of the Prince's cup glistened softly when he put it down.

Not being able to think of anything to say, we made signs of wanting to withdraw. Then the Prince, who had not spoken, returned our compliments and presented us with a worn katag which he drew from under his saddle-rug.

For the spectators, however, the scene was not concluded. They had been falling over each other for fear of missing anything. They were all burning to try the telescope that would enable them to find where their own scattered camels might be. . . .

Reluctantly, as it seemed to me, the Prince took hold of

* Dried dung or droppings, the only combustible in treeless regions.

his new possession and awkwardly tried to open it. We
showed him a notch we had made to mark the point to which
it should be opened to get the clearest view. But the lenses
were a little misty and, worst of all, the Prince could not shut
one eye at a time without covering it with his hand. In short,
the apparatus seemed to give him little pleasure, or if it did
he did not betray it. How were we to know whether we had
made a good impression or not?

Peter went out shooting. I was sitting in our tent mending
a sock. But a crowd of sightseers had collected. The Mongols, nomads who camp only for a rare few days near
Tangar or Lusar, were astonished at everything. They
looked at themselves in the glass. Surprised at its being so
regularly wound, they managed to unwind my ball of wool.
They went into ecstasies over a pair of nail scissors, over a
fork, and a tin box in which I kept the butter. . . My
visitors also included some merchants, Chinese some of them
with a dash of Mongol like Li. These merchants come up
and spend six months selling tea and drills to those of the
nomads who cannot get to town that particular year. They
are more civilized, and those who came to our tent that day
had already seen knives with more than one blade and
electric torches. But I did not like them. They seemed to me
to be rough and coarse, even though they had adopted the
clothing of the barbarians. The barbarians were like great
children, timid, anxious to do nothing to displease me,
and thoughtful on my account.

Tired of trying to entertain them, I suddenly thought of
giving them Lattimore's book on Mongolia to look at. It was
often afterwards to be a source of relief from their insatiable
curiosity. They could discuss the illustrations, knowing what
they were talking about. They had an odd habit of holding a
half-closed hand as a sort of shade before the eyes while they
looked.

Peter returned, dishevelled by the icy wind and dangling three great pearl-grey geese by their necks. The bodies were covered with an astonishing thickness of downy feathers. I felt very much like a cave-woman and proud that our fire was the only one over which game would be cooking that evening. Peter affected a modest air as though such a bag was quite the usual thing with him.

Everybody crowded round. The rifle was inspected and the ecstasies began all over again, over the small size of the bullets, and the marksman's skill. . . . There was a rush for an empty cartridge case when it was thrown away. Li saved us from a disaster at the last minute. Peter proposed to offer one of the birds to the Prince. But the Prince's religion forbade his eating geese. Dear, oh dear! The Mongols barely approved of us—and now perhaps we had committed a grave fault by shooting those birds?*

But a little old Tungan with a beard that blew about a pointed chin, hastened to bleed the goose we gave him, in accordance with Moslem law. He used to chatter like a magpie and we called him the Bo'sun.

The Bo'sun, with nearly a dozen of his co-religionists, had been sent by General Ma Bu-fang to wash the auriferous sands of some Tibetan rivers, at a salary of eight dollars a month. That was exciting. So there we were, travelling companions in a most original gold-rush, wandering the desolate regions of the Koko Nor! Failing ethnographical treasures and rare birds, might we not make a fortune by discovering a seam in the middle of Asia?

Our goose kept us late. Li showed no great enthusiasm about plucking it. It was three hours in the saucepan before it grew passably tender and it was by the light of the candle—

* When they go shooting, Mongols never fire at a beast if it be amongst its fellows. It might be a sacred animal. But if it be alone, there is no need for scruples, for an animal in which a reincarnated spirit is housed is never abandoned by its followers.

another great luxury in the eyes of the nomads—that we drank our tea before going to sleep. Our sleeping-bags were very comfortable, but salt had been used in tanning the leather and it often gave me tiresome fits of coughing.

Koko Nor.

On our right the frozen Koko Nor stretched for miles. It is less than 120 feet deep, but it is ten times as big as Lake Leman, a real sea without any outlet. I had read somewhere that it was salt and in consequence won a bet of a hundred Mexican dollars from Peter, who held that it was not salt. I must admit that I had just lost another bet. Before leaving Sining I had maintained that if we did succeed in getting out of the civilized areas, the authorities would be sure to insist on our having an escort and that we should never manage to rid ourselves of it.

The clear, dry atmosphere gave wrong impressions about distances and though the lake-edge seemed quite near, Peter and I were galloping a good while before we got to it. Blocks of ice covered with snow were heaped up on the shore. We went about taking photographs. . . . That lake had, for such a long time, symbolized an almost unrealizable ambition. . . .

Our rides were sometimes rendered difficult by the intolerable temper of Greys, the pony Peter had bought from the lama. It was a pretty animal but always troublesome when Peter was getting on. Peter put down to xenophobia the special repugnance it seemed to feel for him. One day in particular, the pony made a rush, threw Peter, and, trampling on him, went off at a mad gallop, with the saddle, the saddle-bag and its contents scattered in every direction. I confess I was very much alarmed. Peter dragged himself to a mound of earth and though he did not break down, he was the colour of a cucumber. He had got a kick of a hoof on the ankle. Was anything broken? Such an accident in such circumstances! Imagine what the consequences might have been! Happily he was only bruised. But ever afterwards Li or I always held that black devil of a Greys by the head while Peter was mounting.

On our left, parallel with the lake, a line of hills bounded the view to the south. Sometimes I could see a Tibetan tent, a truncated black pyramid, sheltering there from the wind. I might be able to get the butter we needed over there. . . . Only rare tufts of grass grew on the steppe and in between them crept the wind, incessantly tearing the earth away.

We were now proceeding in a straight line between two banks where water could flow when the thaw came. Probably it was the road that was being constructed to Dulan (or Tulandze), a distant outpost which we meant to avoid by keeping to the south. What Norin had said was right. I could have got to the Tsaidam on a bicycle if only I had had the means of carrying enough food.

Norin had, no doubt, passed along here two years ago, pushing his surveying apparatus before him day after day and keeping up his courage.

Snow still fell as in midwinter. There were no trees and our advance, with heads held down against the wind, was less like a scene out of *The Gold Rush* than a phase of the Retreat from Moscow. Alone, in front, on his white horse, the Prince did rather make one think of Napoleon.

Legends.

It is said that towns are buried under the sand in that neighbourhood. The whole impressive region has given birth to many legends. The waters of the lake are sacred and navigation on it is forbidden. This is why the lamas who live on the island in the lake may lay in supplies only in winter, when the ice makes a natural road.

The origin of Koko Nor is attributed to the anger of a Tibetan god who dwelt very far from there. The inhabitants of the region disobeyed him, and even denied his existence, so he resolved to drown them. Water burst out of a great hole in the earth and gradually covered the whole country. But seeing their pastures submerged, the people repented. Then the god sent his most powerful eagle with a great rock. This it let drop, stopping up the fatal hole and forming the island at the same time. Once upon a time the island was inhabited by marvellous mares that were capable of covering a distance of a thousand *lis* in a day. . . .

CHAPTER XII

LIFE IN THE CARAVAN

DAY after day our existence passed in accordance with the immutable rules of the centuries. Before dawn, without useless fuss or noise, two hundred and fifty camels, thirty horses and about eighty human beings were ready to start.

The camels, which had their pack-saddles left on overnight, slept kneeling in a semi-circle near their owners' belongings. Except for the droppings, round and black like large olives, which they left scattered over the ground, and the ashes of the fires, no traces of our passage were left. Without the droppings from earlier caravans we should have had no fires to cook our supper.

The men and women went about their work with sheepskin coats hanging loose and their brown torsos naked. They would slip a rope skilfully under a camel's belly as it prepared to kneel, then tie up the bags and, with a last girding of the loins, make everything fast. Already the first group might be on the way back to the trail we had turned off the previous day.

The sky was grey, heavy with cold, and the opaque ball of the sun rose over bare hills.

While Li was saddling my horse and Peter taking down the tent, I packed our supplies in the kitchen-box—butter, little cubes of bread as hard as ship's biscuit, cold meat, cocoa, sugar, tsamba and jam. Then, the caravan gone, we would crouch over the still warm ashes, putting off the moment when we must rejoin the slow monotonous march.

86

We swallowed a last bowl of tea. I hung the kettle on my saddle, pushed my mug into the saddle-bag—and there was no more to do but find a clump of earth from which to leap on to the saddle. At a distance from everyone, the Prince might be at his morning prayers, facing towards Lhasa and with a rod stuck into the ground before him.

A gallop, and one overtook the long caterpillar crawling on its way westwards. We horsemen, privileged travellers, free to roam as we liked and at whatever speed we liked, were only a score in all. Our group included a handsome Tungan with the straight nose of an Arab. He became our friend, as did also a jovial Mongol with intelligent eyes. This one wore a round felt hat, like a clergyman's hat. His name was Gunzun and apparently he belonged to the Prince's suite.

As a rule Peter went off early in search of a shoot and I would lead his pony beside my own mount. And very pleased with myself I used to be when, sitting on Slalom, I succeeded in negotiating both animals together in a jump over a ditch. I could see Peter a long way off on the track of his wild geese, sometimes lying down to fire. But however good a marksman he was on occasions when he could be by himself in some one place, waiting to bag something for our evening meal, he was always put out if he had to shoot up and down the line of the caravan. For the Bo'sun insisted on following, dagger in hand, ready, as a good Tungan, to bleed the victims. A complete buffoon—he reminded us of the boatswain in *The Tempest*—the wretch would keep crying out where the birds had settled, with the result that they took flight and Peter missed his shot. Besides, Peter was not used to shooting with the intimidating eyes of two hundred and fifty camels turned on him. He would throw in his hand and there was nothing to do but lead his pony up to him.

87

Sixty Lis *Nearer London.*

Every time I rode behind Peter I wished I could draw
caricatures. The pony was invisible under the military cloak
of its master. And I verily believe that the master's feet
might have been crossed under the animal's belly! However,
for the greater part of the time we rode far away from each
other as though we wanted to be separated for a few hours.
Our states of mind were very different. Peter's attitude was
one of wonder at discovering the ways of the nomads, ways
that are as old as the world. I, on the other hand, was going
back to a chapter in my own history. In a sense I was only
prolonging the journey I had made in Russian Turkestan.
I was familiar with the smell of camels and of their fetid
breathing as they ruminated. I had already joined in the
halt at the watering-place, already seen the gathering of the
dung for fuel. I knew the joy of drinking boiling tea, had
assisted in the search for camels that strayed while grazing.
I knew the silence at night, when one's eyes are burning
after marching against the wind all day. I loved the primitive way of living which gave one back that hunger that
transforms every morsel one puts under one's tooth into solid
satisfaction; the healthy weariness that made sleep an
incomparable voluptuousness; and the desire to get on that
found realization in every step one took.

United in the craving to succeed in our enterprise, we had
come to a perfect understanding. Yet we did not see things
from the same angle. Every night Peter would repeat his
refrain: "Sixty *lis** nearer to London." He did it to annoy me,
and I would tell him to shut up, for I wanted to forget that
we had, inevitably, to return home. I even lost the desire
to return home. I should have liked the journey to continue
for the rest of my life. There was nothing to attract me back
to the west. I knew I should feel isolated amongst my

* A *li* is about seven hundred yards.

contemporaries, for their ways had ceased to be my ways. In London I had thought that Peter was in revolt against town life. Now I saw him impatient to get back to it and I wondered whether he had only been indulging in a well-bred affectation. Yet how was I to know whether he was being sincere now or merely paradoxical, or trying to mystify me? Only his own compatriots, I thought, would be able to resolve these riddles. What is certain, however, is that Peter seemed to be less afraid of finishing up in the depths of an Urumchi prison than of getting home too late to shoot grouse in Scotland. We were about to cross one of the most magnificent hunting grounds in the world. Yet the fact that Tibetan yaks and wild asses, ibexes and markhors of the Hindu Kush were within range would not change his mood. A surprising companion! Or was it only that he wanted to accomplish the unique exploit of shooting, in the same year, "tur" in the Caucasus, duck in Shanghai, antelopes in the Koko Nor and deer in Scotland?

Though we went at a walk, Slalom would gradually reach the head of the column—which was a mile and more in length. An old woman led the file. She rode a slow, shaggy pony and looked like a circus clown in her pointed hat. Her tousled hair hid the wrinkles on her tanned face. In her hand she held a thin horsehair rope, of which the other end was attached to the nose of the first camel, so that he could be led. He was the only camel that had a bell. It hung round his neck and had a dull sound. When the old woman felt cold she dismounted, and, stiff with rheumatism, walked like an automaton, dragging her heavy, down-at-heel boots over the frozen ground. Her huge cloak dragged along the ground also. A tinder-box swung from her belt. The steady, implacable walk of the old Norn fascinated one, produced an impression of inevitable destiny.

Behind every tenth camel or so came a Mongol driver.

Perched high amidst the baggage and muffled up like old women were Tungans, *Hui-hui* gold-seekers and old Mongols with their rosaries of 108 beads slipping through their fingers as they muttered their prayers. Now and then one heard the dry tap of some smoker emptying his pipe against his heel.

Owing to the swinging movement of the camel, the loads often slipped over on one side. Then a Mongol horseman would come up and, still moving, try to lift the load with a heave of his shoulder till the balance was re-established. But most frequently, though very reluctantly, the men had to take stronger measures. The "string" had to fall out, the camel to kneel. The long rope that was bound round the ends of the pack-saddle in a figure of eight must be undone and the load balanced all over again. The camels always seized the opportunity to stretch out their necks, like swans, trying to reach the farthest attainable tuft of grass.

The rest of the caravan having, meantime, continued on its way, the immobilized sector was, of course, behind time. To make up for it the animals were encouraged with a guttural "Oo-ok." Later we were to have only too many occasions of employing that cry ourselves.

After several hours' marching, the rope traces which, at the setting out, tended to hang loose between the camels, would become taut; the heads that had been held high would droop and the tired beasts would slacken their pace.

Smig had said I need not take a heavy coat and assured me that the Tsaidam was not really cold. But it so happened that I had frequently to get down and walk, for, in spite of being almost smothered in clothes, my teeth chattered. In a head wind I was glad to turn down the ear-flaps of my Manchurian fur cap. There was one solitary sign that winter was ending—the wool hung in tufts on the camels' thin legs. They were shedding their coats and the iron-grey smooth skin that began to show was like the rubber of worn tyres.

As they marched along beside their beasts the caravan men would pull out a handful of the tufted hairs and twist them into a soft rope. This they kept in reserve to replace the one attached to the camel's nose, for these head ropes by which the beasts were led wore out quickly.

I often joined the group of Chinese merchants who rode on horseback. From a little distance the long antennæ of the gun-props attached to their guns made them look like crayfish. We often took a gallop together, looking, in our skins of animals, like a horde of savages let loose and giving loud cries as we cavalcaded towards the conquest of the desert. Then we would stop at the first ravine we came to. And, in shelter there, we waited till we heard the bells about the necks of the watch-dogs announcing that the caravan was coming up with us. . . .

It was not easy talking with those merchants. They would ask the price of my nailed boots and of my ski-ing gloves. Then they would express astonishment at my not being English like Peter. . . . And I in my turn would enquire which of them followed *hsiao chiao*—the little faith that was Islam, as opposed to the big faith that was, of course, Buddhism. They were nearly all from the Moslem town of Ho-chow, south of Lanchow. Only the youngest man of them could read Chinese characters. He, however, could also read the printed Roman letters on my visiting card. An alert young man, he asked how far we were from France and I told him:

"The caravan would get there in ten months if every day it marched sixty *lis* as we are doing to-day."

The merchants followed the caravan quietly enough, but the moment they found there were Mongols in the neighbourhood of a camp they bore down on them like vultures, sold them anything and everything, and almost forced them to accept goods on credit. Obviously there were immense possibilities amongst people who did not even know what a shirt was.

We usually finished our stage about two in the afternoon. Only rarely did we cover more than fifteen or eighteen miles in our eight hours' march, as the camels had to be let out to graze for a while before nightfall. Then it was a case of who should be first to have his tent up and the kettle boiling inside. The early arrivals had one advantage: they had only to stoop down to gather up the argols for the fire in the skirts of their coats. Before drinking, the Mongols piously walked the round, each of his own tent, scattering a spoonful of tea as an offering to the four cardinal points of the compass.

For breakfast and the midday meal we ate tsamba like the natives. Into the boiling, salted tea one dropped a piece of butter mixed with toasted barley flour. The whole had then to be kneaded with a skilful hand till it became a solid ball and ready to eat.

It was in the evening after arriving in camp that we had the only real meal of the day. I put such game as Peter had bagged, a cut of antelope, a wild goose, a hare or a duck—sometimes a pheasant—into the saucepan with strips of dough or rice. Occasionally our neighbours brought us a piece of wild ass or tame yak. Or perhaps a man who had had something wrong with him would want to show his gratitude for such care as I had been able to give him, and arrive with a little mutton or a plate of small cubes of the toasted bread that had taken the place of *manto*—town bread. Naturally, I carried my own store of onions and dried fruits. In addition to my saucepan I had a very original frying apparatus. At inns, the Chinese wash their hands and faces in a shining brass vessel with a flat bottom and a nearly vertical rim. It is less fragile and less cumbrous than an enamel basin, so I had bought one. It travelled inside the saucepan. Then in camp we filled it with lukewarm water and bathed our burning faces in it. At meal-times Li brought it to me again and then how the meat sizzled, how delicious the dried apricots became in butter! Never, I told Peter, recalling my earlier journeys, never had I lived so luxuriously as since I threw in my lot with an old Etonian!

Twice a day we had to feed the horses with barley and broken peas as hard as stones. One day when I was removing Slalom's nosebag I discovered one of his molars in it.

Night would come at last and the wind which, all day long, had howled in our drumming ears, and, charged with dust or with snow, had burned our faces, now turned its fury on the tents that were intended more as a protection against its buffeting than against the cold.

To recall that life in this or that western capital fills me with yearning. But there, I was so completely absorbed in the life of the trail, the life of the beasts, of the elements, that it was as though I had always been living it. It was the west that seemed unreal. I so completely forgot it that memory made no effort to bring it back, even in dreams.

I Become a Doctor.

Li told tales of the marvels in our boxes. We had a box that made music! We had numerous medicines! There was nothing to do but satisfy our fellow-travellers' curiosity. My "Mikiphone" gramophone had to be played for them. There were only three records, but the joy of the listeners each time when it came to the sung passages!

Day after day there was a sick parade outside my tent. Some cases were genuine, some not. I treated wounds with permanganate and iodoform. When I found myself in a difficulty I consulted my list of medicaments with a serious air. Those who had stomach troubles were given castor oil, those who complained of being "very hot and then very cold" got quinine. When they had coughs or their rheumatic pains were bad—as, in view of the Mongol fashion of leaving the chest and one shoulder bare, they must sometimes be bad—they received some "Jintan" pills—a Japanese panacea for everything, the chief ingredient of which is liquorice. The eyes of some of the Mongols had long been red and swollen from the acrid smoke of the argols and I showed them how to bathe them with a little cotton-wool steeped in tea. One day I lanced an abscess on a swollen hand with a razor-blade. To get that filthy hand clean I had to bathe it for half an hour in water that was almost boiling.

It is said that the Mongols do not wash themselves for fear of being turned into fishes when they die. They also believe spring water to be full of evil spirits. Does it not issue from the interior of the earth where the female principle rules? That principle becomes good only when it is exposed to the action of the air and the sun, these being part of the male world of the upper regions. However, the unheard-of dirt of the Mongols is not so revolting in winter, for the cold reduces the stink of the rancid butter in which their coats are literally soaked almost to nothing.

CHAPTER XIII

THE TANGUTS' COUNTRY

WE were now, on leaving the Koko Nor, about to cross the land of the Tanguts. In the eleventh century this dreaded people, then called *Hsi-hsia*, played a part in the history of Asia. Their Tibetan realm extended to the south of Mongolia and it was in the course of an attempt to conquer them that Jenghiz Khan, "The Inflexible Emperor," died. According to Marco Polo, his knee was pierced by an arrow. Since then, foreign travellers who have crossed the wild Tangut country have told of attacks made on them or of the precautions against attacks they had to take. They have also described the sacrifices offered to evil spirits by their native servants. Even to-day the Chinese inhabiting the Gobi oases at the foot of the Nan Shan mountains live in fear of the Tangut robbers who hide in those terrifying, snowy regions.

Smig, himself, had told me that the region to the south of the Koko Nor was dangerous. He had been attacked by horse-thieves. It was only in big caravans that one could travel there.

"When you are crossing the Tangut country," he told us, "stow your money away in the flour bags. That is the safest hiding place. At night those daring fellows come creeping round, throttle the watch-dogs, and take the camp by surprise." Sure enough, Li insisted on piling boxes, bags and suit-cases inside the tent in which he also fixed himself up a place to sleep—on the bag of broken peas intended for the horses! The horses' fetters were locked on them, and all

95

night long the watchmen walked up and down the camp, giving raucous cries—I think to show they were not asleep. Peter refused to be impressed. Two minutes after lying down he was fast asleep. But I was obsessed by the stories I had read and I would lie listening to the wind that, like a gigantic bellows, shook our frail tent at every gust. It was a bit like lying at anchor in a small sailing boat, and brought back memories of a few terrific squalls when the mistral was blowing at Porquerolles and at Rosas; and thoughts, too, of the south-westerly gale that drove the *Atalanta* aground off Yarmouth. But here at least I could feel free of that kind of uneasiness. It was much to have the sense of security that the earth gives by feeling it beneath one.

One evening I was writing up my notes when I heard men running and my Mongol neighbours crying out. Outside, sparks were leaping in the grass, a white mist of smoke was spreading and the ground was blackening before one's eyes. Men were stamping with their feet or beating the earth with sheepskins and pieces of felt in an effort to divert the fire from the tents which were in its path. They were not, unfortunately, able to save the dried grass. As if in play, the wind was driving the flames towards the mountains. The camels were staring at the approach of the dangerous thing, and as camels' wool is most inflammable they had to be driven into safety.

It was a week since we had left Tangar. Now we turned our backs on the Koko Nor and set off south, towards strange, smoking mountains with all their grasses scorched and dry. We were coming to regions which were only very vaguely defined in the Indian Survey maps.* For several days we were to come on no human beings, though, according to the map, with its few black dots (signifying camping grounds),

* The indications given by Sven Hedin have never, it seems, been confirmed by the Calcutta Office.

we should be in inhabited country. Going across a deserted world must, we felt, be desolation. The blackened mountains, of which only the ridges caught the light, were like a vision of another universe, like the negative of a photograph of a winter landscape. It was from a hill-top, in pallid sunlight, that I laid my eyes for the last time on the snow-covered stretch of the lake.

Wild Asses.
Peter was right. The Tangut brigands did not find us out. At over 13,000 feet we crossed the first mountain pass. It was pretty steep and was called, I think, Tsakassu. Here and there lay the carcasses of dead camels. Our camels had to stop for breath every twenty paces. Once over, we began to descend again towards the vast desert plain of Dubusun. Far in front a white line quivered like a mirage above the yellow earth. What could it be?

The next day, after a slow advance, I found I had lost a bet. The line was not a salt deposit at the foot of the mountain, but the ice on a lake which is supposed to have an outlet that, after flowing through the land of the Panakas, reaches the Yellow River. The Panakas are Tibetans and it was from them that our friends the Mongols of the Tsaidam copied the fashion of pointed hats with straight brims.

In the bare steppe nothing grew but some furze, the thorns of which had tufts of wool, torn from camels' legs, hanging on them. The light was so blinding and the wind so cold that one of Peter's eyes became inflamed and streaming. He agreed to wear my snow glasses. I did not hand them over without delivering a sermon, remonstrating with him for his imprudence and reminding him of the presumptuous words he had uttered in Peking:

"*I* never wear glasses."

At the summit of the second pass—which was rather low—

our friend Gunzun threw a propitiatory pebble on a great "obo," one of the mounds of stones that, following a custom thousands of years old, are piled up at intervals along the highways of Asia.

Arrived in the middle of the new plain, we waited for the caravan. A little further on, the Prince, facing towards Lhasa, was at his prayers, with Gunzun holding his horse at a respectful distance. Whether because he was timid or whether he was anxious not to commit himself with foreigners whose aims were dubious, the Prince continued to keep himself to himself. Only once had he made any overtures to us, and then only from a desire to handle Peter's gun.

Peter and I were talking.

"What wouldn't I give now," said he, "to see a waiter appearing with a mountain of scrambled eggs and slices of chicken in one hand and to-day's *Times* in the other!"

I agreed about the eggs—but *The Times!* To me Europe seemed so far away that it might as well be dead. I could not understand his wanting *The Times*.

It was very cold and that night I heard wolves. Just as they did all day, the Mongols went about with chest and shoulder bared at five o'clock in the morning when they were loading up the camels. I saw them putting blocks of ice into sacks. It meant that there was no water where we were to camp in the evening.

The horses marched uneasily over ground that, here and there, rose in swellings which gave way under their feet. In every direction there were marks—wide arrows within circles—of the hoofs of wild asses.

For several days there had been talk of these *kulans*. Now suddenly Li, who was riding beside me, cried: "There are some!" At first I could only make out, far away, a series of light specks that might have been antelopes. Then, raising spirals of dust, the pretty creatures fled, but in single file and at a regular distance from each other, their proud heads held high and their manes erect—like an archaic frieze.

A few days later, when I was already feeling glad that Peter had not succeeded in shooting one of them—he would have had to use the heavy rifle, which was erratic—a few Chinese horsemen of the caravan went flying past us like a whirlwind. We followed and came up with a group that had formed round a wounded kulan. It had had its leg broken by a disagreeable old Tungan riding a horse that was fitted with a silvery bell. The wretched kulan had its hoof hanging on by a piece of skin. But with gratuitous cruelty the men were whipping it. They slipped a halter on it and it managed a few steps on the stump of its leg. Then it fell. Its eyes were distended and moving backwards and forwards in a vain appeal for help. It had a great head on a wide neck. The ears were small, the muzzle white. The belly also was white, but the rest of the coat was fawn-coloured. From the short mane, dark and stiff, a brown line ran to the tail, a donkey's tail. In the end the men plunged a knife deeply into its throat. The thick, greasy blood spurted out as from a fountain, continuing for a long time to make a dark, widening pool. To stop the beast's convulsions the men sat on it and at last the legs stiffened suddenly and it died.

Kulans cannot be tamed, but the meat is much appreciated and everybody rejoiced at the prospect of a banquet. Now, also, there would be new leather to tie about the feet of the "Wawas,"* who were doing the whole journey on foot. And there would be bands of thick fur for the ornamentation of the harness, as tradition demanded there should be.

---

* "Wawa" is a name by which Chinese children are called. Amongst us it was applied to the boys who travelled with the gold-seekers.

CHAPTER XIV

Entering the Tsaidam

IT was not long after that scene of carnage that we watered our horses for the first time in a clear river with a gravel bed. No sooner, however, had I put Slalom to cross it than he sank up to the breast in shifting ground. Not to weigh him down, I leaped from the saddle. But I fell into the water. The frightened animal dragged himself out, but of course dragged his trappings with him and my sheepskin sleeping-bag and saddle-bag, with my file of notes, my camera and negatives, were soaked and dripping.

And that night I slept in a violent stink of damp sheepskin. My sleeping-bag was not well tanned and half of it had now grown as hard as an old shoe. And then we were camped in the depths of a gorge through which an icy wind went whistling. But the nightmares I had were, I imagine, due rather to eating the tough meat of the wild ass, of which the men had given us some.

Trees.

Leaving the camels to go round by the valley of the River Tsarsa, we followed "The Arab" up a mountain. There we had an unforgettable surprise. In a little valley sheltered from the west wind we found a strip of pasture grass, green and as fine as hair, growing at the foot of some real trees, the only ones we were to see in the course of that journey to Turkestan. Our joy was so great that we forgot to chase off a magpie which was devouring the red pieces of wild ass meat loaded on a pony. Beside us, the twisted trunks of the juniper trees disappeared up into their greenery and the fire we made of the beautiful wood gave off an odour that suggested a Tibetan temple. I was told that juniper is, in fact, a very precious tree and that the lamas use it for incense.

The morning passed as quickly as a dream. We had to go down the other side of the mountain in a cloud of dust, and then, once more, we were on a blistered, yellow table-land. It was bordered with abrupt, eroded mountains on which nothing grew. The great trail from Dulan to Lhasa by Barun wound through here and I even thought I saw traces of the plough. Yes, I was right. There were field shapes, a wall, an earthen roof. We were at Kharakhoto. The sense of astonishment I felt on seeing the house made me realize that I had not expected to see any houses here in the north of Tibet.

Though I wanted to see a Tibetan hut, I felt unable to go with Peter and Li when they went to buy a sack of barley for the horses. Since its immersion in the river my saddle was broken in two and I spent the best part of the ride sitting on Slalom's hindquarters. Now I was worn out. I lacked even the courage to deal with my patients.

Peter was under the impression that somebody had said we were not far from Dzun, our first objective, and rejoiced. Soon we should be alone on the trail. Camping in the evening we should no longer have to wait for our camels to come up—often they were right at the end of the caravan. And in the morning there would be no more camel-drivers pulling the baggage out of our hands before we had even breakfasted.

Tibetan Caravan.

On the morning of the 10th of April I saw half a dozen poles far away against the sky. Were they telegraph poles?

No. When we got nearer we saw that the rope stretching from one to the other only served to suspend streamers covered with sacramental formulæ which the wind, blowing the streamers, had the task of transmitting to the gods. The shoulder-blades of sheep were fixed to the poles themselves. The trail rose gently and wound amongst these primitive decorations. Then, suddenly, a region without any mountains opened out before us. We had arrived at the Tsaidam plateau! There, on the edge of it, I prayed the gods of this new land to deal gently with two ignorant children of the White Race.

An imposing caravan approached. There were long-haired yaks, heavily loaded, and camels, horses, black dogs, women with babies at the breast. . . . Nearly everybody wore splendid caps of lynx and fox-skin. The newcomers' rearguard was, however, held up at a large irrigation ditch which frightened the camels. They knew their soft, wide feet would slip on the humid clay. One of them just missed leaping it and its hind legs sank up to the belly in the yellow water. It got its knees on to the bank, however, and the owners, a man and woman, proceeded to relieve it of its load. Then, one pulling it by the nose, the other raising the hind-quarters by pulling at the tail, they got the soaking animal out of its distressful plight. Two roguish little girls, with faces the colour of breadcrust, laughed timidly under the broad brims of their dark orange pointed velvet hats. They had their hair in masses of little plaits and like their mother wore big Mongol cloaks. But the mother also wore, hanging down her back, a panel of embroidered material on which a dozen hemispheres, the largest of them as big as soup-bowls, were worked in *repoussé*. These primitively luxurious ornamentations which visibly incommoded the good lady when it came to loading the camel must have constituted a fair part of her fortune.

I galloped off to rejoin my own caravan, which was already so far off as to look like a moving frieze away to the southwest. But in the yard before a mud hut which had Chinese lattice-work windows I saw Li's horse. And, sure enough, there, in front of a Mongol yurt, was Li, smiling through his half-closed eyes, and inviting me to join two women with kalpaks of white lamb on their heads in a bowl of tea with milk. In another yard adjoining, a young Tibetan girl with a long beautiful face was spinning, her eyes, however, fixed on me. She had a tent of brown woollen material, quite different from the felt yurt of my two hostesses. Hers was kept spread out tight by the hair-ropes that held it, and looked like a great pinned insect.

Then turning aside for ever from the road to Lhasa that ran left, I trotted away through meadow land. Partridges ran to cover amongst the grasses. A lark sang. But Slalom fled from some big dogs which, in spite of Gunzun and his horse-whip, attacked us.

From now on everything was going to be different. We should have to cross a *gobi* (desert) in forced marches. Once again we collected blocks of ice from a river bank in anticipation of waterless ways. There was beautiful sunshine and at the midday halt we were able to unsaddle and make cocoa to drink with our tsamba. Usually I flavoured the tsamba with sugar and raisins, but that day Peter made an innovation and seasoned his strips of dough with vinegar and Worcester sauce.

The Prince and his wise men had just instituted a court of justice, for during the morning there had been a quarrel in the course of which a Chinese horseman had been attacked with a whip by a Mongol. I had thought it was some cruel game cherished amongst the children of the steppe. But there was more than that to it. Somebody was accused of stealing a horse. At that very moment "The

103

Arab" (whom, it appeared, I had cured with castor oil) was defending his compatriot. I understood nothing of what was said, but it appeared the Mongols had been mistaken. The Prince, who, as always, kept his dignity, was obliged to hand over two pieces of material as compensation for the wrong done by one of his suite. After an exchange of katags and salutations, everybody went away content, but I wondered whether the Prince had not, against his convictions, cut the case short, knowing that it would be unwise to alienate the Chinese merchants, since everybody owed them money.

No sooner was the trial over than we set off on our difficult march again. Our horses were sinking in the sand and to spare them we got off and walked. The march lasted all day and part of the night. It was tiring and I envied those who were riding on camels. The Prince was bandy-legged from riding, and when he walked the many folds of his short cloak gave the impression of a man wearing a kilt. About the beasts and also around some tamarisk bushes the dust created a cloud that the sunset transformed into a rainbow-tinted veil.

It was near midnight when we got to sleep. For once we had not the tent between our eyes and the stars. The dry air of the high table-land made these latter look as though they were streaming over the sky.

The next day our forced march was continued through a landscape of scrub and brushwood: high tufts of yellow grass, stunted bushes, and ground heavily cracked by the drought. There was no water for the animals. This state of things disagreed with Slalom. He was growing thin before my eyes and his saddle-girth now buckled at the last hole. Nor was Peter's eye improved by the dust. I tried to blacken the glasses he had bought at Sining with a candle. Most of our Tungan companions wore yellow Chinese spectacles.

Our great caravan was breaking up gradually, though

nowhere did I see any sign of the thing suggested to my mind by the words "pasture land." Then, unexpectedly, the wind brought a damp, slimy smell, the smell of a seaport. And near two felt yurts I was surprised to see the yellow waters of the Bayan Ho flowing between their flat banks. The fording point was discovered, and we crossed. We camped on ground that was uneven and white with salt. Sheep trailed over it dismally.

CHAPTER XV

The Houses at the End of the World

IT was two months since we had left Peking, sixteen days after leaving Tangar, that we reached Dzun. A windowless cube rose out of the plain. "That's the Dzun cinema," said Peter. "We'll have a gay evening there!" But it was a deserted lama temple. There were a few huts about it. We were to spend four days in one of them, for Li had to find camels to take us to Teijinar.

Dzun* is about two miles from the edge of the great marshy plateau of the Tsaidam, which is over 400 miles long and about 125 across. The earth there is saturated with salt, and rare groups of Mongols find pasture land only at the foot of the surrounding mountains, where a few rivers opportunely descend. To the south rises the chain of the Burkhan Buta, constituting a buttress to a huge uninhabited region of Tibet.

Our Mongol travelling companions set off for their invisible camps. The horses disappeared in quest of some better pasture than was provided by the bare plain of Dzun. But the gold-seekers remained settled by the walls of our habitation. They also had to get camels to go on.

A tall, toothless old man often came to see us. For hours he would absently turn his prayer-wheel, all the time watching Peter copying out his notes of the journey on the typewriter. *The Times* special correspondent preparing his weekly column of news from the Tsaidam!

---

* The name means "left," having the same etymological derivation as Dzungaria, the name of the country to the north-west of Sinkiang.

HOUSES AT THE END OF THE WORLD

The mud huts of Dzun were used as a warehouse by some Chinese merchants during the good business period. One of the merchants was a young man who had a seven-years-old abscess on his thigh and whom I had treated every day. He rode with his bad leg turned back on the pommel of the saddle and I had not been able to give him more than temporary relief. He invited us now to eat mien with meat, and we gave him some letters to send by the next caravan going to Tangar. The stores here included bricks of tea, flour, cloths, needles, thread and coloured silks for embroideries, wooden bowls, sugar and boots. The bricks of tea cost six Mexican dollars, two more than at Sining. Money was still in circulation.

In summer there is a going and coming of people at Dzun, and some of the huts are used by nomads who come for supplies. As I chanced to explore the ruins I came suddenly on two shrivelled old men sitting at their one-day fireside. They offered me the customary tea with milk. It was a pity we could not talk. They would doubtless have been able to tell me of the splendours of the Panchen Lama's caravan which had passed near here some years before on its way to Peking.

In winter, only three old women stay at Dzun. I passed one of them, a gnarled old thing with shrunken naked breasts outside her sheepskin coat. Her chocolate skin, with the marks of cuts showing violet, made a Gauguinesque colour scheme . . .

On the edge of the desert rose the only storeyed building of the settlement, the abandoned temple. I collected the contents of a prayer-wheel there. They consisted of a roll of paper made from rind on which the printed characters jostled each other irregularly. On the roof, over the entrance, two sacred antelopes adorned the Wheel of the Law. The metal in which these symbolic figures were cast glittered in the sun. I sat by them a long time, dreaming in the brilliant glare.

The mountains on the south had disappeared behind a veil of dust and, as from the poop of a ship, I could see the whole circle of the horizon. In that vast desert, beneath that vibrant sky, the soul seemed to become concentrated within itself and for a moment I had an extraordinarily intense feeling of being remote from everything and everybody I knew, as though I were at the uttermost limit of my own being.

A deep, lugubrious sound broke in suddenly on my contemplations. I got down. Before a house a bareheaded lama was blowing into a shell. A few aromatic twigs were burning in a bowl on a whitewashed earthen pedestal. The tails of yaks hung on metal tridents placed on the roof, at the four corners of the house. I followed the lama into a big room where four wooden pillars supported the ceiling. The lama sat down on the ground, Turkish fashion. The only furniture was a stool in front of him with the instruments of the ritual placed on it. On the wall hung a delicate painting on silk of a Buddhist pantheon, the colour scheme being in pink, blue and green.

The lama prayed in a quick chant with well-marked rhythm. He punctuated the phrases by, in turn, striking cymbals, ringing a bell, and tapping a drum, or simply by making gestures with his fingers. He had delicate hands, a conjurer's hands, which he held in imitation of the Buddha gestures, but he did not feel bound to refrain from holding out one of them for an offering, and did so with a smile. Then he went on with his ritual. From time to time I noticed that he threw some grains of corn behind him mechanically.

Having examined the room, walking round on my toes, I went further and found myself in a small court where there was a ladder. I climbed up and came to a tiny recess full of the perfume of incense and with the walls covered with banners and paintings on silk. Butter-lamps glimmered on two little altars. Suddenly, with that oriental gesture of holding the hand with the open palm downwards and then closing the fingers on it, the lama summoned me. I came down and he escorted me out, courteously, but commanding silence by putting his finger to his lips.

I did not need to waste much time on the surroundings of the settlement. There were pack-saddles in tatters, dead dogs and old shoes—battered tins are not yet to be found on the Tsaidam. And I was soon back in our dark, smoky interior. The Urechs had given us several enthralling crime stories. It was fortunate, because Peter is not very good at waiting about. And I was myself exasperated by the roof which seemed to be weighing down like a tomb on my head. Gunzun, who came with a katag and some milk from the Prince, asked for the cover of one of our story-books. It depicted a beautiful blonde lady flying along in a motor car. The Prince had reached his yurt and his fathers. He had given his last sign of life so far as we were concerned.

The Winds as Monarchs.

After a wait of four days, the gold-seekers went away with some ten yaks. But it was not long before Li turned up with four camels for us. I called them the negroids because they had black frizzy hair on their foreheads. But they were lanky and also they were casting their coats which, it is well known, greatly reduces a camel's strength.*

We returned to the trail, thinking joyfully that in a fortnight we should probably be with Smig's partner and getting news of what was happening in Sinkiang. Now and then we marched beside ledges of hills of loess that looked as if they had been cut with knives. In the hollows of them one could see trees twisted and dead of thirst. The mighty

* See note, p. 301.

wind which produces these hills raises great columns of sand that move before it.

The next day it was cold again and with some of the gold-seekers whom we overtook we burned some bushes to warm our hands. Li seemed to know the trail and announced that we should reach his brother's house that evening. He persuaded us to gallop over a desert of sand as flat as a hand. A "black gobi," he called it. After that there came tamarisk bushes not yet in leaf, a trickle of irrigation water, deserted fields, some sheep, a yurt . . . We were there.

All would have been well if only the camels, now unloaded, stayed with us as we expected they would. But no! They were going back to Dzun and Li informed us that new ones had to be found. . . . That was a disaster . . .

CHAPTER XVI

THE TAMARISK CAMP

IT was a disaster, because we were not the first travellers to try in vain to hire camels at that oasis of Nomo Khantara where there were so few inhabitants. Our immediate predecessors had also failed.

First there had been the chief of the gold-seekers, a thick-lipped Tungan, very carefully turned out. At Dzun he had said it would be a pleasure to travel with us, but then went ahead in order to secure the camels at Nomo Khantara before we could get them. However, even with a recommendation from the governor of the province, he had failed. Now he was extra polite to us and invited us to eat mutton with him. For he thought that on account of having special passports we must surely succeed in obtaining some pack animals.

Yet there were two lamas who had arrived from Lhasa a whole fortnight before and still unable to find means of getting to Tcijinar. If, in spite of the great respect that everything pertaining to religion inspires in the Mongols, camels could not be found for these holy men, what hope was there for us? The lamas were staying close by us, in a canvas tent decorated with beautiful patterns in black. Near a tamarisk their two horses were resting in an improvised stable consisting of a square ditch about five feet deep. One descended to it by a narrow sloping path closed with a great log of wood.

As if we had not troubles enough, Li announced that he was coming no farther. He had, he declared, carried out his contract, since we were at the first of the oases of the principality of Teijinar. And he added that if he were to come any further he would not dare return alone across the Tsaidam. Decidedly things were going wrong. And Peter and I used one argument after another on our serving man.

"Big brother, Li," we pleaded, "do you see that letter? At Lanchow we undertook to deliver it to Borodishin, who lives at Arakshatu near Teijinar. If we do not take it to him we shall to a serious degree 'lose face.'" (We had to be very careful not to suggest to Li that he knew he ought to guide us the whole way, for it would be betraying clearly that we thought he was tricking and good breeding does not allow such a suggestion to be made.)

"Listen, Lig'o! When we have spoken with Borodishin we shall know whether we can go hunting the wild yak in the mountains or whether we ought to go back to Tangar with you."

No doubt the lad had been got at by somebody, for until then he had been very proud to introduce us amongst the Mongols—explaining to them that we took such masses of photographs because the Tsaidam was utterly different from our own part of the world where the houses were so high that they hid the sun! Did Li guess that we had secret plans which might lead to his getting into trouble? And was there anyone else who was speculating uneasily about our plans?

The next day, taking care to keep out of the way of the thick-lipped Tungan, Peter went off with Li to interview the natives. He took all our passports with him. The Mongol Elder told him straight away how the matter stood. All the camels were in distant pasture lands and would not be in a state to take to the road again before the eighth moon, for the soles of their feet had been softened by the marshy soil. For the rest, the passport which had been given us at Sining, and of which Peter was so proud, was, in the eyes of the natives, useless, since it did not include the Tibetan translation that was obligatory.

Could it be that those charming people at Sining wanted to see us sent back towards civilization and had deliberately left it out?

In the end the Elder decided to hold a conference with his neighbours about us. Peter promised him a good present, either in tea or money.

Once more we had to wait. Patience was the quality of all others we were to acquire in that world.

Society Gossip.

Li's Mongol sister-in-law was a superior woman. Wisdom was written on her face and she was practised in the care of horses. Greys had developed bladder trouble and for two days he rolled on the ground in pain. The good woman managed to make him swallow a few drops of alcohol which she administered through the nostrils. It was a Chinese drink we carried in a cask and of which Peter imbibed half a glass each day at cocktail time.

The woman also brought us goat's milk and I called on her to express our thanks. Her fingers were heavily beringed with barbaric jewellery, but nevertheless it was with her fingers she stirred the fire under the tea-kettle. I played with three bleating newly-born lambs. Their droppings made a carpet as thick as it was odoriferous at the back of the yurt.

Gumbo, a baby boy, two years old, crawled round me on all fours. I shall always remember his astonished face and the burst of laughter with which he greeted the gay, syncopated rhythm of our American gramophone record:

> *The sun has got his hat on*
> *And is coming out to-day . . .*

When it was time to go I took off a necklace of red pearls

I was wearing, and to my hostess's delight gave it to her. Throughout the entire journey I travelled elegantly adorned with some piece of jewellery of that kind, so as to have it to offer any woman whom there was occasion to thank. When I was in the tent I was often interrupted in the course of my housekeeping by visits from our lama neighbours. At our first encounter they enquired whether we were not Japanese, and we of course hastened to correct any such impression. As early in the journey as Lanchow a policeman took us for Japanese. I can only suppose that in Central Asia the term Japanese is applied to any overseas foreigner.

One of the lamas, who had his head shaven and wore moustaches, was big, fat, jovial and as garrulous as a Marseillais. The other, his assistant, I imagine, had darker skin and was tall and thin. They would squat Turkish fashion on our felt rug and we exchanged politenesses with them.

"*Lo-t'o yo meyo.*"

("Are there camels or are there not?")

The invariable answer was that they had no camels. And then the fat lama would insist on pointing out Lhasa and Galin Kutta (Calcutta) on the map of Asia. He had stout fingers, but he could read the map and he had been to India. He begged to have my mirror as a souvenir of our meeting, but I put him off with an empty tin that had once contained tomato extract.

The first mosquitoes of the year appeared at Nomo Khantara and as I killed one on my arm the lama sadly reproved me. To show me how to act in such circumstances he took a sand-louse that was marching on to my rug and, handling it gently, deposited it outside the tent. Still I did see him scratch himself on occasion. He must certainly have had lice on him, and I wondered whether he took pains to treat them with such pre-eminently Buddhist gentleness.

The fat man was incapable of bending sufficiently to get out of the tent with ease and always as he departed I had to hold on to the centre pole lest he should bring it down completely with his behind, which his ample skirts and the folds of his russet toga enlarged from "full-size" to "colossal."

In his own tent, which smelt of butter and burnt pine-needles, I satisfied his craving to be photographed in ceremonial dress. Squatting before the sacred vessels which were worked in Derge silver, with a high mitre of yellow satin on his head, and holding leaves from the sacred books in his hands, he made an imposing figure. The vessels included bowls for offerings, a skull lined with silver for libations, a bell, a *dorji**, a little drum, peacock's feathers and a wreath with velvet petals, worn on the head. In his hieratic posture he was astonishingly like a Buddhist divinity.

As they could not obtain the camels they needed, the lamas decided to return to Lhasa, which was a bare forty days' journey away. It seemed like a chance for us. Why should we not set out with them if it proved to be impossible to proceed into Sinkiang?

Then, just as the lamas and I were leaving the tent after they told me of their decision, up came Peter with a hare and a pheasant he had just killed. Hm! I had grave doubts as to whether the lama would care for us as travelling companions, seeing how very much our customs clashed with his.

Dead City.

A drama developed. Two days before, one of the Wawas had gone out to look for wood and did not come back. At the gold-seeker's camp there were no lamentations—etiquette forbade it—but each day mounted men scoured the country and in the evening a great fire was lighted. On the third day

* Or sceptre, the masculine symbol and emblematic of Method. The bell is a feminine symbol, emblematic of Wisdom.

all hope was abandoned. The lad must inevitably be worn out and was doomed to die of inanition in the vast oasis where yurts were as rare as water. We knew nothing about him, whether he had parents, whether there was anyone to mourn for him, to weep over him.

I went, walking with Peter, to examine the deserted fortifications. And it was then I realized what a dangerous place our oasis was. Over miles of land, tamarisk trees, all exactly similar, rose every twenty yards. The ground was covered with a veritable network of sheep-tracks. Only with a compass could one be sure of finding one's way through such a labyrinth. The only presence in the innumerable, deserted alley-ways was that of the Demon of the Sands, who took the shape of a thick whirl of dust, an immense column, opening out to the sky and turning on its almost compact base, as, with a sinister noise, it moved along.

Rising abruptly from the ground was an embattled fort, the walls and posterns of which were in an excellent state of preservation. From the height of the inner parapet we looked down at the interior, a huge square, empty save for a few bushes. The annals mention that "long ago there were towns in the Tsaidam." But there was nobody to amplify that bald statement. The inhabitants of Nomo Khantara could give no help. "There used to be more *shinko* (barley) here," was all they knew. The walls seemed to be Chinese. Perhaps they were constructed in the course of some military expedition in the Tarim Basin. Or it may be that at some period Mongol incursions made the ordinary roads dangerous and a general chose to get to the west by the little-known Tsaidam. Or again, some columns might have been sent on ahead to prepare and gather in a harvest, and built the fort to protect themselves against bandits.

*   *   *   *   *

We had not abandoned hope of being able to continue on our way, even though Li held to his opinion of the Mongols of the country ahead. Li's brother, and then Li's brother's friend Tsogo, had, in turn, decided against acting as guide for us, and in the end Li himself agreed to remain in our service and come with us as far as the centre of Teijinar.

In preparation for our departure, which we insisted in believing would ultimately be arranged, I boiled five hares. Alas, the next morning, my store of cold game had disappeared, stolen, no doubt, by a cat. One or two backs were all I had to show for my labour of the previous evening. My vexation may be imagined. What made things worse was that, without knowing how, I had tried to make a lye-wash with ashes, and, instead of whitening our linen, had blackened it.

Peter was in as dark a mood as I. In his impatience he proposed leaving our stores with Li's sister-in-law and riding to ask the Prince of Teijinar for camels. The Prince lived a fortnight's ride away. We used to make bets as to when we should get off, and then Peter would return to his "Patience" as to a drug.

However, there was some hope that our last scene with the Elder of the oasis might bear fruit. Peter threatened that if we were not given the beasts we asked for everybody concerned would have cause to regret it. He would certainly lodge a complaint with the Governor. It was a dangerous game to play, possibly the game that, played in Northern Tibet in 1927, had cost the members of the Marteau expedition their lives. The Mongols might well strike at us so as to make sure that no complaint was lodged.

CHAPTER XVII

M O N O T O N Y

ON the 23rd of April I woke for the last time to the frantic bell-ringing of the lama performing his rites in his tent—it used to be our joke that his servant rarely seemed to take any notice of his summons. I say "for the last time" because the four camels we had ordered were at the door. They were hired to us only for six days and cost us our last three bricks of tea and all that was left of our *daliembu*. (Daliembu is dark cotton cut in squares. The shirts of the rich are made with it.) We wondered how we were going to manage without these commodities in regions where they constitute the only small change.

However, I was happy to be setting off again. The gold-seekers also were leaving, but on foot, and driving yaks laden with their flour before them. As we left the tamarisk oasis I could not but grieve for the fate of the poor Wawa. He had trudged along so bravely as far as that.

A few miles to the west of the oasis we were surprised to see a small mausoleum in the Turkish style rising out of the desolate plain. It was cubical in shape, built of brick, and surmounted by a half-ruined dome. Nomogon Khoto, they called it. The doorway looked south-east and the dome had collapsed on the north-west side. Legend has it that in the days when Gessar Khan was at war with the Khan of Shiragol, the latter was helped by an invincible sorcerer, whose prayers were all-powerful. But Damdin, Gessar's guardian spirit, resorted to stratagem. He sent two celestial crows to quarrel with each other on the sorcerer's roof, and the latter was so distracted by them that he broke off his incantations. Gessar was then able to attack the chapel and the sorcerer was killed by the falling bricks.*

Our trail was marked through marshy clay and as we went along Slalom dragged his feet out of it with an alarming noise as of suction. I was afraid of getting stuck and would only go on at the heels of some other animal of the caravan. How I wished that Slalom had webbed feet! The miry plain was dotted with pools of water and at the edge of each one a crust of salt glittered. I had no difficulty in collecting all I wanted for kitchen use.

We got on to drier ground. Now the path zigzagged between innumerable hillocks higher than a man, each one saved from erosion by a dead tamarisk. Then again it was the desolation of bare land extending as far as the eye could see.

Peter Gets Lost: The Dumb Wife.

With its back to the wind and open to the east, our tent let in the first rays of the morning sun. Breakfast over, Peter, with his gun under his arm, usually set off on foot in front of the caravan in quest of game. It would be two or three hours before I saw him again. But riding at the head of the column so as to escape the dust, I could make out his tracks on the ground. I envied him the sensations of the hunter, and the only distraction I had was tracking him from the column. But one day I lost his tracks. No doubt he had taken some other path. No doubt, either, he must have gone north, where it was very marshy. At the end of a two hours' march, as the caravan was going to be hidden by high dunes, I grew uneasy, so I made Slalom climb the highest dune and there I stayed, planted like a signal, until Peter appeared, at first no bigger than a black speck, moving slowly towards

* Tsybikof's *Journey to Lhasa.*

me across the flat immensity. He was dragging along the haunch of an antelope—the whole animal would have been too heavy. And that evening, by the banks of the muddy River Tukhte, we ate the most delicious roast I have ever tasted.

We were approaching the River Naichi, where we must find new camels. I was thinking about this when our cameldriver, whose sad face I had already noticed, began to speak of his wife. A year before she had suddenly been stricken dumb. If we could cure her, his camels and all he had were ours. We should be passing within a few hours' march of his yurt. He would go home for her overnight and bring her for me to see.

A wild hope rose in me. I had no remedy for the stricken woman. But was it not possible, seeing that her dumbness had come on her suddenly, that she might, if some nervous shock could be produced, recover her speech in the same way? A poor Mongol who had never seen a foreigner! She would have faith in European medicines. What else is cure by suggestion? I expounded my idea to Peter. Everything depended on him and me. If we made up our minds that we were going to succeed, we must inspire confidence in the patient from the moment she set eyes on us. A dose of any one of our remedies—it did not matter which—would carry the day.

Alas! No sooner did the patient put her foot on the ground than I realized how vain were my hopes. She was not only dumb but had her right arm paralysed. She wore a blouse inside her sheepskin cloak. And her body was clean. Impassive of face—she had regular features—she slowly took in everything that was happening. Not to disappoint her completely, I gave her a pill, and hoped she could read from my face the sympathy I felt for her.

With resignation the husband came on with us, the wife returning home alone.

*   *   *   *   *

Meanwhile the days were becoming warmer and warmer. Peter's nose grew sore from sunburn, and the Tungans protected their lower lips with pieces of paper. It made them look like clowns. Li made himself a visor out of a picture of a top-hatted detective called "Victor of the Smart Set," and held it in place by stuffing it in under his skull cap.

I let the caravan go on ahead, for I wanted, without getting off my horse, to take my first sunbath of the year. The scent of my burnt skin brought back certain summers of my life, just as the mountains, a long spur of which jutted out into the plain, brought back the north coast of Majorca and Port Soller—only the previous summer I had had such difficulty in steering my sailing boat into that harbour. Suddenly I descried one of our camels. He must have fallen out of the column when nobody was paying attention. Remaining in my saddle I rode up with a view to taking him along on lead, Mongol fashion, but just as I was about to seize his halter, Slalom took fright, reared, threw me, and bolted off by himself. Now I had two beasts to catch. Fortunately Li had dallied also—with a smiling Mongol woman who was minding lambs—and he came to the rescue.

But we were not at the end of our troubles. That same day Peter killed a hare and, sitting on the edge of the trail, smoking his pipe, waited for his pony to come up. But he was not into the saddle before Greys, taking fright at the dead hare, bolted and threw him on his head to the ground. It took Li and me a long time to capture that black devil of a pony.

Except for these rare incidents, the monotony of the

journey was extreme. To the south there were great mountains but only twice did they reveal their snowy summits. I believe that if there had been flowers or pebbles on the ground I should have collected them for no other reason than to occupy my time.

Gorumu.

Our camp on an island in the river Naichi was delightful. For once, we had running water, so to speak, laid on. Our Tungan acquaintances were going to stay on to prospect in the region. Their headman always called me by my Chinese name, Ma Ya Na, whereas the others always spoke of me as "The Frenchwoman." Li called Peter *Musseh*, the form of address always used in speaking to missionaries in China.

I have, regretfully, to declare that Musseh did not think it worth his while to follow my good example and take a bath in a natural basin near our tent. The farthest he would condescend to go was to allow me to wash his shirt in it.

Li went off to make enquiries and came back with the news that our new camels would not be available for three days. I quickly decided to turn the delay to account. The Naichi issued from the mountains to the south and one of the trails leading to Lhasa wound up the river valley. Ever since we reached the flat solitude of the Tsaidam those mountains had been beckoning to me, but there was no persuading Peter to sacrifice a week to exploring, and I had given up the hope of getting to know them. Now, with my rucksack on my back I could spend three days in going, at any rate, some little distance, up the valley. It was a way of becoming my own master again, of ceasing to be a mere fragment of a caravan. Of course Peter was chivalrous and pretended that I was very useful, but he could not realize how much I longed to shake off the inertia that had taken hold of me since I began travelling with him. I no longer took the lead, no longer shouldered any responsibility. I was one of a group, and my capacity for decision was blunted.

But it was no use. Peter returned from his hunting, happy at having had a good day while I minded the house—for Li too had been away. Peter said he wanted to get on. He cherished a dubious theory about luck and at every stop he invented variations on it. He held that it was reasonable to anticipate a favourable turn of the wheel of our fortunes, that in view of the numerous difficulties we had had to overcome since we set out, we must inevitably and soon strike a series of strokes of luck.

Peter had just been seeing a lama in a tent where—a by no means normal phenomenon—there was a watch. The lama told him that the Prince of Teijinar, whose name was Dorji Teiji, had gone away, to Ghass. Now Ghass Kul is the last oasis in the west of the Tsaidam on the trail that leads to Turkestan. The Prince's setting out on such a journey implied a possibility that communications with the great adjoining province—the goal of our journey—were being re-established.

Amurh Saïn.

The next day we paid a visit to the Sleeping Beauty, a laughing Mongol woman whom Peter had discovered asleep in the sun beside her sheep. The Mongols of the Tsaidam, when they arrive at a yurt, utter the greeting: *"Amurh saïn,"* which means "Good luck" or "A blessing on your flocks." Then the guest sits, Turkish fashion, on the ground, to the left of the fire, which is the noble section of the habitation, for there, set against the wall, is the bracket on which are placed the sacred book and the little cups of offerings filled with butter or water. That bracket and its burden constituted the only difference between the Mongolian Buddhist yurts and the Kirghiz Moslem yurts which I knew so well.

The Beautiful Mongol was pleased to satisfy my desire to see her jewels. They were coarse things, rings and long earrings. She kept them in a chest. A widow, she must yet have been comfortably off, for she had sugar candy, which she broke for us, and biscuits from Sining. As a good hostess she served enormous quantities of tsamba, but I did not feel equal to taking much of her butter, which was several months old and which she kept preserved in a sheep's stomach. It was the colour a jelly-fish goes when left derelict on the seashore and it tasted like cheese gone wrong.

Peter behaved as if everything was perfect, but for once it was not easy to swallow the tsamba we had learned to like so much.

False Start.

Within two days, and contrary to my prognostications, we were once more following the road to the west behind a couple of camels and a small boy. A third camel was waiting for us somewhere. Peter was enjoying a modest triumph. This time we were sure of making Arakshatu, where Borodishin ought to be.

But after two hours' going our baggage was dumped near a lonely yurt and there a comedy on classical lines was gone through.

The boy disappeared in search of the third camel—it was quite near.

Day turned to night and night to day again.

In the morning, a woman came to say that the cameldriver's tsamba and clothes were not quite ready. About eleven o'clock word was sent us that the camels had strayed. Peter was at his two hundredth game of "Patience."

There was one consolation, however. Peter was discovering that he had a genius for trading. He had just swapped our only glass for two squares of pink satinette which would come in useful for Mongols from whom we wanted to buy *chorma*—white, faded crumbs of milk and dried butter.

At last, an elderly Mongol carrying a bag of tsamba appeared out of the noonday light. A few drooping hairs on either side of his mouth constituted a moustache—as in modern illustrators' ideas of the Huns—and I christened him *The Tom Cat*. His eyes rose at the corners and he kept them half closed against the glare of the light. He was naked to the waist. The rite necessary for good fortune had to be gone through. He moved, burning pine-twigs that smoked aromatically, backwards and forwards under the camels' noses, reciting some sacramental formulæ at the same time.

Meantime Li with an air of great consequence was busying himself about his latest acquisition, a young in-calf camel. Her legs were so crooked that it was impossible to look at her without laughing.

The six following days we spent crossing a land which frequently had the aspect of a desert and which was of a deadly monotony. My only amusement was the study of Slalom's shadow. During the morning it moved slowly from the left to the right of his head, for our course was what sailors call north of west. We marched practically all day and I must have been tired because I remember that one day I felt I could not bear the interminable chatter (in mile-long sentences) of our good Li, though he was exchanging confidences not with me but with a Mongol. I would willingly have done something drastic to the latter.

There came an evening when, contrary to his promise, The Tom Cat could not find a watering point. After wandering about till nightfall we had to pitch our camp tea-less. This led to an innovation. We used brandy in mixing the tsamba. The result was exactly like bad *baba au rhum*.

Another day as I was preparing a duck for cooking I found

six yolks of eggs inside it. They were graded in size and in perfect alignment. I don't think there were ever fresher or more delicious eggs than those. It was on the same day we discovered that we had spent Easter at the tamarisk oasis.

The first couple of hours' ride was always beautiful. The early morning sun played with the deep shadows of the mountains. Then the light would grow whiter and everything turned to boredom. I had to have recourse to various pastimes. First I would let the reins hang loose on Slalom's neck and manicure my nails with the greatest care. Then I combed my hair and made a long job of "doing" it. Yet still there was time to kill. I had some ideas that I wanted to work out, such as estimating the loss of time our journey represented; or comparing the advantages and disadvantages of a Mongol's life and a Parisian working-man's life; or the relative values of our civilization. But I could not reason. My brain was not functioning well. When I realized this it depressed me. I said to myself that a really clever person ought to be able to get as good work out of his brain in the Tsaidam as in prison. How often had I not anathematized life in Europe because in the rush of it I could not think! Now I found that only the preoccupations of material existence counted for me.

At last the long anticipated moment for the "ten o'clock" would come and I took a pellet of tsamba, saved over from breakfast, out of my pocket. I made that last as long as possible. Peter would come along to see whether I had kept a few raisins for him. But they were not enough to satisfy his gnawing hunger and by eleven o'clock we would find ourselves launched on the daily discussion about our evening meal. Peter had a passion for curry and I could get anything I wanted from him if I promised to have it for supper. He would get the nails out of the cases. He would grind the pepper. He would let me use the cleaning rod of his gun as a skewer in cooking. But one's hunger was not always lulled to sleep by deciding about the menu. When that happened we would recall the savour of meals eaten at such and such restaurants in the past. And then it was not long before memories of exquisite dishes gave place to those of colossal "gorges" enjoyed in childhood. Peter would remember "high teas" consisting of mountains of sausages with mashed potatoes, followed by such cake and such chocolate as exist only at Eton. And I would elaborate on the *roschtis* with eggs and bacon I had devoured in Swiss inns after ski-ing tours.

Slalom had all my sympathy at such times. For he too was hungry and would snap at an odd blade of dried grass as we went along. It was hard that he should have to trample on food, that I gave him no time to gratify his appetite.

At midday we halted, made tea or cocoa and had it with tsamba. I might also have the distraction of plucking a grey goose or a brown duck. After riding through deserted regions for a day or two the sight of a camel's hump showing above a bush would suddenly give me the sense of returning to a civilized country.

Getting Nearer.

Li was kneading flour to make mien when a group of well-dressed Mongols came to call. We were in the midst of our smiles to each other when one of them, admiring my frying-pan, uttered the Russian word *kharacho,* meaning "good." Here in the depths of the Tsaidam he could have learned it only from Borodishin, the one foreigner in the country. We were approaching our goal.

But there was still a plain to be crossed, a plain of earth that was as grey, flat and bare as the sea. It was a cloudless morning and I felt myself at peace with the world, asking myself what could be as satisfying in a perfectly empty immensity.

The next day we were at the middle of a patch of vegetation

when I noticed two camels disguised oddly as ladies in petticoats. Going nearer I saw that each had a bag sown into the wool of its hump and hanging to the ground over its hindquarters. Li explained that they had both given birth to Wawas and were now convalescing.

Then we were in pasture land where there were sheep and where hares, wild duck and storks ran about. They were so plentiful that Peter would not shoot any more, on the ground that it would not be sporting.

From a shepherd we learned that we should find our Russian's yurt at Arakshatu, twenty *lis* further west. Here, we were at Hajjar in the territories of the Prince of Teijinar.

The plain was cut by numerous trails. I saw groups of yurts, and traces of them—great circles of beaten earth surrounded by thick layers of goat droppings. Dogs answered the barking of other dogs.

To dissimulate the feeling of anxiety that gained on us both as we approached one of the crucial moments of our journey, Peter cracked jokes. At last he was going to meet the blonde Russian countess hung with jewels whom the agents of the Third International would not fail to send to meet him at the capital city of the Tsaidam. . . .

Our fate would depend on what Borodishin said. We should know that very day. We must, before he had time to dissuade us, make it clear that, no matter what it cost, we meant to go on. But would he be the man to face it? Would he understand our craving to get to Sinkiang? And then we wondered whether, supposing that war still raged round Cherchen, it would be crazy of us to try and cross Tibet instead of returning over the lugubrious Tsaidam.

We were nearing the end of the first part of our journey—the Russian yurt at Teijinar which, at Peking, it had seemed to Smig the simplest matter in the world to reach. Beyond was the unknown. But echoes of the political situation in Turkestan must surely have filtered through. We were going to find out.

PART II

THE UNFORESEEN

CHAPTER I

BORODISHIN

W E found out nothing—nothing more than we had known at Peking three months earlier. We rode, at a trot, round a marsh full of molehills and turning green under the first spring grass. At the other side two yurts were planted on the rounded back of a bare patch of earth. A felt curtain in the doorway of the smaller one was raised by somebody coming out, and without realizing I was doing so I cried out:

"*Borodishin! Zdravstvuite!*"

He was a little man with a black, square-cut beard and kind brown eyes, dressed as a Mongol except for the little Tatar cap perched on the top of his head. His partner, Wang, came and stood beside him, a Chinaman with a face like a squirrel and wearing a working-man's cap—truly an odd figure.

The horses were unsaddled, fettered and turned out on the fresh grass of the marsh.

Inside the yurt, over a fire of brushwood, Boro—as we came to call him—was soon cooking *aladis** and at the same time reading Smig's account of his set-back at Lanchow and of our plans. Shimi, the speckled cat, was dozing beside me.

"So you want to go on to Sinkiang and India," Boro observed.

"That would be impossible," Wang interrupted.

"No," Boro said, "not for them. They have all the passports they need."

* Strips of dough fried in fat.

131

What should we not have given for the honest man's statement to be true? But, fearful of alarming him, we left it so. What we wanted most to know was his estimate of our chances of getting on.

The sum of the information he could give us amounted to the fact that, since the Moslem rising two years before, nobody except Norin had come through to Teijinar from Cherchen. Cherchen was forty-five days' march from Arakshatu on the main caravan route, formerly the well-known Silk Road, which was a considerable distance away. It was not known whether the civil war had ended. Nobody dared to travel. Two Chinese traders had been killed by huntsmen in the mountains when they went to try and collect what was owing to them. The people had withdrawn, every man to his own camping ground. Nobody dared cross certain areas. The Mongols—whom our host called Kalmucks—distrusted everybody.

But if Boro found he could not get us a guide, he would himself help us out of the Tsaidam. He did not, however, disguise the fact that it was a bad season. The beasts were thin and there was still next to nothing for them in the way of pasture. The ordinary route had no water-points, and it led to Ghass on the frontier of Sinkiang where there was an outpost from which we might easily be sent back. It would be better to go by the lonely mountainous region to the south where there must inevitably be water. That way we should reach a camp of Turki hunters at Issik Pakte (Mongolian, *Mokshan*) in twelve days. The Moslems, it appeared, had not left the place after the rising, though their co-religionists had evacuated the Mongolian lands on which they usually lived. At Issik Pakte we should, doubtless, be able to find a guide to take us to Cherchen—Boro, as a Russian, would not be allowed to go there. In fact, all the southern oases were in the hands of Ma Chung-ying's Tungans and these were at war with the Russians who had come to the assistance of the Urumchi Government forces. As for finding out where we could buy camels, we must make enquiries in the neighbourhood the following day. Nobody would hire out camels for an expedition to regions into which one simply did not go.

In spite of the sense of uncertainty it brought, the day had been satisfactory beyond all hope. It ended with a dinner of *canard au riz* and the good Boro lamenting the poorness of the reception he was able to offer us. Not even a sheep killed in our honour! A caravan had brought him word a few days before that two friends of Oross Baï were on the way to Arakshatu.

The Story of a Cossack.

Smoking his little Chinese pipe—which held the wherewithal to produce about three puffs of acrid smoke—Boro told us how he commanded a *sotnia* of Cossacks under Annenkov, and how, when his chief abandoned the struggle against the Bolsheviks and decided to ask the Chinese to intern his starving, typhus-stricken troops, he, Boro, was given the task of arranging about accommodation for them. He knew the Kirghiz language, which bears a close resemblance to the Turki language spoken by the Moslem population of Dzungaria. It was also his business to recover the money deposited by Annenkov with the Tsarist consul at Chuguchak. He had no passport and found it very difficult to slip unnoticed past the Chinese and Bolshevik patrols at the frontier. Two Cossacks who were sent before him had been killed. In China he was arrested, but insisted on having an explanation at the yamen before going to prison. It was there he had met our Sining friend Lu Hwa-pu. By talking only of his financial mission he succeeded in obtaining his release. Then he fled, I think to Kucheng, and without wasting time on the over-greedy Chinese entered into negotiations about quarters for the troops with the chief elder of the Turkis. This man bought five hundred sheep, and rice and flour sufficient to feed between three and four thousand men, at the market price, and the internment was then carried out. It was some little time later that Annenkov left for Urumchi and, retreating across Mongolia, was assassinated. General Feng had sold himself to the Soviets and betrayed him. Boro, however, was not with his chief. He had set up in business at Tunghwang, the village where Stein and Pelliot explored the famous Grottoes of the Hundred Thousand Buddhas, and it was there, fifteen days' march from Teijinar, that Smig met him and brought him to the Tsaidam, where apparently no permit to take up residence was necessary.

Unfortunately, when the Khotan Moslem revolt broke out and Smig decided to fly with Norin, Boro was away in the mountains. So it was Wang who took charge of the account book that Smig left behind. Now, the foxy Wang, from being partner, had become boss, and as he had not the art of making himself liked by the Mongols, business was slack.

Boro was born at Akmolinsk in Siberia. His wife and children were still there, and he was extremely uneasy as he had not heard from them for four years. His pipe was now his only real companion. The poor fellow suffered from heart trouble and the high altitude of the Tsaidam made it unsuitable for him. He wanted to move to Tientsin, which is a kind of metropolis for all the men of Central Asia. His regrets were, however, somewhat modified when I told him how Chinese trade had declined since the Japanese gained the supremacy in the north of China, and of the tens of thousands of Russians who wander up and down the coast in search of a livelihood.

BORODISHIN

A Princely Yurt.

In the morning word came to the effect that, his father being absent, the young Prince of Teijinar was ready to receive us. The invitation was welcome, for undoubtedly the Prince would be able to help us to secure good camels. Wang, so as to be seen in good company, I suppose, insisted on coming to act as interpreter, though we found it very difficult to follow his lisping Russian, and his knowledge of Mongolian was less good than Boro's. We rode at a trot to Hajjar, rejoicing at the thought of the sheep which, in accordance with the laws of hospitality, must be served in our honour. Once more I took Peter over his lesson in behaviour. He was very lazy and had never mastered the art of gnawing a bone. Nomad etiquette insists that a guest must not abandon a bone till it is bare. Only thus does he show the high value he places on that precious animal, the sheep.

The women and children watched us dismount and enter the great yurt. Inside, the elders of the tribe, squatting in rows, made an imposing assembly. The young Prince sat, impassive, facing the entrance. With a disdainful pout he accepted the modest presents proffered awkwardly by Peter, a packet of cigarettes, a pocket-knife and a pack of cards. The unsmiling senate brightened a little when a great plush rug representing a dead tiger fell from where it hung over a pile of chests behind me. The bracket supporting the sacred books and the eight offertory cups was decorated with paintings, as was also a wardrobe—it was the first time I had seen such an article of furniture in a yurt.

But my attention was mainly centred on the white-bearded Mongols round me and on a woman with very fine features—no doubt she was of Tibetan origin—who, like ourselves, sat near the door. Beyond question, it is in Teijinar that one sees the finest types of the Tsaidam region. Probably our hosts were descendants of the

135

thirty-three nobles or "Teiji" who have governed the province since 1725.*

So far we had been given nothing but buttered tea. The inevitable tsamba, placed, out of reach, on a low table, had not been offered. It was now midday and these people knew we had had a two hours' ride. As the tsamba remained untouched I assumed that we were going to banquet off a sheep. My neighbour on the left had a magnificent head with a hooked nose, like a Sioux warrior. I passed the time admiring him while Wang—at last—embarked on the question of buying camels with one of the men, the one we afterwards called the "Prime Minister." However, as they would not let us have any beast for less than seventy *lan* (a weight of silver equivalent to 105 Mexican dollars), we rose to go.

And still no food was offered. I felt disturbed about this and we both wondered whether it was to be interpreted as a sign of hostility towards us, as foreigners. We learned that, in August, 1933, Norin had given the Prince a present of twenty-eight dollars. Doubtless, we were looked on as very penurious travellers . . . but that was the reputation we wished to have.

Exploited.

Li was returning to Nomo. We took leave of the devoted lad and thanked him for all he had done for us. He was a born trader and had just bartered his packets of tobacco for two fox-skins. He also borrowed twenty dollars from Peter, to help him to buy another camel. His master, Ma Shin-teh, would answer for the loan—by the way. It would be paid back in September, through our friends the Urechs, at Tangar.†

* The five principalities of the Tsaidam are divided into twenty-one "banners." See note, p. 301.

† The promise could not be kept, for in September the Urechs had to fly before the Communist advance.

Before he left, Li told us that the Prince had forbidden all camel-owners to sell to us. Probably the Prince wanted us to go back to himself. The elders had, no doubt, made him realize that it was a mistake to lose the chance of extracting good dollars out of us. As a matter of fact, all the Mongols were in want of money to pay the interest that Sining exacted on unpaid taxes.* And as they rarely had money, the foxy Ma Shin-teh advanced it for them to the Governor. The Governor happened, as though by chance, to be Ma Shin-teh's son-in-law. Ma recovered usurer's interest on his money by sending his agents to seize the Mongols' finest sheep. Other dealers did the same and the Mongols, after bartering their wool for an equal weight of flour—a deal in which they were scandalously tricked—had no alternative but to lapse into debt. It was agreed that a dollar's worth of merchandise should be counted equivalent to one sheep. But the dollar itself was not, of course, paid. And so, the following year, the dealer would claim, as combined capital and interest, two sheep for each dollar advanced. It is a typical example of the system of penetration cherished in China.

This method of acting explains the assassination of the two Chinese traders and the precipitation with which Outer Mongolia seceded from China during the revolution of 1911. And so, at the heart of Asia, where I expected to find myself amongst poor men but free, I found economic slavery and national antagonism as strong as in any part whatsoever of the present-day world. At Peking the students were ready to rise against Japan. At Sian the Nanking Government troops were risking their lives against "Communism." In Kansu the Tungans revolted periodically and put North-West China to fire and sword. Now, here, it was the exploitation of the Mongols by the Chinese.

* The annual tax of ten dollars per yurt, calculated on a basis of 3,000 sheep, 300 horses and 200 cows, must be handed over by the fifteen hundred or so yurts in the Tsaidam.

Ignoring the orders of his Prince, the "Prime Minister" came and offered us his finest camel. He declared that the animal had not yet been at work that year and was fit to take us to Kashgar if necessary. (Was it possible that even already they knew what we were up to?) As a Mongol never haggles and as the Pearl of the Tsaidam—that was the name we gave him later—was nice and plump, we paid the seventy dollars the "Prime Minister" asked. Then and there Peter, anxious to get on and fearing that we might be suspect, decided to buy the best three of ten camels that Yanduk, the handsome half-caste, was offering us to choose from. They did not limp. Two had good teeth. The "Old 'Un" had not. We might have to feed it from the nosebag. The beasts had already crossed the Tsaidam once that year, but Boro said their feet would be the better hardened for that.

Our Cossack friend now set about the preparations for our departure. He looked about for pack-saddles, bought barley, onions, bricks of tea (twice as dear as at Tangar), daliembu and white flour. We still had supplies of rice, sugar and jam as well as of the usual spices. Instead of butter we were taking some delicious sheep's-tail fat preserved in the stomach of the tail's owner. . . . The laying in of provisions took time, for the tents were very scattered. Peter, at a loss for something to occupy his mind, sighed the sigh of an exile deprived of his *Times*, and resignedly asked me for his *History of England*—Macaulay's. I kept my boxes of matches packed between the little volumes.

Just then, incidentally, I was full of admiration for Peter. At over four hundred yards and with his small rifle he had shot an antelope. It came most opportunely for my larder.

We were staying in the larger yurt, the Smigs's yurt. This was the place they recalled when, at Peking, they spoke of "home." Now it was we who were there, and our fondest dreams seemed to be coming true. But they, where were they? They had left quantities of the bank-notes issued during the Kerensky and 1905 revolutions in a big chest here. Derelict bank-notes! They lay beside old medicine bottles which had labels marked Bombay, Moscow, Tientsin . . . enough in themselves to make us realize that we were at the very centre of the continent of Asia.

CHAPTER II

LOST TRAIL

ON the 15th of May we set out for the unknown, for the south. Here, at the centre of the Tsaidam, we were between thirty and forty days' march from the nearest town. Sining, from which we had come, was to the east. On the south was Lhasa and, to the west, Cherchen, which we wanted to reach.

Beyond the Nan Shan mountains, to the north, stretched the desert sands. Immediately behind us were the camping grounds of Teijinar, grassy plains spotted with yellow dunes. In front of us rose the Kuen Lun mountains, their shadows so blue as to seem like so many parts of the sky. There we should come to the high, bare Tibetan lands where we hoped to find a guide to lead us to the gates of far-off Cherchen.

We were only three. We could not find a Mongol to come with us, money or no money. Three Europeans, two of whom knew not a single word of the Mongol language, and knew of the region only what they might make out from an incomplete map! Truth to tell, however, Borodishin was not so much a European as an Asiatic, a nomad at heart, at home anywhere. But he was fifty, and when it came to loading up the beasts his heart grew troublesome. And we were as yet only nine thousand feet up. We should have to climb to about sixteen thousand. . . .

Were we imprudent? I did not think so and I could not help feeling that danger, if it arose, would but allow of my drawing, at last, on my dormant energies. I was always asking myself how I should behave if any difficulty arose.

And though Peter and I had confidence in each other, I could not help asking myself also how he would behave. These questions added a certain piquancy to our departure.

Life was beautiful. . . . But it was too hot, and we were following no trail, marching into a sheer desert of hard grey earth like the bed of a dried-up lake. Peter asked ironically whether I was afraid of the cold, for I did not trust the climate of Tartary and had all my warm clothes packed on my saddle. But he laughs best who laughs last. Now we came to the diverging arms of the Boron Kol, the course of which we were to ascend for ten days. The thick, yellow water had the oily tints of the colours in which I had often painted the decks of my boat. Then we struck a region which hardly seemed real. It was covered with crescent-shaped dunes, their ridges streaked like tiger skins.

Suddenly an icy blast of a crazy violence broke from the west. The black earth was covered with a veil of white sand moving forward like sheets of spray on stormy lake-waters. Even the pebbles rose. The rocky mountain, which, like an island, we were using as a landmark, disappeared. And it was my turn to shout to Peter: "Are you warm enough?" He was in his shirt-sleeves, wrestling with the difficulties of putting on his jacket in the wind. Then Greys took fright at the flapping coat and, with his cavalier, disappeared in a whirlwind. That evening, worn out, breathless and with our faces burning, we set up the tent against a cliff at the foot of the mountains. Happily, a joint of antelope was not long in restoring our good spirits.

The next morning, numbed with cold, I put my nose outside the door and found our tent covered with newly-fallen snow. Yet, so utterly sick was I of the flatness of the Tsaidam, that I could not take my eyes off the austere black walls that now rose on every side. We rounded the Kitin

Kara—the Cold Black Mountain—in a hailstorm. The mountain itself was wrapped in mist and all day, up and down, we followed the Dantesque defile through which rolled the yellow Boron Kol. My heart stood still when, crawling along above an abyss, a camel knocked one of his cases against a rock. At the foot of one of the steepest passages there was an obo—evidence of the pious fears of travellers. It was surmounted by a curious piece of wood, sculptured, as well as I could make out, in the form of a flower.

The Boron Kol Valley.

The second day the valley grew wide. But it was a desert. The river flowed, invisible, at the depths of a canyon. We advanced along a wide terrace of reddish gravel. Immense dunes of yellow ochre protected the foot of the black mountain. The tender, snowy summits* glittered against the blue of the sky. Antelopes and kulans seemed to be the only inhabitants of the region, though Boro said we might expect to meet shepherds.

There was water in plenty but provender was scattered and Boro had his work cut out getting the beasts back to camp in the morning and evening. Another tiresome fact was that the Pearl of the Tsaidam was decidedly vicious. He would stop abruptly and tear out the wooden peg passed through his bleeding nose. He kicked and spat when anyone got busy about him. I was afraid to go near him. Peter's pony also gave grounds for anxiety. He was ill. He stopped frequently, head down, lifeless, and we could only get him on by using the whip. Peter walked.

On the fourth day, where a little of last year's grass survived along the river bank—less shut in here—we came on sheep again. There were two splendid-looking Mongol

* The Bokalik Tagh or Marco Polo Mountains.

shepherds sitting between the humps of their camels, each carrying a lamb in his arms.

That evening a Mongol whose yurt was near our tent came in and sat by the fire. Boro, as it happened, wanted someone to help him with the animals and he also wanted a camel for his own return journey. The man was nervous about coming, as he would have to find somebody to lead his hungry flocks to pasture, and just then grass was difficult to come on, for nothing was growing as yet. However, by using all his powers of persuasion, Boro succeeded in overcoming the man's hesitations and he entered our service. His name was Akpan.

His arrival allowed Peter to put the most important part of the day to whatever use he liked. After breakfast he might now smoke the first pipe of the day in peace. It was a source of perpetual wonder to the Mongols that a wooden pipe should not be burnt away. They had only brass pipes usually filled with a neighbour's tobacco. Peter lent himself with a good grace to the polite custom, but it was not without some apprehension that he saw his supply of "Edgeworth" diminishing as a result.

We had halted for a day, but it was not sufficient to restore Greys to health. Neither was an extra ration of barley. Probably the first grass of the year which he had had at Arakshatu was too much for him. We were obliged to tie him with a rope to the last camel while his master went off on foot to shoot antelope. As for Slalom, he was still in valiant form and had thrown me twice, more roughly in fact than seemed, at the moment, good for my head. The first time I was trying to overtake one of the camels from which a bag was falling, and we were in full gallop when Slalom suddenly shied at a little mound of earth. The second time he reared at the sight of a dead goose which Peter was handing me to pluck as I rode along.

FORBIDDEN JOURNEY

Another Asia.

Quite suddenly we saw five or six tethering poles and the tails of yaks blowing in the wind on top of a hill. Then I recognized a Turki Moslem grave the moment I laid eyes on it. My emotion may be imagined. I was in Turkestan once more. Not far from there, within a structure of dried earth, was a bread oven. . . . Bread! What would I not give to have some bread instead of our hard old biscuit? But the Turkis had evacuated the valley after the recent troubles and only the desert welcomed us.

We were at the border of a new aspect of Asia, with new ways and new peoples. Here the corpses would not be abandoned to the birds of prey as Mongol corpses were. Here flour would be baked in an oven instead of being mixed in tea. Here prayers would rise to the invisible Allah instead of being muttered before terra-cotta Buddhas. A simple grave, and Mongolia, the yellow world in which I had just passed so many long months, vanished behind me!

But in the desert landscape nothing had changed. Flocks of antelopes still gambolled gaily before us. They were almost white in colour and wore their long black horns, shaped like lyres above their heads, with a distinct "air." Peter had just shot a straggler from the herd, for we were running short of meat. But there was a deception in store for us. When we cut him up we found that, beneath the hide, his hindquarters were being devoured by a whole colony of worms as big as nuts. It seems that in springtime stinging flies deposit their eggs inside the skins of the attenuated animals. The pretty antelope, the incarnation of bounding joy, capable of effecting its escape from all the dangers it meets, cannot escape this slow torture. Here, doubtless, was the explanation of the numerous carcasses I had noticed in the desert these last days. We were nervous and did not dare

144

to eat the meat. But a week later, impelled by hunger, we had grown less fastidious.

Peter was still walking. He might have ridden on Akpan's second camel, but Akpan pointed out that we had only hired the animal for Boro's return journey, and besides she was carrying his prayer-book.

Astray.

It was a week since we set out from Arakshatu and that morning the air was stimulating. The atmosphere really was the atmosphere of high places. We had spent a freezing night near the source of the Boron Kol. Unlike the sources of water-courses in the Alps, the "Valley" here was only an immense plateau with scarcely any slope, and the mountains seemed to have disappeared.

We set off towards the north-west, leaving a thin stream of frozen water untouched, for Boro said there was a spring where we were going to camp that evening. It was about sixty *lis* across a gobi. Akpan brought a supply of roots in a bag because, away from the trails, there are no argols with which to make fires. The track had not been used for two years and had practically disappeared. Only antelopes seemed to frequent the region. Here and there antelope carcasses were drying in the sun. The heart-shaped prints of antelopes' feet showed on the ground where the herds had passed. The shape also reminded one of two almonds together, of an undivided philippine. We made our way without landmarks. Since leaving the Tsaidam I had picked out the route with the help of Norin's compass, playing at being an explorer—for there had been few, if any, travellers here since Carey followed this same valley in 1886. That day I noticed that when Akpan took the lead he kept more to the north than Boro did, but when I grew uneasy, he said it was deliberate.

The deep blue sky was not unlike the ocean when the compact squalls of the trade-winds are blowing. At regular and uniformly equal intervals, swelling white clouds were putting out, as it were, more sail, in a race to the ends of the horizon. About midday at last the black summit of a pyramidal mountain appeared in front of us, like a little island. We took it to be the Karachuka where our spring was. But three hours later we were at the foothills of the "mountain" and realized that it was not what we thought but the towering Karyaghde mountain chain. Boro had made the journey only twice before and could recognize nothing here.

To get a more comprehensive idea of the lie of the land we climbed up a stiff little valley to a col. Greys could only be persuaded to go on by lashes of the whip and we ourselves were dead beat. The air was pretty rarefied at sixteen thousand feet. We had scarcely reached the top when snow and mist came about us. We sent Akpan on a scouting expedition, but he came back defeated. He had never been here before and there was no doubt that the mountain on our right could not be negotiated. Boro was an object for compassion. "*Shto takoi?*" ("What can it be?"), he kept repeating, and tried vainly to imagine how it had happened.

We came down again. Boro wished to go back further west. Akpan went south to reconnoitre. Peter and I unloaded the camels and set up the tent on the bare ground. We resigned ourselves to an encampment without grass or water, for we had been twelve hours on the march and the ill-nourished animals did not want to go on.

Furnished with the luggage and its own felt carpet, our little tent did not fail to produce the sense of comfort we valued so much. But that evening Boro was too restless to enjoy it. He suffered from thirst to the point of not being able to swallow his biscuit. The man had a heart of gold. He had gone to a great deal of trouble for us and we loved him well.

It was not only that he was somebody new to talk to. I think we were all three just as much drawn, each to the others, by our common feeling for order and cleanliness.

Boro would take nothing but a gulp of cognac. Peter thought he might try tsamba with cold mutton fat. The result was that he had a very bad night. I was out, in my shorts, to salute the rising sun and proceeded to harvest some of the light snow that had fallen on the tent. But I need not have troubled. Boro and the Mongol were off on a reconnaissance and came back announcing that they had found our famous spring less than three miles away and that it was almost frozen. Within two hours, our little caravan, all intact, was encamped beside it.

Searchings.

But a tent-pole had been lost *en route*. There was no timber in the region, so it could not be replaced, and I went off to look for it. Walking along at an even pace I felt in great form, filled with such joy as I used to experience setting out on my skis on very dry winter mornings. There on the high table-lands of Asia I was singing, *I'm sitting on top of the world*.

I even laughed at the wide heavens. It was an odd situation Peter and I were in together at the centre of that continent. Indeed, it was like a situation in a novel, and if I were writing a best-seller, it should be that very day or never that the hero and heroine fell into each other's arms in mutual love and gratitude for rescues—on one side, rescue from the results of poisoned food, and on the other, rescue from a dangerous mist. Well, the novel-readers would have to go without.

Peter was the best of comrades and I had found that I could be absolutely frank with him. It is true that our enterprise bound us to each other to such a degree that, living as we did, like two castaways on a desert island, our conversation at supper, evening after evening, revealed the fact that the same thoughts had struck us simultaneously in the course of the day. But it was only our egotisms that worked together, each helping the other. I could see clearly where we parted company. We both liked to spend our leisure in the open air, he shooting, I ski-ing. . . . But then? Peter thought me too serious and I did not understand British humour (as serious a fault in the eyes of an Englishman as it is for a Chinaman to "lose face.") I had the bad taste to lay down the law about the art of living. Peter was bored by my craving to understand the thousands of diverse lives that make up humanity and bored, too, by my need to relate my own life to life in general. How could anybody be so crazy as to want to find out whether men's efforts brought about an improvement in human nature? Peter was troubled by none of these things. In his imperturbable wisdom he looked on human beings as characters in a comedy. As to his deeper self, his timidity usually made him hide it beneath a facetious dignity. Except at rare intervals, he seemed persuaded that his concerns were of no interest to anybody. . . .

I found the tent-pole. That was what mattered just then. And success made me sing as I returned to Peter, who stood waiting for me to appear in the plain he dominated.

CHAPTER III

The Men at the World's End

ON the tenth day we came in sight of Issik Pakte—a few yurts set down on a patch of earth in the midst of marshes. To the north, the peaks of the Karyaghde rose abruptly. The first Turki we passed was a ginger-haired shepherd with clear eyes, a straight nose and a face burnt by the sun of these altitudes to the same mahogany colour as the Mongols' faces. But instead of skins of beasts he wore garments of native cotton and he had bands of cloth wound round his legs. Boro called him a Sart. It is the name given in Russian Turkestan to all Turki Iranians who live a settled life. The Chinese call these Moslems of Central Asia *chantos*, meaning "turbaned-heads."

We went on, poor Greys still needing a touch of the whip, and being hauled, much against his will, by Slalom, who was very lively. Even Peter volunteered that Slalom was a valiant creature, and withdrew all he had ever said about his ugliness and stupidity.

On our arrival, some Turkis recognized Boro and made quite a fuss over him. They carried him off, we staying behind to pitch the tent. Nobody invited us to drink tea. . . . What exactly might be the meaning of that?

It was not long before we knew all there was to know. So far as entering the dreamed-of province of Sinkiang was concerned, our chances were no greater now than when we were in Peking. In two years, since the fanatical Moslem revolt in the oases of the south, we were the first arrivals from the outside world amongst the Turkis. During all that time they had not seen any stranger except one Mongol who had been sent by the Prince of Teijinar to find out whether his lands at Issik Pakte were inhabited.

Having no news, these Turkis—some fifteen in number—had not dared to return to the lowlands for provisions. And then, after the murder of the two Chinese traders, they were afraid of reprisals, so continued to sit still where they were. Also, though the land at Issik Pakte belonged to the Tsaidam, the inhabitants depended for their livelihood on the oasis of Charklik, at the eastern edge of Sinkiang. This oasis was at war with Cherchen and it was to Cherchen we wanted to go. The Turkis hesitated about acting as our guides and in no circumstances would they take the risk of going further than Toruksai. Toruksai marked the frontier of Sinkiang. It was in the Altyn Tagh mountains, six days' journey from Issik Pakte, and it was possible that there might be a military post there. Boro's position was as we had expected. He must not go to Cherchen. It was in the hands of the Tungans, who were hostile to all that was Russian. That was not very reassuring. And as for these isolated mountaineers, they were paying dearly for the calm of their retreat. They had no tea left and were drinking an infusion of black pepper, which they were shy of offering to us. They had had no flour for a year and lived exclusively on meat. But our arrival filled them with a somewhat interested joy—we had done well to provide ourselves with tea.

Two dignified women called on me, bringing their grey wool with them and continuing their spinning. They wore little round fur toques which served to hold squares of cotton on the head. A fold from the square of cotton fell in front of the face to accord with Moslem custom. Their dress was the *chapan* worn by all Turki people in Central Asia, a real caftan of padded cloth. Their faces might almost have been European—I mean, they had no definitely Asiatic character.

I even called one of them "Phèdre," so much did her carriage and her profile suggest a classical figure.

"*Onn? Onn?*" they asked. "Had I any flour?"

And by means of expressive mimicry they gave me to understand that flour was the one remedy for the headaches brought on by their meat diet. I could only spare them a plateful, for I had to keep enough to last us at least a fortnight, even without allowing for a delay at Issik Pakte itself.

Actually we needed to rest for two days for the sake of the camels. There was pasture for them here. Greys, once so full of life, would not be able to go on. The thin Slalom, on the other hand, had never at any time refused to carry me. He had even succeeded in dragging Greys along as a tug drags the dead weight of a barge. The good brute was so willing that I was afraid he might go on till he collapsed.

One of the men who, with his hooked nose and "collar" beard, reminded me of a figure in a Persian miniature, came with two fillies. Peter called them "the amphibians," because they had been brought in from the marshes and were all muddy. He exchanged Greys for one of them. She had a brown winter coat that was coming out in patches and looked like a moth-eaten rug. While they were filing her hooves, which, as a result of inaction, had grown to an extravagant length, Peter found a name for her: Cynara. Peter yearned over Greys and Boro asked the Persian miniature "to be good to the little black horse, so that he should not be sad in his heart at losing his master."

There were three wretched yurts near our tent. In one of them a man with a pointed nose and a gay laugh was preparing us a supply of little strips of dough with our own flour and our own mutton fat. His brother, Tokta Ahun, was to accompany the elder of the camp, Assa Khan, who was coming as our guide. Tokta Ahun brought in two antelopes Peter had killed, and in his own yurt I had occasion to admire, for the first time and with some alarm, his prowess in eating—we had had to undertake to feed our guides in order to persuade any Turkis to come with us. Tokta Ahun stuck some cuts of wild ass meat against the iron bars of the stove and they were only beginning to be grilled when he swallowed them whole, without any chewing. It was in that yurt also that I saw smokers putting little fragments of a greenish paste into the bowls of their pipes. This was *nasha,* made with the juice obtained by cutting stalks of hemp—hashish, in fact.*

Hecatomb and Preparations.

In my "canteen" box, which contained all our riches (medicine chest, gramophone, and two typewriters which we had brought specially in case we had to face the tedium of prison), I packed supplies of food for ten days. I melted down mutton fat, ground sugar, broke up a brick of tea—it smelt like hay; I put in rice, tsamba, a box of cocoa, another of jam, a packet of candles, a bottle of curry, another of brandy, and some cloves of garlic. Everything was ready to hand when the time for feasting should come. The canteen box was a present given us by Mr. Keeble at Lanchow. It still bore the name of a Yangtze missionary, but it played a major role in our journey. Without it I should have been nobody, for in it were all my resources as doctor, as musical director, as cook. There were two keys, but Peter had lost one of them long ago, so I alone had access to all the riches it contained.

As the sportsmen at Issik Pakte were short of ammunition we succeeded in exchanging twenty-two of the bullets which could only be used for the big rifle, and were therefore no good to us, for two wooden spoons. At Dzun a wooden spoon was as valuable as a sheep. The acquisition of the new ones was very important, for, all the others having been broken,

* In China it is called *mayan* or *bong;* in India, *sharrs.*

poor Peter had been eating his soup out of a teaspoon, which meant that I, who had a patent pocket-set of cutlery, got on twice as fast as he. Also, in exchange for an empty bottle, a packet of boxes of matches and a piece of soap, I secured five lengths of admirable mountain homespun cloth. The women themselves spin the wool and make the men's cloaks out of it.

I still had a day's washing to do before I could feel that I was ready to start off again. Peter, optimistic as ever, remarked that he had been wearing his shirt "only" a fortnight. I called him a barbarian and would not listen to any nonsense. . . . Then, as I was putting the shirt out to dry, I suddenly noticed a pale tiny speck in a pleat—a louse! Soon I had eight grown-ups of the same family to show to their owner and also a hundred and seventy nits which, pitilessly, I counted out for him, one by one. By way of thanks, the half-confused Peter deplored the solitude he was going to be left in without the little beasts.

And now we had to pass to intellectual work of a most valuable kind. Before he left, Boro was to teach us about forty words of the Turki language, so that we should be competent to face major eventualities. Boro had been admirable. He overcame the last hesitations of our guide by exploiting the flour shortage. Everybody wanted flour and he pointed out to Assa Khan that if he led us to the camp where we were to find someone to take us on to Cherchen, he could buy flour with the money we paid him. If the Cherchen oasis ahead was still at war, Assa Khan was to see that arrangements were made for us to be taken round to a more westerly point on the caravan trail. And to discourage any likelihood of attacks by robbers, Boro spread the rumour that we were at this moment spending our last dollars, that for the money that would be needed after Cherchen we counted on the sale of our camels. The animals must, therefore, since they represented our entire capital, be taken great care of.

That evening, Boro squatted in our tent smoking his pipe for the last time. From his cloth tobacco pouch hung a nutshell into which he emptied the last embers from the smoke he was finishing. As soon as he had his pipe refilled he lit up again by turning the embers over, back into the bowl. It was a clever device which made it unnecessary to use his Mongol lighter. The lighter consisted of a half-moon-shaped iron and a flint with local tinder.

By a curious coincidence, a messenger arrived on foot in the course of the night with the news that the civil war was over. Charklik had fallen into Tungan hands and those who dreaded the new masters were in flight across the desert towards Tunghwan.

CHAPTER IV

THE CARAVAN IN DANGER

WITH the little nutshell attached to his tobacco pouch swinging with the movement of his camel, our friend Borodishin, whom no doubt we should never see again, set off with Akpan on the return journey to his lonely yurt in the Tsaidam. We set out in the opposite direction, sure now of getting back on to the oasis trail within a fortnight. The trail was the old "Silk Road" which led to the land of the Seres.

Our guide, the foxy Assa Khan, was smiling because of the good news of the night. And Peter was radiant, happy to be on a horse instead of pulling with all his might at a halter. We had little fear for the future. And as if to emphasize the auspiciousness of the start, we found ourselves within two hours eating a marvellous omelet made with wild duck's eggs. This was in a yurt that took on an air of comfort from a central earthen fireplace and excellent rugs which were piled on chests as amongst the Kirghiz. It was a very warm yurt. We were surrounded by the numerous family—the children playing with my compass. On leaving I made a present of my necklace to the mistress of the house. And then, once more, it was good-bye to all human habitations. I did not expect to see another for twelve days.

Once one feels sure of being able to get away, the Issik Pakte region is of an unforgettable beauty. Along the middle of the plateau stretched the intense blue of a lagoon set in the beige-coloured earth, itself dominated by black mountains with snowy crests. The Torhut Mongols going on pilgrimage to Lhasa sometimes used a trail that wound along there to the south, over a ramification of the Kuen Lun, and through a desert like the one we were crossing. Without water, wood or grass, covered with salt, and flat, like an unused aerodrome, it is certainly one of the most desolate regions in the world. And yet antelopes lived there—I could see them bathing in an arm of the lagoon—and wild asses—we used their droppings for our fire every evening. The antelopes surveyed us from a distance, as if astonished at the sight of animals moving on foot yet not grazing.

The second evening, after a march of nine hours, we came on a hole which other travellers must have dug and, scooping further with the frying-pan, we found that enough sweet water to make tea trickled through. But the animals were restless, and Slalom, who looked like a living interrogation mark, was not satisfied with his small ration of barley. He had a charming trick of putting his head in at the tent-opening when we were at supper, and that evening I saw him crunching an antelope bone I had just thrown out.

On the third day we marched along by an immense salt lake, the Ayak Kum Kul. Its waves, of a Mediterranean blue, were a delight to eyes fatigued by the colourless table-lands. On the edge of it we found a trickle of sweet water rising in the hollow of a little patch of green grass. We widened the hollow to make a drinking pool and watered Slalom at it. As the water in the pool went lower he stretched his neck so far that his legs were trembling. Then, several times, he fell on to his knees in the effort to quench that insatiable thirst.

Tokta Ahun went on foot, leading the camels. From a distance, he looked as if he were wearing a dressing-gown. Assa Khan sat, perched on his beast, taking no interest in anything. The happy humour of our departure had disappeared, for the camels were getting on badly. The oldest one often knelt down and had to be beaten before he would get up. Perhaps his worn teeth were not fit for the *buturga*—dry, twisted tufts of little creeping branches which the camels ate on the way. But should we have to abandon him in case he could not keep up? We had ten-hour marches before us each day. . . . The Pearl's incisors were broken. Boro had said it was because he had fallen on ice the previous winter. We were now of opinion that the "Prime Minister" had tricked us.

The Animals Abandoned.

Again on the fourth day we watered the animals and filled our cask at a spring on the bank of the salt lake. Assa Khan gave us to understand that there would be grass for the horses behind some low hills that now broke the line of the horizon. We were in serious need of fresh grass, for the bag of grain was almost empty and I had even begun to stiffen Slalom's ration with my share of tsamba mixed with morsels of raw antelope. As for the filly, she still had reserves of strength.

To turn my mind from these anxieties, Peter declared that if we searched carefully we should find caviar on the lake edge! But I could not get away from the thought of the animals and of the road that was still before us.

Once again the old camel knelt down, and this time, though we tried beating him, he would not get up. He grew stiff. Lost in far-away thoughts, he seemed to be looking into the other world. . . . As he was no longer loaded, there was nothing to remove except the pack-saddle and the nose-peg. Assa Khan collected them and went on as though nothing had happened.

I was trying to imagine myself as a fatalistic old camel-driver. It was true that we had seen many carcasses along the frequented routes and I asked myself why it should not be our turn to lose a camel. The abandoned animal grew smaller and smaller behind us till he was no more than a speck amidst the sparse buturga.

Though Tokta Ahun had made a gesture which seemed to imply that all was over, the beast was not dead. Peter longed to shorten its agony with a bullet, but it would have been a breach of the law of the desert. An animal that is "thrown on the gobi," as the caravan people say, may be saved by a miracle. If he be killed his troubled soul will follow the other camels and bring them bad luck. The camel-drivers make it a point of honour to abandon a camel with a careless air. Should they, Lattimore tells us, betray any sign of attachment to their beasts, a maleficent power will attack the rest of the caravan.

That evening we camped in a melancholy hollow. Flakes of snow fell on the tent with a whispering sound, like elytra. Even the smell of cooking could not cheer us. Another camel was ill. Unable to go out to pasture, he was kneeling motionless beside the tent. He had almost brought our shelter about our ears as he knelt down, but I saved it by working at his haunches with the ladle until I had shifted him a little.

Already our caravan was distinctly below par. If things continued like this, we would be on all fours before we arrived at the next inhabited point. . . . Truth to tell, we were feeling conscience-stricken. Why, on our account, should these camels die? And after being beaten?

It was very tiresome, at the end of such a day, to have to keep an eye on Tokta Ahun. He stole some flour, then pilfered one of the cutlets he had to boil. The very idea of food was an obsession with him and he ate ravenously. At the end of a colossal meal he begged me, with the look of a beaten dog in his green eyes, to give him more. *"Talkan, bar?"* ("Have you any tsamba?").

To stop his begging we divided what was left into two parts —one for ourselves and one for him and his master—and left them to settle the subdivision between them.

On the morning of the fifth day the animals had got scattered in their search for buturga and it took two hours to get them in. We spent the time trying to revive the sick camel by putting menthol crystals in its nostrils. This was a remedy Smig had recommended. The Mongols believe that, at great heights, spirits hostile to travellers produce plants, the mere presence of which causes mountain sickness.

The previous afternoon we had turned our backs on the splendid lake, and ascended to a sloping plateau, bordered, very far away, by high mountains. That day we continued to ascend, Peter towing the sick camel along by pulling with the whole weight of his body on the nose-rope. I called out: "*Oo-ok!*" to encourage the animal, and flicked the bare skin of its thighs with the whip. The brackish water must have caused this unforeseen weakness, for it urinated unceasingly as it went along. Suddenly the creature collapsed again, as though every nerve was gone. Assa Khan went on, without taking any interest—perhaps, I thought, because it was not his camel. Were we going to lose this one as well as the other? I revolted from the idea. I made a double half-hitch with the halter so that Peter could get a better pull on its head. At last it rose—but only to take the last few steps of its life. . . .

Then, at last, I understood. This was what the gobi existed for. And what use was it to protest? You paid out money for animals simply to "throw them on the gobi." We went on without unnecessary delay. Slalom had to take the second castaway's two cases. We followed the Turkis' tracks. They had not helped us. They were not interested in us except at meal-times. And now Slalom began to show signs of weakness. His load had to be removed. Peter called with all the strength of his lungs: "*Tokta!*" Assa Khan waited and put the two cases on his camel, handing over two small suit-cases instead. These we balanced on the filly, though, as a result of her recent shoeing, she was limping slightly.

The Turkis went off first and got further and further ahead, so that we did not see them again till that night. Unceasingly we watched for their tracks, though, as the ground was hard, they scarcely showed. We had already been marching five hours. It was only midday and it was essential to go on till we came to water.

Slalom dragged his feet and stopped every couple of hundred yards. I would speak to him gently when he stopped. And he would look at me miserably before starting off again. Impatiently I kept looking for some change of ground and promise of water. Now Peter, with the leading-rein passed over his shoulder like a Volga boatman, was pulling Slalom on with all his might. I handled the whip. At last, a gully seemed to be opening out in front. It was the beginning of a little valley which widened further on into a broad, mountain valley. Down there, there must be water. Surely the camping ground must be there! But at five o'clock we were at the other end. It was black and bare and there was nothing, nothing at all. Where had our Turkis gone? Had they climbed the little pass that separated us from the next valley?

Peter—I could not think exactly why—shouted as loudly as he could. The men must surely have gone on with their camels till they came to water. And water was far away. We found their tracks at the foot of the slope. But Slalom would never be able to get up there. What were we to do?

"One . . .

"Two . . ."

Peter had the bridle wound round his arm. I leaned my

shoulder against the emaciated hindquarters of the horse.
At "Three" we managed to move the stiff mass that was all
Slalom was now. Every hundred yards we sat down without
a word, to get our breath. I was afraid of the halts, anxious
each time lest Slalom should stick for good. At seven
o'clock in the evening, from the top of the pass, I saw the line
of a frozen river in the distance. Peter would not dare
believe it was true and opined that it might only be salt
deposit.

It was still a long way off and the question was whether we
should leave Slalom and bring him back some water later
on. No, I decided, never. It was as though I held on only by
a single idea—to get my horse into camp before he collapsed.
Pulled and pushed, Slalom was got down, exactly like an
automaton, an emptied hide, in and out of which the breathed
air only barely passed. It was to be hoped that our men had
not crossed the river and gone on still further in the night.
No. There they were at last. . . . What a victory!

The men unpacked and I was surprised to find we had the
strength left to set up the tent, to plant the poles well into the
ground, and to get everything inside: the heavy "canteen"
box, our hold-alls, the guns, glasses, cameras, our sleeping-
bags which we rolled tight so as to have them at our backs for
the time being; our suit-cases, which we put along the lower
flaps of the tent—we could write our notes on them, play
cards on them, use them as dressing-tables.

Then suddenly I felt utterly worn out. I was stiff and sore.
I gave in and let myself rest. I had ceased to believe in rest.
I thought Assa Khan had made a mistake and that we were
going to have to wander about all night.

We had just enough strength left to drink a little cocoa
and some brandy. Peter was half asleep in his clothes,
and for the first time went without his evening pipe. But
before he went right off I extracted a promise that we

should take a holiday next day and let Slalom rest. As a matter of fact, my own back was stiff and my knees were painful.

Slalom.

We were on the bank of the Toruksai. Here there were no gold-seekers, no military posts. Absolute calm reigned in that desert region between the black mountains. Only the clear water plashed against the bank where a few tufts of fresh grass were showing. The filly was grazing diligently, but Slalom, run down and worn out with fatigue, stood inert, his head hanging, the bone of his hindquarters pointing skywards, his ribs sticking out. Only his hearing was still sufficiently keen for him to turn to me when I spoke to him.

I thought the rest would put him right. But he would not eat and I feared the worst. It might have been the Ayak Kum Kul water that made him ill, or perhaps the Issik Pakte marsh had given him worms. He needed several days' rest and castor-oil treatment. I knew one thing that could save him—an armful of hay from the alp at Evolène. There the hay would be ripe to-day, and perfumed, full of dried flowers, with the flesh colour of the wild pinks showing brilliantly. . . . But we had to start off again the next day. Our provisions were running low.

At least we must try not to lose the two remaining camels. The second, "Number Two," was ruminating solidly, but the Pearl was squatting with an air of disgust of the whole world and he stank of rottenness. Raising the strip of felt that covered his back—he had not had the pack-saddle off for a long time—I discovered a purulent sore between his two humps. And then I had no more fear for the Pearl. All he wanted was care. I dressed the wound, Tokta Ahun holding him and he moaning. Then I arranged a mattress of felt, thinned out at the middle, over his back.

Peter kept to the tent while we were in camp, for his eye was hurting again and he had to bathe it. We talked over our impressions of the previous day, the most fatiguing of our journey. Yet I had often felt just as worn out after a long climb on skis, arriving at the hut at my journey's end feeling utterly done and with my back scored from my heavy pack.

Yesterday had left me with the marvellous sense of having put forth all my strength and of having been of use in pushing Slalom as far as the water's brink. If, to-morrow, my horse would not go, we could leave him here, where, should he get better, Assa Khan would be able to trace him on his way back from Tokuz Dawan in a fortnight's time.

The next day I gave Slalom a breakfast of well-softened dried pears, tsamba, raw meat and some sugar. The gentle creature clearly ate the mixture with more pleasure than he had got from the lid of our last tin of marmalade, which he had appropriated. I was the last to saddle up and was happy to be setting off again on his back. The camels were in front and, timid as always, nervous of crossing the Toruksai. The filly absolutely refused to be the first to enter the swiftly-flowing stream. I took the nose-rope of the Pearl in my hand and Slalom and I drew the caravan after us.

And then, fifty paces beyond the bank on the opposite side, Slalom stopped.

"Come on, Slalom! Come on, little horse!"

The camels had passed me, Peter also.

"Slalom. . . . You are at the end of your great journey. In a few days you'll be eating lucerne grass in a green oasis."

Slalom looked at me. His eyes had become very large. The eyelids were puckered up like circumflex accents. He was as though rooted to the ground. All that he could do he had done. He knew we needed him and had brought

163

us across the river. But now it was time to say good-bye to him, to say good-bye to the friend on whose back I had spent so many never-to-be-forgotten days. I kissed his nose and called to Peter. We transferred my old Chinese saddle to the filly. And I went away, leaving my little horse motionless in the solitude behind me.

CHAPTER V

ADAM DJOK! ADAM BAR?

IT was sad, that first day without Slalom. However, as it was the fourth of June, the date of studious Eton's annual spree, Peter was determined that we should stick to a decision he had made earlier and have a *tamasha* ("party"), celebrating at the same time our entry into Sinkiang a hundred and nine days after leaving Peking.

It appears that on the fourth of June all the boys at the famous school (founded in 1440) dress up. Amongst other amusements there is a boat race on the Thames, with the oarsmen wearing their top-hats. Well-known men and women come to spend the day with their sons, and within the historic walls famous men of letters are pleased to make speeches. I listened to Peter, noting that an unwritten law has decreed that it shall be considered a sign of good breeding for an old Etonian never to speak of "Eton" unnecessarily but always of "School," without saying what school.

I, in my turn, spoke of Home, describing how on the first of June the school children celebrate the anniversary of the entry of Geneva into the Swiss Confederation, which event followed the landing of the Helvetian troops from Lausanne further up the lake in 1814. Napoleon's troops had been in occupation up to a few months before. Peter also learned that day that Berne was the capital of Switzerland! But it was his turn to mock when I found myself unable to say who was the President of the Swiss Republic.

Apart from this sudden orgy of words, the celebration was mainly gastronomic. The curried rice was unsurpassed and our one tin of crab—a present from the Japanese Consul at Vladivostok—was considered worthy to be sacrificed on such a day.

As a termination to the proceedings we regaled the assembled multitude with a gramophone concert. Then we settled down to discuss our itinerary with one half of it, Assa Khan. He knew all the Kuen Lun passes as far as distant Khotan. But the map was vague and we had difficulty in tracing the route already covered. That very morning we had come over a pass and down into the flat depths of the Guldja valley, but according to the map, this was part of the depression in which we were to find Tokuz Dawan and its encampments.

Four endless days still separated us from our immediate goal. Thanks to the melting of the snow that covered the round backs of the barely visible Achik Kul Tagh, we found every evening a trickle of water in some lateral valley or where little patches of grass were beginning to show. But our marches by day were so monotonous that they seemed centuries long. Peter protested against the monotony in his own fashion. Often he would stop for half an hour in some ditch, sheltered from the wind and smoking his pipe. Then the business of rejoining us kept him occupied for a while. I took good care not to stay with him, for though the camels did not go very fast, they never stopped, and I knew how difficult it would be to find them again once one lost touch.

In the morning I rode Cynara, so as to be able to hand her over to Peter at the end of his Asiatic Marathons. The hours round midday were always hard to while away. Being tired, one grew impatient for the halt. I got into the habit of saying lines of poetry over and over to myself and walking to the rhythm of them. In the middle of those vast stretches of yellow earth dried up by the sun and the wind, none pleased me as much as:

ADAM DJOK! ADAM BAR?

Midi là-haut, midi sans mouvement,
*En soi se pense et convient à soi-même.**

Once two o'clock was past, we began to come alive again, for since they had not given way we could make a contract with our legs for another few hours.

One morning about half-past five, as we were preparing to start, it proved to be impossible to catch the filly to saddle her. At first this was a most welcome distraction. However, she followed the camels, though, in spite of all our efforts to surround her, she kept out of reach. Assa Khan very kindly offered me his camel and I tried to throw the lasso over the horse's head. I think I may assert without boasting that if I had a week's practice I should certainly have been able to manage it. . . . To make a long story short, the game had quite ceased to be amusing when, after seven hours of effort, coming to a low cliff, we managed, with the help of a long rope, to bar the road to the little wretch. And I promise you Cynara got the thrashing she deserved.

Other surprises were in store for us that day. The plateau which we had tramped since morning scarcely seemed to have a ripple, let alone a hill, rising on its surface, but there, flowing westwards, was one of the thin streams that constitute the sources of the Cherchen Darya. Without realizing it, we had left the Guldja valley which faces east and were now at the edge of the immense Tarim Basin, which is Turkestan. Assa Khan was contemptuous of the little stream that scarcely appeared before it was lost again in the gravel, and he promised us something much better. That was about two o'clock. . . . At six o'clock we were still on the march. Lashed by an icy wind, I held on to the slight shelter provided by the camel's load. One of our boxes, an old petrol-

* High noon, motionless noon,
In itself thinks itself and is in accord with itself.
(Paul Valéry.)

tin case, had a red shell design which finished by becoming a positive obsession . . . We were going along a water-course, but a dried-up water-course. That was all, so far. Certainly he would be a clever man who found water in that water-course. Peter had just torn the entire sole off one of his shoes and came up in great distress. What was the good of wearing out man and beast by marching vainly for four-teen hours on end? I put my foot down, and insisted that, water or no water, we pitch the tent before nightfall. That evening Peter went asleep all of a sudden, letting his pipe fall from his mouth. It had been drawing badly and tasting bitter . . .

In the middle of the night I was awakened by the dull roar of a far-away torrent. I thought I could see Assa Khan. Yes, it was he. He had gone off and come back with our kettle full of water. The snows only melted during the day and it was night before the water, absorbed at first by the parched sand, arrived at the great valley. We were not long in making tea over a fire of roots we had brought with us, and the low-browed Tokta Ahun did not fail to ask for tsamba, declaring that we should be amongst human beings the following evening at a place called Dimnalik. But I did not believe him. In the dim dawn we could see the camels eating the only vegetation visible, a few tufts of old grass near-by.

It became clear, some hours later, that we had finished with the monotonous table-lands. As we went down, the landscape became transformed. The river reappeared in the depths of the valley. It would lead us to Cherchen. Further along in the shadows the water was still under a coating of ice. The mountains on either side almost touched and we had to climb over a flank of the southern chain because the water flowed between two sheer cliffs. When we got to the top Assa Khan espied the slopes of

ADAM DJOK! ADAM BAR?

Dimnalik and gazing at the bare country before us observed
—as he had observed at Toruksai: "*Adam djok!*" ("No men!").
In a vast circus our river joined the Patkalik, flowing from
the south. There were no human habitations, though fuel
was plentiful. The plain was covered with buturga, so we
threw away our stock of roots. We were following a path
now and I found myself moved by the sight of the first flower
of the year barely peeping above the sand. It was the three-
pointed blue star of an iris. The desolate stages really were
behind us.

Peter lent me his rifle. I was very pleased. This was only
the second time I had been so favoured, for ammunition was
scarce. On the first occasion, which was amongst the
tamarisks at the dead city of the Tsaidam, I had missed two
hares and now I was burning to revindicate my marksmans-
ship, more especially as we were short of meat. For once,
it was my turn to go on ahead, well in front of the animals
and keeping a sharp look-out. I reached the edge of a ridge
without making any noise and rejoiced to find a little
antelope grazing down below on the other side. I lay down
and fired. The bullet passed over its neck and was lost in
the sand. The antelope was surprised, but it could not see
me and stayed where it was. . . . I had, however, been
given only one bullet. By the time Peter and the caravan
arrived it would be too late. . . . So ended my shooting
exploits!

In the evening, having pitched camp after marching
twenty-three hours out of thirty-three, and our guide declaring that next day there would be human beings at Bash Malghun, I used all the flour that was left to make a pot of
mien.

The Riches of Nature.
It was eleven days since we left Issik Pakte and we were

all anxious to arrive. But the camels were hardly able to accelerate their pace.

Though tired, we were cheerful. Had we not got over the melancholy Tibetan passage? It was too bare, too rarefied. . . . Peter was saying that there would be champagne at Cherchen. The prospect appealed to me. But to tell the truth, what I craved was an assurance that I should drink at Kashgar within the year, were it but a glass of water.

From his perch on his camel Assa Khan at last saw something, for he proffered an *"Adam bar!"* ("There are men"). Since the day before we had descended from over 13,000 feet to 11,000 feet, and now, at a bend in the path, we came on a huge yellow patch of the previous year's grass. Then I had to salute an old shoe lying on the sand—an infallible sign of a settlement in the neighbourhood. Next there was a dark back which became a donkey, and at last a little girl in skimpy rags running into a canvas shelter to announce our approach. We were at Bash Malghun.

We pitched our tent on the bank of a limpid stream. Women, wearing long, straight linen garments, came with wooden bowls of sour milk and, in a cloth, yellow bannocks of meal bread hot from the oven. If ever I have had a moment's unmixed happiness it was there, surrounded by kindly faces and with those sweet-smelling, savoury, natural gifts before me. I noticed light-coloured hair and eyes here and there and had a sense of finding myself amongst hitherto unknown, distant cousins. The notion was not absurd, for at the beginning of our era, the oases of the Tarim were inhabited by Iranians of white race who had a language of their own— *Saka.* Now, in spite of the Turkish invasions, some traces of the older stock still reappear.

When they came up they said: *"Aman kelde!"* ("Welcome!"). Then they took my two hands ceremoniously in their two hands and pressed them. Then they touched their foreheads and chins, at the same time uttering some formula in a low voice.*

Peter, who tried always to speak for both of us, had made great progress in the Turki language. Here he gathered that we were only four days' march from Cherchen'and that things were peaceful. The *aksakal* ("elder or ancient") of Bash Malghun had just gone to Cherchen, because of the military authorities having commandeered the camels. It seemed as though these people did not like their Tungan masters, but the Turkis had no desire to expound their views and passed quickly on to other subjects. There were "Engleesh" at Cherchen. They even had an aksakal there.† He was not, of course, an Englishman. But we should be in luck if he proved to be able to speak English. He was a British subject from India and would be able to help us if there were any trouble. It was the best news we could have received.

We decided that we should have a guide and some donkeys to take us to *our* aksakal.

Small Shopkeeping.

We took advantage of a day's rest at Bash Malghun to get rid of everything we could do without between there and Cherchen. So I made a counter by turning our cases upside down, and in exchange for rice, a lamb, sheep's fat and actually a little compressed gold-dust, we traded matches, soap, thread, old saucepans, empty tins and bottles—bottles were considered more valuable out there than anyone in Europe can conceive—pepper, cotton, bags of horsehair, horseshoes and coarse nails. I was also able to give some sweets to the children and ointments to the sick.

---

* I had seen this salutation practised as far away as the shores of the Aral Sea.

† Literally *aksakal* means "white beard," which is to say "chief." At the head of every village there is an aksakal who is elected by the aksakals of the trade guilds. Similarly foreigners in the country had an aksakal, who, to defend their interests, was invested with consular authority.

A transformed Assa Khan was the lion of the occasion. His puckered nose twitched, he winked maliciously, and all day long he cracked jokes which sent his audience into shouts of laughter. Happy at being back amongst his own kind, he made up for the time he had lost, cut off from the rest of the world, in lands that even the Mongols will not inhabit, and where, for two years, he had seen nobody outside of his own immediate circle.

We went to a primitive but extremely clean tent in which a family of shepherds lived, to fetch some wheaten bread that was being prepared for us.

A noble, white-bearded old man gave a banquet in our honour, in the course of which Tokta Ahun had at least three antelope cutlets more than anybody else. When it was over we said good-bye to Assa Khan. I shook him warmly by the hand—it was an unknown gesture and created great hilarity. My parting words to our guide came to something like: "My sick horse, very good horse. At Toruksai, seek thou and take my horse."

The Gorges of the Altyn Tagh.

Our equipment was loaded on the donkeys, so that the Pearl could take the road travelling light. The sore on his back should consequently heal more quickly.

Tuzun, our guide, was charming. He had white teeth that gleamed through his black beard and he had a bubbling laugh like the laugh of a child. With him came a man whose mouth was all wrinkled from the frequency with which he uttered his sonorous "Kirr! Kirr!" in order to make wayward donkeys get on. I was, myself, riding a donkey now. It was not very pleasant, for he was a lame donkey, and kept stopping all the time. However, I vaunted the delights of donkey-riding to Peter, and with his usual good grace he ended by handing his mount over to me.

We were two days descending the valley of the Cherchen Darya. I was deafened by the roar of the grey, tumultuous water. Such water! Such grass! Three days earlier the thought of such abundance would have suggested another world. To cross the Altyn Tagh chain, however, the river plunged into a defile that, for us, was impracticable, and on the third day we had to climb two passes in succession over the bare, steep mountains. The summits had been enveloped in mist for two days and now suddenly it set in to rain. Peter's suitcase was shaking with the donkey's trot, and in that first downpour since our departure from Peking the labels of the Hôtel Adlon and the Hôtel Lido began to peel off it in bits.

In ravines sheltered by the flanks of the escarpments were flowers that charmed the eye, little irises in quantities, and sweet-smelling globe flowers with their golden balls—after being on a diet of leathery buturga the Pearl found them very delectable and made regular banquets off them—and then tiny, climbing rosaceous plants, compact beds of them forming great green patches on the ground.

A decided-looking and heavily-laden young mother joined our caravan a little way out from Bash Malghun. Her baby was given to crying at night and to vomiting; in short, "did all that the dear little things do." Thus the somewhat peeved Peter. He went so far as to predict all sorts of difficulties. He did not like women. "You have to be always helping them," he said. "The moment they appear, complications begin." And he was afraid that this one might turn the men against us. However, as he looked at the child, tied on the donkey and getting shaken, Peter finished by observing: "Poor little chap! He hasn't much of a life." My compassion, on the other hand, went out rather to the mother.

Our stage that day ended in the depths of a narrow ravine. The milk I was carrying in a bottle had turned into a hard mass of butter. And we had to make our tea with brackish water drawn from a dark grotto.

Throughout the whole morning of the fourth day we were staggering down the ravine which, as we descended, turned into an awe-inspiring gorge not much more than twenty yards wide. Down we went, and down, until it seemed as if we should end up in the bowels of the earth. Choughs croaked from the cracks of the gigantic walls of rock and the place reverberated with echoes.

And then at midday we quite suddenly emerged into brilliant sunshine and on to the desert of gravel that stretched along the foot of the mountain. We were at the edge of the Takla Makan, the sea of sand which extends for over five hundred miles of Eastern Turkestan. At Muna Bulak, a little spring, we were able to fill up with water in the shade of misty tamarisks in full bloom. The flowers were masses of pink shoots that had just opened.

But we were in an absolutely desert region and the heat as well as the change in altitude upset us. It was mid-June, we were only about four thousand feet up, but we had to make a halt.

Setting off again at six o'clock in the evening, it was not long before we were following the trail by the light of the stars. It became necessary to proceed on foot for the animals' sake. . . . We were intensely tired. . . . Once again it was only a question of endurance, of killing time for an hour, for another hour. . . . A little after midnight we settled ourselves to sleep on the ground, somewhat comforted by drinking each a mug of brackish water with a little brandy in it.

Having scarcely slept, we were off again at four o'clock on the morning of the fifth day. A sustained roar assailed our ears. No doubt, I decided, it is the great desert wind rising. Beyond that distant hill of small stones it was probably flattening out the dunes. But I was wrong. It was running water carrying shingle along with it, our river rediscovered once more. We were thirsty by the time we got to it. It was necessary to cut steps in the sand of the abrupt dunes, for it gave way under the camels' feet.

What was to Happen to Us?

We were to arrive in the oasis of Cherchen the next morning and found it difficult to imagine what it would be like. There would, no doubt, be maize, cotton and mulberry trees. But we did not feel sure about big trees. "Oasis" was a lovely word suggesting rest and abundance, but for us it meant disquiet and new dangers.

What was in store for us in this our first Sinkiang community? Ought we not, at any and every cost, to send word by courier to the English Consul at Kashgar, announcing our presence before the possibility of our being arrested arose? At the very least, we were in danger of falling into the hands of minor Tungan officials, who might well put us in prison while waiting for orders as to the treatment of foreigners. And, on the other hand, supposing the situation were still strained and the atmosphere one of suspicion, our European passports were liable to be taken for forgeries and we for Russians trying to find out the strength of the Tungan forces. If I were addressed in Russian, ought I to act as though I did not understand?

Of course two people ought to rouse less suspicion than one solitary man. A spy rarely encumbers himself with a woman. My presence might be of primary importance in its effect on any decision taken with regard to us. If our travelling through Sinkiang seemed too inexplicable, I could say I lived at Lanchow and that my father was lying ill at Kashgar. That would be the quickest way of getting there.

Peter took it that, as an Englishman, his presence would not be displeasing to the Tungans. They were hostile to Chinese

175

and Russians alike and were therefore liable to turn in friendly interest towards Great Britain.

Under Arrest.

Standing on top of a dune in the light of the setting sun, Peter focused his binoculars. Then, "Poplars!" he cried as a sailor might greet the sight of land. In the distance the soaring tops of trees could be distinguished in a mass of verdure that, with the mist of evening, was taking on a bluish tint. It was too late for it to be convenient to arrive that night, and we camped amidst the tamarisks on the bank of the Cherchen Darya.

Next day—the fifteenth of June, four months since our departure from Peking—we crossed the arms of the pale gold river. I saw sheep amongst the reeds, then, solitary on the bank of a canal, a willow. I could not help touching the trunk. "Adam bar!" With a turn of his spade, a bearded man opened a passage in a dyke to let the water flow into a field of maize. Cocks were crowing in every direction. We should have eggs. A cuckoo called. Such wonders! . . . In the deep shade of a sunken road smelling of honeysuckle, I was surprised by a curious noise repeated from moment to moment. It was the mighty symphony of thousands of leaves trembling in the indefatigable wind and I saw above me:

> *Vibrant du bois vivace, infléchi par la cime,*
> *Pour et contre les dieux ramer l'arbre unanime.**

We came to earthen walls shaded by trees and Tuzun led us into a courtyard. The filly's ears rose in her fright at crossing the first doorway she had ever crossed in her life. We were amongst friends and they offered us mien. Once they realized that, in spite of my breeches and my tanned face,

---

* Vibrating in the quick life of its timber, bent at the top,
The tree, at one with itself, pulling with and against the gods.
(Paul Valéry.)

I belonged to their own sex, the women took possession of me. . . . They asked me for face cream! Tuzun brought me a huge heavily perfumed rose from a neighbouring garden. I could not keep back my tears—partly because I was tired perhaps: who is to say? But it was when I saw all the beauty produced by the world that the tears came.

Our aksakal lived an hour's journey away, so we set off again, I on a donkey this time, for a lady of quality might not go on foot, and Peter, as head of the expedition, had to go on horseback. As we were crossing a big field in which camels were grazing, two soldiers appeared riding at a gallop. My heart thumped and I felt sure they were out after us. They seemed to be Chinese. Their caps were decorated with the Kuomintang sun. But I was fascinated most by their mounts, enormous horses, twice as high as our filly, short-necked, as fat as whales under their shining coats, such horses as I had forgotten existed.

The officers asked us to hand over any arms we had and then made the camels turn off from the direction we had been following. Tuzun gave them a baleful glance, and Peter summed up the situation by observing:

"We may consider ourselves under arrest."

CHAPTER VI

CHERCHEN CELEBRITIES

WITH forced smiles on our lips we followed the two horsemen. They made us pass through the middle of the village. In the main street, which was shaded with straw matting, the populace watched us in silence. Soon we entered the covered courtyard of an empty house.

A crowd that grew steadily in numbers examined us, murmuring "Oross." They thought we were Russians and it was clear that our declaration "Oross, djok! Engleesh!" was received with reserve. The donkey stables were too small for the Pearl and his companion and, suddenly out of their depth, they considered the situation with outraged faces.

Our passports were taken from us.

We sat on our suitcases and pretended that we were enjoying the rest. But we felt anxious. This was no inn and it was useless ordering the traditional tea—we were given nothing. We were in the rebels' power and if they chose to arrange it so, this house might well become our prison. We hoped that the authorities would examine my Peking passport first, since it was the one in which Sinkiang was mentioned.

The crowd made way for a young man of Iranian type. He was Abd Rakhman, confidential servant to the British aksakal, and the onlookers waited for Peter and him to engage in conversation since they were both "Engleesh." And they looked suspicious that we had only smiles to offer in answer to the questions he asked. But he was asking them in Hindustani, in Persian . . .

At the end of what seemed an interminable wait our papers were returned to us stamped with the official seal. For the moment we were out of danger. That was a comfort. A rug was quickly unrolled and we were given tea, sugar and fresh bread. Then the aksakal appeared. He carried himself with dignity, had a white beard, thick lips, and the dark skin of the Indian. He invited us to stay with him. Like the rest of his rare compatriots in the region, he wore the English flag on his coat. It was a distinctive sign and would be a protection in the event of a rebellion breaking out. He did not know English.

He led us across the oasis. The countrywomen fled, hiding their faces with a fold of their white veils. Only well-to-do Turki ladies wear the horsehair or lace veil. The men rose and joining their hands on their breasts salaamed to us. Those who were on horseback hastened to dismount as a gesture of respect. There were ripe apricots on the branches above our heads and I had my first taste of fruit that year.

Groups of peasants, in garments of white cotton, were weeding in the cornfields. Here and there one of them wore a rose over the ear. As they weeded, two of their number made music with a viola and a little drum. Under the shade of a tree in a courtyard further on, a dying man lay on a divan rug. His family knelt round, silent, fanning him, looking on him for the last time. The cemetery was very close by, its tombs surrounded by a wooden palisade and surmounted by a horse's tail.

Comfort.

Once more under a roof, we stayed five days as the aksakal's guests. Though the windows were large, I felt the lack of air at every turn. We were put in a guest-room decorated with Persian flower patterns and furnished with thick modern rugs on which we slept and ate. To Peter's great joy, Abd Rakhman brought us a folding table on which a typewriter could be placed. The typewriter itself was to send our visitors into ecstasies. The aksakal despatched a courier to his chief, the Consul at Kashgar, announcing our arrival. I seized the opportunity to write a reassuring letter home. But it never arrived. And in consequence of Peter's craving to get on quickly we ultimately reached Kashgar before the aksakal's message.

The aksakal himself waited on us every day, bringing rice with fat, chicken, eggs, sour milk, very sweet tea, dainties of one kind or another, and piles of bread, round and flat like pancakes. We stuffed ourselves shamelessly. During dessert one day the aksakal did us the honour of bringing out his gold for our benefit, for each year he sent two men into the Altyn Tagh to bring him back gold dust, and what they brought he had made into ingots. He had a little pair of scales and we amused ourselves weighing our tiny bar against the smallest fragment of his store. Our host also introduced me to his wife. Her face would have caused me no surprise had it been in Paris we met. Of uncertain age, she was a morose Turki woman, not very good at conversation in the odds and ends of various languages at our command.

An uninterrupted procession of visitors passed through our room. Leaving their overshoes in the ante-room they knelt in a semi-circle round us and passing the bowls of tea from one to another, asked us a thousand questions the sense of which we tried to guess, though in reality we understood nothing.

A group of charming old men in turbans and ample khalats* assured us that the Russians in power in the capital of Sinkiang were bad people, whereas the English who ruled over India had all the virtues. The world would be so much

* The khalat is a kind of caftan or outdoor cloak.

easier to study if it were thus clearly divided into good and bad.

During our long march through desolate lands, Cherchen and civilization had become synonymous terms for us. But it was not long before we realized that here, in a country without telegraph or postal communications, two months' journey from India, it was we who were expected to provide news of the great world. The people about us found it difficult to understand how we came, and when we spoke of the Kuen Lun Mountains they simply stared. We might just as well have dropped from the moon.

They all rose when one visitor was announced, no less a personage than the Ssu Ling.* His bodyguard heralded his arrival with a flourish of trumpets and, according to Peter, who went out to receive him, they also brought a machine-gun mounted on a horse to add to the solemnity of the occasion. The General brought us presents, a chicken, some eggs and a sheep. He was a little Tungan with a cynical mouth. His very Chinese, beardless face radiated liveliness. He had no difficulty in realizing how we had got to Cherchen from the Tsaidam and could easily make sense of Peter's attempts at Chinese. The Ssu Ling had fought the legendary Turkestan campaign under Ma Chung-ying, and when we asked what had become of that hero, he answered without the flicker of an eyelid:

"Ma Chung-ying is in England buying aeroplanes."

The unconvincing assertion really meant: "Let us talk of something else," and the little general embarked on the main object of his visit. For several months he had been suffering from trouble in the groin and found riding painful. Perhaps one of our ointments might give him relief. As simply as an infant with its mother he revealed an enormous gland, protected by a pad of raw cotton—doubtless gathered in a

* General, Commanding Officer.

field that same day. I gave him some iodoform, avowed my incompetence and once more defended myself against the implication of being one of "those who study diseases." But I hastened to disinfect the boils and abscesses of the soldiers he presented to me.

I learned later that my patient was no other than Ma Ying-piao, who, under the name of Little Chung-yang (Colonel), enjoyed an unenviable reputation. In 1932, at the head of several thousand men, he had wiped out numerous Chinese villages in Kansu. Then under Ma Chung-ying he held the command of the oasis of Barköl, in Sinkiang; and in February 1934 it was he who escorted Sven Hedin to Turfan when the explorer had landed himself right into the civil war.

Court of Miracles.

The Ssu Ling had scarcely gone when the aksakal asked if I would see some sick people who had come a distance. What the people had in mind was doubtless the last English expedition. The leader, they said, was a marvellous doctor who travelled with forty camels. He knew every language and his name was Ishtin Sahib. It was, we discovered, Aurel Stein they meant.

Peter was acting as my interpreter and, seeing the crowd of people of all classes at the door, he took charge of operations. I had a basin of permanganate, some talc, vaseline, iodine, bandages, ointments, quinine and of course castor oil and the useful Jintan pills. As each patient entered the room Peter asked the same questions: "What is your trouble?"—"How long have you had it?"—"Do you eat well?"—"Do you feel very cold—very hot?"

Sometimes the patient was disposed of quickly. One said he felt ill whenever he ate hot food. "Eat cold food," Peter commanded and beckoned to the next. For the most part the questions were unnecessary. Beneath their lambskin caps the children had heads covered with sores. One woman had no palate left. Another's nose was gone. A third had fallen into the fire and, raising her horsehair veil, revealed a frightful face with the eyelids all inflamed and hanging down to the middle of the cheeks. Under trousers stiff with pus, a man revealed a haunch eaten away by an ulcer. Peter grew impatient with me and could not understand my hesitation in recommending this or that treatment for, in reality, I was not competent to deal with these complaints, which were of tubercular and syphilitic origin.

Day after day, the procession continued, though I persisted in explaining that I was not a doctor. The news had spread like a train of powder that there was a foreign woman with medicines. And as it did, suffering people who, up till then, had no doubt felt resigned, began to hope. . . . And I had no alternative but to extinguish the piteous light in their eyes. A mother turned away with her burden—a little girl who had diphtheria, with the death-rattle escaping from her purulent mouth and her stomach sagging down her emaciated thighs. A girl was carried out on a stretcher. Her legs were enormous and the transparent skin of the ankles, swollen with water, was like a toy balloon inflated to bursting point. But what I shall remember more than anything else is the man in the prime of life who, taking off his turban, revealed the pink skin eaten away, leaving bare the spongy tissue of the greenish cranium bone. It was like some nest of frightful bees.

I had to close down. I could do no more. Because at the same time, I wanted to rest, to enter up my notes for the day, to lay in new supplies from the village, and to make myself a light garment for the broiling crossing of the Takla Makan which lay between us and Khotan.

Cherchen Visits.

In the market at Cherchen, to which I had looked forward with joy for so many weeks, there was no soap to be had, no mien, no spirits and no dried apricots. All the commodities I could see on the dusty shelves of the booths were Soviet sugar and matches, English muslin, old Austrian needles and some pieces of native silk. But most of the stalls were closed. There was no saying what riches might not be available on the weekly market day.

We had to call on the notabilities of the town. As was fitting, we went first to the Little Colonel. He received us on a shady platform near a sheet of deep water and accepted our present of revolver bullets with pleasure. He treated us familiarly and it was thanks to a word from him to the mayor that we got beasts to take us to Keriya, the next oasis, twelve days' journey from Cherchen. He also gave us a letter of introduction to Ma Ho-san, the Commander-in-Chief of the Tungan forces at Khotan.

His soldiers wore white piqué hats like those little girls in Europe wear at the seaside. We were amused by the heterogeneous and international collection of old rifles on the rack in the guard-room. The history of any one of them would doubtless furnish material for a novel.

We were scarcely out into the street again when Chin-pan, another military chief with some mixture of Tibetan in him, led us off to visit his barracks. He wore what looked like white satin pyjamas and his barracks were very clean. Tea was, as always, served in our honour, here in bowls of Russian earthenware, and with six pieces of Russian sugar. And we were offered Russian cigarettes.

Next a dealer in rugs invited us into the fresh courtyard of his Chinese house. He spoke of a blond young foreigner who, a year before, had arrived in Cherchen, but becoming suspect, got sent back under escort to Kansu. He had not known Chinese any better than ourselves, but they gathered that he came from Khotan, where he had been refused permission to take the road to India. Who could he be, the poor lad who met the fate that we had been fearing would befall ourselves?*

We learned also that the Tungans at Cherchen were commandeering camels. That was why nobody would buy our camels. But an embassy sent to Khotan by Ma Bu-fang had recently criticized the exactions system so severely that the delegates were being kept in isolation until they got back home to Sining. The Ma dynasty at Sining then claimed the right to intervene in the affairs of the Tungan administration in Sinkiang, though it meant braving the desert of Lop Nor on the trail followed long ago by Marco Polo. Ma Chung-ying had been under orders from Sining some years earlier. This latest news meant that, though the Tungans were counted as rebels by Nanking, they were not totally isolated from the rest of the world. Was it not even possible that in case of war they might he helped by their co-religionists of Kansu?

Their chief, however, the terrible Ma Chung-ying, was far from Cherchen. Our host said he was in Moscow and claimed to have seen a snapshot of him that was taken in that city. It was said that a messenger had been sent to him there. These interesting titbits of gossip sharpened our desire to learn what was really happening in Chinese Turkestan.

---

* I learned later that he was a Czech named Sedlacek and that it was he who, meeting us, had said "Caput" as we were leaving Lanchow. For nine months he lay ill in prison at Tunghwang, but in the end was tried and acquitted.

CHAPTER VII

ACROSS THE TAKLA MAKAN DESERT

HAVING given some small presents to the aksakal in token of our gratitude, we left his hospitable house, and for the last time I admired the English flag above the door. It was made locally and the impassive Peter had been not a little moved at the sight of it.

Custom ordains that travellers must be escorted on horseback to the edge of the oasis. It was there we took leave of our courteous host and his secretary. At the last canal, in the shadow of the last tree, we had a drink of water. It was midday. The desert danced before our eyes in the glare. We had twelve days of hard going to get to Keriya, the next oasis.

Now we were on the famous Silk Road, so frequented in the past. I had imagined—I do not know why—that somehow we should travel it in a cart, during the freshness of the night for choice. But in the deep sand, tracks got levelled by the wind and without the light of day one was liable to go astray.

In reality Cherchen was a dead spot of Sinkiang. Very little traffic went through it, not only because of the recent political troubles but also, and chiefly, because of the barrier of the Lop Nor to the east which made the journey between Cherchen and Tunghwang difficult.

Before recounting the salient incidents of this stage of our journey, I must introduce the protagonists. First of all, there was Absalom, the only horse we had been able to hire through the authorities. He was a handsome stallion and out of generosity I left him to Peter, for in Moslem countries it is fitting that the man should be well mounted. I was perched on a donkey with my feet dragging on the ground like a native woman. We had once again set out with the two camels and the scraggy pony, but we were hoping to sell them at a profit at Keriya. And now a thing we had not foreseen happened. Absalom fell in love with the awful-looking filly. Throughout the entire journey he paid her assiduous court and day and night the descending arpeggios of his powerful neighing resounded in our ears. He grew thin of his passion, he could not sleep, at every stop he tore at his reins, and Peter, who constituted himself Cynara's protector—perhaps because he judged her to be a minor—had to be perpetually on the alert.

From the second day on, I enjoyed the privilege of riding Absalom, and I became aware of the fun the filly got from provoking the poor stallion— though the moment he came too close to her she roared as though her throat was being cut. The fact that I was on horseback again was because one day on a trotting donkey, and also, perhaps, the greasy food we had been having at Cherchen, brought on an attack of lumbago so bad that for several weeks the slightest movement caused me acute pain. Peter took pity on me and gave me his horse, whose movement was less fatiguing than the donkey's. Sometimes I tried to unstiffen myself by walking, but in the soft sand I found the effort exhausting.

Good Great Man.

The donkeys that carried our baggage also played an important part in the march across the desert, for at night they were tied up near us, they had bells on their necks, they were amorous, and they got so agitated that we found it impossible to sleep, however tired we were. An honest fellow named Aziz was in charge of them. We found him amusing —a consummate playboy who, from the very first day we saw him entering the aksakal's reception room with his father, addressed us in a tearful voice. He had moaned because he could find no maize for his asses at the bazaar and would not therefore be able to leave on the appointed day. Now he never ceased imploring us to have pity on his tired donkeys. Peter he addressed, in Chinese, as *Ta jen* ("master" or "great man"). The gentleman addressed did not fail to point out to me that nobody would ever pay me such a mark of respect. When Aziz had a particularly important supplication to make he played such variations on the theme, *Hao Ta jen* ("good great man"), that the hardest heart must have melted. One evening at the end of the stage and with several people standing round, I caused much hilarity by addressing a most melancholy *Hao Ta jen* to Peter when I wanted a match.

Some Turki travellers joined up with us on the outskirts of Cherchen. We groaned, for inevitably it must lead to complications. And, sure enough, Aziz helped them to load up their donkeys every morning. That meant that we were not the only people to whom he had engaged himself. But, in fact, the fellow-travellers thus imposed on us provided some diversion. There was an old woman, all wrapped up in veils, with her son. There was a father with his son. When the latter got off the burning sand and leaped on their ass he left his old sandals for the father who had just dismounted from the animal.

Then there was a fellow, another Tokta Ahun, a high-spirited, unsympathetic creature who wearied our ears with the unchanging song he bawled from dawn to dark. In our exasperation we called him every name we could think of—and that, after all, was a way of occupying our time too. After prolonged negotiations this Tokta Ahun had ceded one of his donkeys to Peter in exchange for Cynara. He was extremely proud of his bargain and in the evening gave her vast quantities of maize to make her fat. But meanwhile

Peter's new donkey, which he had mounted with ceremony, turned out to be far inferior to what had been claimed for him and often lay down on the way. Peter wished to cancel the bargain and it was only 'after an epic discussion that he won—by insisting on the question as to who was to pay for the maize eaten by the filly. The term *ahun* added to most names meant "reader of the Koran" or "literate," but I think it is used as a courtesy title. I doubt very much whether our hungry Tokta Ahun of Issik Pakte, for instance, had ever read the sacred book.

Travelling with us also was Tuzun Ahun, a silent, noble figure. He was deputed by the Cherchen yamen to accompany us as far as Khotan and he pushed condescension to the point of leading our two camels by their halters. One day I overtook him and was asking him how many hours' marching we still had to do when his horse, jealous of Absalom, let out a kick that got me on the shin. The pain of it, on top of the pain I was already suffering with my lumbago, was so great that I felt constrained to lie down on the sand. And I waited there till Peter should come up and be company—and therefore distraction. As I observed to him, uninteresting little accidents like that were always befalling me. I did not get lost in cyclones at sea, in the deadly sandstorms of the desert, in encounters with Manchurian bandits, or in bivouacs at the bottoms of crevasses—though such experiences would be very useful when it came to satisfying the passion of stay-at-home Parisians for tales of adventure.

To divert my mind from my misfortunes, Peter recounted the tribulations of an English nobleman whom he had accompanied on a journey to Soviet Caucasia the summer before. . . .

Day after day we forced ourselves to talk, in order—so far as I at least was concerned—to keep some check on the imbecility that grew on one in the monotony. Thus, we went over the films we remembered, criticizing them in detail; and then books; and writers; and the lives our friends led. One day we ran out of subject-matter and I asked Peter to give a dissertation on London clubs. . . .

Brackish Water.

Now that we were no longer fearful of finishing up in a Sinkiang prison, now that we had well-marked-out stages to follow, and were sure of finding more and more modern comforts at each oasis we came to, our principal distraction consisted in speculating about the quality and the nearness of the next water-hole.

Mosquitoes were welcome messengers, forerunners of humidity. The wind brought me—I say "me," for Peter admittedly had no sense of smell—a scent of pinks that came, in fact, from clusters of pink flowers like little bells. Then the reeds in the sand would become more dense. And suddenly, in the shadow of ground that was itself whitened by salt, there would be the dark water-hole. We would get down on our knees and fill our bowls with cool, sometimes magnesian, water. Afterwards it would be the animals' turn.

We were so used to eating and drinking things as they came that we were not at all incommoded by water that had quantities of insects floating about in it. Similarly, we went bareheaded for months, though it was against every canon laid down in the manuals of Asiatic travel. We used to take water from the holes in gourds attached to the packs on the donkeys' backs, but it became hot and nauseating very quickly.

In the course of that trek across the desert we saw some clumps of a queer type of tree—queer, for it had long lamellæ of willow leaves and trembling poplar leaves growing on it at the same time. This is the *toghrak* or wild poplar of the Tarim Basin. But there was a weird silence as of a cemetery amongst those green powerful-looking trees. And death was, in fact, everywhere. The tree-trunks were already partly submerged by the sand, the level of which would inevitably be raised by every fresh storm. The cry of a bird struck one as an anomaly. One day we made our way between huge cones of sand immobilized, each one, about a regular armour of roots and dead branches. This was exactly what the flourishing trees we had been seeing would come to look like in time. On another occasion I had to admire the curious terracing of the ground caused by wind erosion. I felt as if I were visiting the crypts of long-buried temples just beginning to appear under the shovels of excavators.

Aziz did not seem to be very clear about the lengths of the stages and I was usually surprised at the sight of the great pole that marked the end of the day's march standing up against the horizon. There would be a solitary hut made of boughs and branches and a man to keep in the fire. Supper, the only meal of the day, no longer gave us pleasure. The weather was too warm. I dreamed of the fat strawberries that, now it was June, must be ripe in Europe. The only food I appreciated where I was was the refreshing *k'tak* produced by Tuzun. It was solidified sour milk which he had brought in a cloth bag. One mixed a spoonful of it in a bowl of water.

The night we were at Aghe we fled from the fleas, the donkeys and the incessant chatter of the hut, and in spite of the mosquitoes, against which we wound scarves about our heads, went and lay down on the sand in our sleeping-bags. In the middle of the night I woke with a start and in the darkness made out the head of a baby camel resting on my knees. I could not believe my eyes and put out my hand to stroke the woolly head. But it proved to be Peter's hair. Still asleep, he was trying to protect his face against mosquitoes.

191

Veterinary Practice.

Before we and they separated definitely, the camels were again to play a part in my life. On the fourth evening we came to a lonely but deliciously verdant stretch, where the ruins of great wells, strengthened with enormous beams, were still in existence. On leaving Cherchen I had noticed some blood on the Pearl's nose, but attached no importance to it, feeling convinced that he had been well cared for during the five days we stayed with the aksakal. But the Turkis are donkey men and know nothing about camels. Seeing the animals we had brought from the mountains getting on so bravely, with never a groan, I had developed an affection for them. Tuzun Ahun made them go faster than they were in the habit of doing and when Number Two did too much stretching of the neck, I was not afraid to encourage him by scratching him behind the ears. When a wooden peg fell out from his sore nose I knew how to put it back.

Now it was the Pearl that was complaining. Obviously he was suffering, and not merely from the numerous ticks that hung on to his belly and gorged themselves on his blood. When we got into camp I lifted off his pack-saddle and noticed that the first thing he did was to plunge the point of his nose-peg into his wound. It had become deep again. There was a cavity as big as a man's fist just below the spine, and this cavity was crawling with maggots massed so closely as to constitute a kind of whitish stuffing—like the core of an artichoke.

Neither Aziz nor Tuzun knew what to do. But I was not going to let the poor brute be devoured alive in such fashion even for the one week of our partnership that had still to run. Peter and I forced Tuzun to help us to tie up the great creature's legs when we had got it kneeling. But I had to give up the attempt to operate with my knife, for the moment I touched the raw flesh the Pearl would roll over and escape from our hold. So I treated the wound with concentrated permanganate and threw xeroform into the open mouths of the uneasy worms. Within a few days we had the pleasure of seeing the swarming little brutes stiffen and turn black, and then they fell for ever from our good Pearl's back.

As for Number Two, Tuzun had been pulling so hard on his nose that it bled, and the flies had quickly gathered for the feast provided. I was not able to dislodge the worms that gathered as well. But a little later, at the first village we got to, I went to an old camel-driver for advice. He made me buy some black pepper and pound it up. With this he filled up the wound, and in three days it had healed. Peter thought it praiseworthy of me to go to so much trouble with the animals every day. He could not realize what joy it was to feel that I was being really useful about something.

The fifth evening saw us at Endere, which was just a farm in the midst of trees near a muddy river. It reminded one rather of an English park. Far down from there, at a point where the river disappears in the sand, Sir Aurel Stein had carried out his extraordinarily interesting excavations at Niya and Dandan Oilik. Seventeen centuries ago, the Silk Road ran well to the north of the present trail, through regions that were then irrigated. The texts which have been discovered, written in a North Indian language—Kharosthi—prove that there was important transcontinental traffic in those days.

On the seventh day, the heat though dry was very trying. As the hut at our station was beside the river Yartungaz, I managed to get a bathe, but not until I had made several vain attempts, for there were steep banks of deep mud between me and the water.

Five-o'clock Tea.

We were coming near to an inhabited area. Travellers sometimes appeared on the trail. The great desolate spaces were left behind and now there were clumps of greenery. The next day about noon we came to the caravanserai of Yangi Darya, situated at a point in the middle of a grove of willows. Some dozen Tungan soldiers were there at the same time as we. They were not at all timid and flung themselves on my Leica camera to see what it was. Their little officer invited us to drink tea in one of the rooms of the stage-house, and as he had learned Russian at Urumchi we were able to talk as we had not done since we parted from Borodishin. The officer had come from Khotan and was taking home the wife and son of the rebel chanto who had tried to set up as an independent commander at Charklik. The suppression of the revolt by the Tungans had been thorough-going, a hundred inhabitants being executed. This happened just at the moment we arrived in Sinkiang. The officer who, like Ma Chung-ying, was a native of Hochow, told us about the battle of Tutung, to the south of Urumchi, some seventeen months before, at which he was present. The Government troops were suddenly reinforced by five tanks and by Soviet bombing planes, with the result that the Tungans, who thought the day was already theirs, were wiped out. The planes had made a terrific impression on our host. He believed, or wanted us to believe, that Nanking was no longer hostile to the Tungans and was even now sending troops against Urumchi. They would be at Hami very shortly.

The officer was offering us delicious rolls made at Keriya when he asserted, in answer to a question from me, that Ma Chung-ying had not been forced to cross to the Russian side of the frontier. Ma Chung-ying, he said, would soon be returning from Moscow, where he had gone of his own free will to study the mysteries of aviation.

Niya and the Last "Gobi."

The next day we reached a prosperous village where
apricots, sour milk, rolls and quarters of meat were displayed in front of the booths in the shaded street. We found
the inn very clean. The Turki notabilities of the oasis,
wearing the silk chapan, came and paid their compliments,
but it was not, apparently, altogether on our account that
they put themselves about, for they had the doors at either
end of the crowded courtyard locked and proceeded to get
on with what seemed, as far as I could make out, to be a
count of the cattle belonging to the men thus penned in.

It was only with the greatest difficulty I got permission to
have the doors opened for our camels to be led out to
pasture. Being Tsaidam beasts they did not realize that the
cut lucerne grass we had offered them was edible.

*   *   *   *   *

Three days' journey and, according to Aziz's account, a
terrible desert still lay between us and Keriya, the big town
where we were to change our caravan. We left the shaded
road with regret and then we came to a delta of gravel before
striking the burning waste. For hours we escaladed waves of
sand on which the trail could barely be made out. A cart,
the first we had seen since Tangar, was drawn up at one
point. The owner lay sleeping in its shadow while waiting
for his beast to eat a bundle of straw.

Hour after hour one's eyes went on searching, but nothing
appeared except some little donkeys being beaten by their
masters. These latter wore a smock of coarse white cotton
tied round the waist with a scarf. The dryness of the atmosphere created optical delusions. I thought I saw a rocky
mountain chain on the horizon, and suddenly I was beside a
pile of dark cases on which a man lay asleep, waiting doubtless for new animals to come up and be loaded. Further on,

in the limitless plain, a solitary man stood beside a dying donkey whose back was all one sore. Carcasses abounded. The poor little donkeys with which the roads of Asia are strewn—though they know how to be very exasperating at times—ought to have a ballad written about them.

I rode as fast as Absalom cared to go, so as to get in a couple of hours' sleep somewhere while waiting for the others to come up. From the top of a dune I saw a pole standing up and then suddenly, gleaming like a jewel, a sheet of water beside some century-old mulberry trees. It was Ovraz and its solitary house. I found a detachment of Tungan soldiers there. Their bearded officer invited me to sit on his rugs, which were lined with white sheeting. I did so—and slept for an hour.

The soldiers had six handcuffed prisoners in their charge. These had been captured during the rebellion at Charklik and were being taken to Khotan to be tried. The soldiers were well-built fellows and roared with real guard-room laughter when Peter, jumping off his donkey, managed to tear the seat of his trousers. I did not laugh so hilariously, for it was on me the job of mending that tear must fall. But indirectly my sewing brought us an omelet for our supper. The pretty daughter of the *saraï* keeper assured me she had no eggs, but a moment later she saw my needles and produced four eggs in exchange for two of them.

That night we slept blessedly on an earthen platform at the foot of a tree. Enormous white mulberries splashed on our faces from time to time, but they hardly disturbed us. I did, however, wake up suddenly out of a nightmare in which I had been lying on a shore lashed by storm-driven waves. It was already morning when I woke. The great sandy wind had risen, the *shamal* which turns day into night. At every turn I made, the sand that had been heaped up on me fell off. There was nothing for it but to take refuge in a dark room until the storm died down, and so we fled indoors.

After Ovraz the sandy plains had narrow baskets filled with stones and very high, as landmarks—like desert buoys. We passed the three caravanserais of Yesulghun, slept in the charming house of the *Shang-yi*, or mayor of the village of Uitoghrak, and at last, on the first of July, came in sight of Keriya. But not before Absalom discovered the bright idea of rolling over some fifteen times on the ground, with the result that my wooden saddle was now more battered than ever.

CHAPTER VIII

LUXURY AT KERIYA

ON a wide, well-made road, we passed cows and sheep. Near us little half-moon-shaped fields of rice, terraced and inundated, glittered in the sun. At last we reached the town, passing along streets bordered with fruit-stalls. Women with uncovered faces wore voluminous robes of silk ornamented at the breast with five bars like stylized wings of eagles. The bars were a sign that a woman was married.

At the end of a paved and winding street we entered a little courtyard which was ablaze with oleanders. Here was the home of the aksakal, Rholam Mohammed Khan. Peter and I were led into a room that made us open our eyes very wide. There was an umbrella hanging on a hook, several paraffin lamps, an electric torch, a deck-chair in a corner and several clocks on the walls. But the climax of luxury was to be reached in the evening—we were to sleep between white sheets on a raised platform that ran round the court-yard. In a room near the one we were in, a sewing-machine was humming. A young man with a cough was making masses of the caps worn under the turban by the chantos.

Our host was of Afghan origin. His black beard made his fine face look longer than it was. He carried a cane and wore a fez, splendid yellow shoes—only half-laced—and over his light suit of clothes of European cut, a khalat of silk. He pressed honey on us, and rose jam, rolls, Russian sweets (*Stratosphere* brand), biscuits and even cold duck. And all the time we were carrying on a conversation with him in halting Chinese.

Then, dressed in our very best—which is to say that we wore clean shirts—we set off, accompanied by the aksakal, to pay calls on the civil and military authorities. Brigadier-General Ma Fu-yang had a shaven head and a low, wrinkled forehead. He was unable to read the Chinese visiting cards we presented, so his secretary, an elegant young Chinaman, was called in. This "literate" from Lanchow had heard of *The Times* and he knew where Switzerland was, even Geneva. That was a surprise. Having exchanged civilities we managed to turn the conversation on to the subject of the renowned young chief, Ma Chung-ying. We wanted to know where he was. It was difficult to hide our astonishment when they told us that Ma Chung-ying was at Khotan. We were going to be there in five days' time. But no, we should not see him. He was there incognito. We followed our hosts' example, smiled politely and affected to believe what we were told. Was it bad for the Tungan cause, then, to have Ma Chung-ying in Moscow? Otherwise why not admit that he was there?

The barracks were cleanly kept, as were also the hundreds of old rifles arranged in their racks. We were escorted ceremoniously to the outer door. In spite of the extreme heat several awkward-looking young recruits were playing basket-ball on the barrack-square.

The aksakal next presented us to the mayor. We reached him at the end of a series of courts which formed an imposing yamen. He was a handsome Turki dressed in a khalat of green taffeta. Though he dared not complain openly, we gathered that he was not allowed to resign his office, nor could he emigrate to India (taking his fortune with him), for want of a passport. When he was saying good-bye he promised that we should have the five donkeys and two horses we wanted to hire.

Rholam Mohammed Khan took us to lunch at a country

house he was building for himself. We must eat *palau*, the national dish of Turkestan. It turned out to be rice cooked with fat, and made savoury with carrots, pieces of fried lamb and raisins. A pitcher of hot water was brought in. One washed one's hands both before and after eating. The aksakal ate in the traditional way, with his fingers, but covers were laid for us. The wide windows gave on to a beautiful orchard. The women's quarters were at the end of a corridor, in a low wing of the house, and I was taken along to meet the aksakal's wife. Though he was old, she was a pretty young woman with a smiling face, and seemed to be happy living there with her children and her old mother. . . . How should I know anything more? Beside her she had a dear little girl, Meradj, whom I had met with the aksakal the evening before. Mrs. Rholam Mohammed Khan and I examined the different materials of which our dresses were made. Her muslin veil was held on her head by an embroidered cap. Her voluminous dress was of the white silk of the country—silk that, according to legend, was first brought to Turkestan by a Chinese princess who came to Khotan to marry the king. Though it was forbidden by the Chinese emperors, she managed to hide some of the precious cocoons in her turban when she was leaving her own country.

Our way back to the town lay along little sunken roads. Then we came to such a parade ground as I had never yet seen. There were parallel-bars and cross-bars, these with knotted ropes hanging from them; and then an astonishing wall of planks, no doubt representing a wall to be taken by assault. On a canal bank near-by and in the shadow of some willows which had shaggy red roots, hundreds of pot-bellied army horses were in training. . . . It appeared that during the preceding days the authorities had requisitioned eggs by the thousand, mutton fat and bricks of tea from all over the oasis, with a view to producing a stew as a variation to the diet of maize which was making the horses too fat.

We found Aziz at the house awaiting our return. He immediately threw himself at the aksakal's feet, embraced his knees and over and over again cried: "*Hao Ta jen.*" After some time we gathered that the yamen wished to send him on with us to Khotan, whereas, according to his contract, he was free to return to Cherchen once we were safely delivered at Keriya. What was to be done? Fortunately a lieutenant-colonel arrived precisely at that moment, to return the call we had paid his General. He immediately scribbled a note to the yamen of the civil authorities, countermanding the order, and the incident was closed. The officer, who was charming, had sent us presents beforehand: two bottles of Téjé eau-de-Cologne from Moscow, a packet of sugar and a black sheep. The odd thing was that, while we were out, the mayor had called and left similar gifts. With sugar, which is the essence of luxury in Central Asia, descending on us like an avalanche, I could easily afford to give a packet to the sad young man who never seemed to leave his post at the sewing-machine.

At Keriya we at last carried through a most important piece of business—the sale of our caravan. It was imperative that we should get rid of our three animals this time. A friend of the aksakal's was so good as to offer us a thousand *lianzes** for them. We were never to find out the exact value of the dirty bank-notes that circulated in the Tungan republic, but it was clear that our camels were surrendered at a ridiculous price, for at the bazaar a pair of Russian tennis shoes cost a tenth of what we received for our beasts, a bottle of eau-de-Cologne cost thirty lianzes and a box of Russian *Nasha Marka* cigarettes, seven lianzes.

* Bank-notes.

From One Oasis to Another.

At two o'clock on the afternoon of the 3rd of July we left Keriya, both of us on horseback. But Peter's rejoicings at having an animal suited to his height were of short duration. He had to finish the stage on foot. The authorities had hired us thin animals that they had no use for themselves. Next day my companion left Damaka mounted on a donkey once more. Peter made no complaint, but he had to admit that donkey-riding as a method of locomotion kept one's mind at a very prosaic level. In every village after Keriya we were to find it difficult to hire animals and to obtain food supplies.

And the new donkey would not go! Urging him on with backward kicks on the flanks became wearisome and Peter preferred to walk. The weather was very warm and every time we came to an "ice-cream" man sitting at the foot of a tree, we stopped. During winter, ice is buried, and then in summer it is exhumed and sold in small pieces mixed with sour milk, the mixture constituting an admirable drink from the point of view of relieving thirst.

On the road we passed donkeys laden with lucerne grass, faggots and bricks, commandeered by the authorities. That same day, a troop of camels barred our way near a tank of fresh water and there we saw how a three-year-old camel is tied up while its nose is being pierced with a wooden peg for the first time. This one could now be easily led and he was of an age to become a beast of burden. Noticing us, the officer decided to find out who we were and insisted on our going in to drink a bowl of tea in the court of his house. Tuzun had no love for the Tungans and came with us reluctantly.

On the evening of the 4th of July I arrived in advance, Tuzun with me, at the rich oasis of Chira. The soldiers we met took me for an "Oross." As I went by an exercise ground, a cavalry regiment was practising the manœuvre of making all the horses lie down simultaneously. An officer standing on the top of a wooden tower was in command. A little later, Peter, passing the same spot and covered with dust, was to be interrogated by the same officer. He wanted to know the identity of such an unusual kind of tramp. The situation might easily have taken a nasty turn, but the Old Etonian succeeded in extricating himself with flying colours. He got the laughs on his side by addressing the officer on his high perch, not inappropriately, as "*Do Ta jen*" ("very great man").

The bazaar in the main street was a lively scene, with its baskets full of green and yellow cocoons. A group of people had collected round a Chinaman, who was trying his best to sell them silver dollars at forty-five lianzes each. Peter listened carefully and, having made sure that he understood, suddenly produced a silver dollar from his pocket and offered to sell it to the Chinaman. How the crowd laughed when the money-changer refused to pay more than thirty lianzes for it!

On a little bridge a few steps along I bought a hundred apricots for a lianze.

At the inn where every square inch of our tiny room was covered with flies, several Tungan soldiers came in, and in almost incomprehensible Russian, and very roughly, asked us questions: "You Russian, yes? How old are you? Give me your camera!" We pretended not to understand. But one of them who had a pink-and-white face and slanting eyes, spoke perfect Russian. He, I discovered, had two years earlier been *komsomol* in Frunze, the capital of Soviet Kirghiztan, where I had been in 1932. We talked of the school which he had attended for three years, then of Frunze's cinema. He said that life there had become too difficult, so he took his mother to Kuldja and, leaving her, came on here himself. "I wish I could see her," he said. "My heart is not easy when I am away from her." Being a Tungan, he had joined Ma

Chung-ying's forces. "But," he added, "it will not be long before things are as difficult at this side of the Tien Shan as on the other. Shops are closing down, everything is commandeered and money goes down in value every day." He had food, of course, and he was paid thirty lianzes a month, but he complained that he had no time to himself, what with all the gymnastics they had to do—accompanying the movements with military songs repeated over and over again. There were several who, like him, had succeeded in escaping from the U.S.S.R. It was one of them—his name was Pashkoff—who had trained the horses in the Mongolian exercises. My komsomol declared also that Ma Chung-ying had gone to Moscow to ask for Stalin's help. When he came back he would make war on the nerveless Chinese and the Russians would allow him to take Urumchi.

I have been continually writing of revolts, of civil war, of the vanished commander, and I write of Sinkiang as inaccessible. It is time I gave some particulars of things that, seen from Peking, seemed incomprehensible. Besides, as the obstacles liable to make a trans-Asiatic journey impossible were mainly political, it is only by discussing them that I can make it clear why our expedition was hazardous. And as we were now approaching Khotan, the Tungans' capital, it may be of interest to see how their republic was created.

CHAPTER IX

Sinkiang

SINKIANG,* which in area is twice the size of France, is shut off from the rest of the world by the highest mountains and the greatest desert that exist—the Celestial Mountains, the Pamirs, the Karakorams, the Kuen Lun and the Gobi. The one normal line of access to this vast country is by Siberia.

To the south Sinkiang consists for the most part of the Takla Makan desert, with the Tarim and its tributaries flowing through it—the fertile oases extending over less than a sixtieth part of the surface. The province, which is the largest in China, has scarcely more than three million inhabitants, most of them Moslem Turkis. It would appear that a region of the kind offers nothing likely to appeal to the greed of conquering nations. And in fact it is its strategical importance that has always made it an objective for its ambitious neighbours. Only why was it always at their mercy?

The inhabitants are for the most part of Iranian origin but "Turkified" at the beginning of our era as a result of invasions by the Uighurs in alliance with the Huns. They are a settled agricultural people and peaceable in their ways. Their fields have to be irrigated as well as cultivated, so their time is completely occupied, and they have never manifested warlike tendencies. Nor are they bound by national feeling. As each oasis is separated from the next by desert land that is not easily traversed, so each village lives isolated in a closed economic system. Until recent

* The name, meaning New Dominion, was given it in 1759.

times the people have never been stirred to action except when the fanaticism of Islam was outraged by Buddhist and Chinese oppression.

In the Past.

For two thousand years China was Sinkiang's only powerful neighbour and every time that China, after a period of disorder, wanted to affirm her hegemony in Asia she found it necessary, for strategic reasons, once more to reoccupy the far-off land. This was the only means of forestalling attacks by the barbarians who, in spite of the Great Wall—constructed about the third century B.C.—made incursions into the middle of the Empire. In addition, Chinese supremacy in the Tarim basin ensured the safety of the caravan traffic along the Silk Road which for a long time was the only means of communication between Cathay,* as China was then called, and Europe.

The Chinese were already masters of Sinkiang under the Han dynasty in the first century B.C. After periods of eclipse, China again conquered and reconquered these western marshes, under the powerful Tang (seventh century) and under the Mongols (thirteenth century). Finally, in 1759, it was the turn of the Manchu Emperor Chien Lung to extend his power as far as the Pamirs. And beyond the frontier, Kokhand, Badakshan and even Baltishan recognized the suzerainty of China. But the native Moslems, discontented by the heavy taxation imposed on them, fled to Kokhand.

In 1826 and again in 1846 the Kokhandis attempted to invade Kashgaria. But it was Yakub Beg who, in 1865, helped by a Moslem revolt against the Chinese, succeeded in establishing himself as master of all Turkestan. This new Turki conqueror was the son of a Tashkent judge and had

---

* From Kitah, the name of the Mongol tribe that reigned over northern China in the eleventh century.

fought against the Russians before he became Captain of the Guard to the Khan of Kokhand, whose help had been sought by Kashgar. When a Chinese army under the Governor of Kansu, Tso Tsung Tang, marched against him in 1877, Yakub Beg, knowing that he could not get Russian support, and foreseeing defeat, committed suicide. Tso Tsung Tang, who had declared war against him on his own initiative, restored Sinkiang to China and it became the nineteenth province of the Empire.

To-day China has again lost the mastery of these distant provinces—of Tibet, Sinkiang, Mongolia and Manchuria. But the circumstances of the dismemberment have not hitherto been retailed, and a brief sketch of them will show the present importance of Sinkiang for the future of Asia.

The Dismemberment of China.

Hitherto, China had known, from long experience, the kind of diplomacy that was necessary when she had to reconquer any province the loss of which had shaken her own power. But in the nineteenth century the attacks of the Occidental nations by sea constituted a new factor to which the decadent Manchu dynasty was unable to adapt itself. The old Chinese method was to oppose one enemy nation against another, but in her attempts to apply it now China had to acquiesce in the most disastrous encroachments, concessions, loans, foreign control, naval and military occupation.

In the present period, continental greed has become more acute than ever. Japan, crazy for the dismemberment of China, is master in Manchukuo. The U.S.S.R. controls Outer Mongolia. Outer Tibet is under British protection and Yunnan is in a zone of French influence. Inside this ring the still nominally Chinese territories of Inner Mongolia, Sinkiang, and Inner Tibet are torn between revolts and the greed of their neighbours. And the slightest incident that occurs in any of these territories to-day is of more than local interest. Like the tap of a probe on an abscess that is ready to burst, it reveals the distribution of forces to those interested.

Sinkiang's Neighbours.

Allies but not subjects of the reigning Manchu dynasty, the Mongols seceded from China during the revolution of 1911.

Outer Mongolia, to the south of Siberia, has about a million inhabitants. After various ups and downs, it was evacuated by the Red Army and had its independence recognized in 1924. But Soviet advisers remained in the "Popular Government" formed by the Young Mongols, who advocated numerous reforms.

Manchurian Mongolia, with two million inhabitants, was constituted an autonomous province of Hingan by the Japanese of Manchukuo in 1933. These Mongols form a conservative group about certain princes who seem to be attached to older customs.

Inner Mongolia has one million inhabitants. It is very close to China and in theory still forms part of it. But its nomad Mongol inhabitants appeal in vain to the Nanking Chinese to protect their interests against Chinese farmers who, day after day, advance implacably, encroaching steadily on their pasture lands. Naturally these "planter" farmers are supported by the authorities, and the nomads, grouped about Teh Wang, get nothing. Too feeble to be independent, the Mongols might have chosen between two opposing tendencies. On the north were the Sovietized revolutionaries, on the east the conservative Japanese. Had they opted for one or the other, the balance of power would be upset. Either the U.S.S.R. or Japan would have found enemies on the other side of great stretches of its frontiers in case of war.

The strategic importance of Inner Mongolia, which is on the borders of Sinkiang, increases as the continental encroachments of Japan extend beyond the bounds of Manchuria. According to the latest news from Peking, Teh Wang has no longer any choice in the matter, for in reality the Japanese are in control of practically all Inner Mongolia.

Tibet, to the south of Sinkiang, broke away from China at the time of the 1911 revolution. It has been under British protection since 1904, when armed intervention at Lhasa succeeded in its object of opening up the country to British trade and at the same time combating Russian influence, which had been growing in Tibet. The Dalai Lama died in 1933 and nobody knows what influences will dominate in the next reign. As for Inner Tibet, which is a dependency of China, it was divided in 1929 into the provinces of Hsi-kan and Koko Nor (or Chinghai) in order to control it more easily.

Forces Present in Sinkiang.

Sinkiang is the largest province of China and is very difficult to govern. On the one hand, the civil administration is supported only by an insignificant military force, and as Sinkiang is from two to three thousand miles from Nanking it is almost impossible for it to receive any help from there; on the other hand, the Turkis, Kirghiz, Mongols and Dzungarian Tungans need to be governed carefully through the intermediary of native chiefs; for the Governor of Sinkiang, who resides at Urumchi, the Moslems of the province constitute a permanent menace. If they got into the hands of foreigners, they might unite against Chinese domination. We have seen Yakub Beg taking advantage of a Moslem revolt. In addition, account has to be taken of the Tungans occupying the neighbouring province of Kansu, who have always been mixed up in Sinkiang disturbances. They number about three millions—there are in all some twenty million Moslems in China—and wield very great influence, being energetic and having, therefore, secured all the important posts.

The Tungans have the reputation of being cruel fighters, and in their periodic rebellions north-western China ran red with blood. The country was only barely recovering from the devastating troubles of the years 1862 to 1877 when the 1895 revolt broke out. (The slightest pretext, such as the carrying-off of a Mohammedan woman, sufficed the Tungans to give the signal for a massacre of the detested Chinese.) Sven Hedin tells us that in 1895 no less than eighteen thousand Tungans were executed as reprisals in the village of Tangar alone.

Finally, it was at Hami, in Sinkiang, that the 1931 Moslem revolt broke out. The consequences of that were still visible to us. I shall try to explain what happened.

* * * * *

Up to 1928, the province had been governed by Yang Tseng-hsin, who was clever at surmounting the difficulties that threatened Chinese authority. But Yang was assassinated at a banquet held in Urumchi, either by one of his ministers or by the man who succeeded him in office, the famous Chin Shu-jen. That was the beginning of the trouble.

But in reality internal as well as external difficulties had already begun to show themselves.* The settled population had increased as a result of several decades of prosperity, and "planter" farmers were emigrating to the lands of the nomad Mongols in the north. As peasants are easily imposed on, the planters were supported by the Governor. On the other hand,

***

* *The Dismemberment of China*, by T. A. Bisson. (Foreign Politics Reports, New York, 1934.)

the subsidies previously paid to the nomad chiefs to maintain order were no longer paid. Further, Communist propaganda developed from 1922 onwards, vaunting the agrarian reforms introduced in Russian Turkestan, where the settled population is similar to that of Sinkiang. In 1920, four years earlier than in China, the Russians of Sinkiang had abandoned their extra-territorial privileges.

In 1925 the Russian consulates were reopened as Soviet consulates and trade with Russia was resumed. (Even under the Tsars, the province had been open to trade with Russia ever since the Treaty of Kuldja, made in 1851.) Trade so flourished after 1925 that it was not long before Russian money became the standard of currency. Chinese officials gained less and less out of the caravan traffic with China, and as their gains grew less they increased the taxes, much to the discontent of the population. The orientation towards Russia became more pronounced and in 1928 the Sinkiang consul at Semipalatinsk announced that his province would act in its own interests and not in those of the Chinese Government. Finally, in 1931, came the opening up of the railway service between Turkestan and Siberia. (I travelled by it in 1932.) This could only have the effect of strengthening the commercial importance of Russia, now so near. Governor Chin Shu-jen, who, by that time, had succeeded Yang, accordingly made a secret commercial treaty with the U.S.S.R.

Chin was not so intelligent as his predecessor and, flying in the face of the most elementary good sense, nominated his compatriots from Kansu to all the government posts. And then he oppressed the people as never anybody had dared do before. He closed the frontiers of the province to prevent news from spreading. That was why he held up the Citroën and Sven Hedin expeditions. But events were gathering momentum.

The ban on the carrying of arms was raised in China in 1929. Urumchi bought rifles and, well armed, marched on Hami to establish a directly controlled administration over the principality—the Prince had already been deposed. But at Hami, the Turkis had just been expropriated from their lands to make way for Chinese peasants who had escaped from Kansu, and what was more, a Moslem woman had been carried off by a Chinese clerk. The clerk was killed, as were also the Kansu peasants, and, in March, 1931, Hami rose. Government troops occupied the town. The Turki inhabitants fled to the mountains, and their chief, Hodja Nyaz, called on General Ma Chung-ying for aid.

Born at Hochow, this young Tungan general, on whom the name Ga Ssu Ling was afterwards bestowed, became famous when he was only seventeen, during the Moslem rising in Kansu in 1927. The most moderate estimates of the number of victims of that revolt put it at 200,000. It broke out because the Tungans, crushed under the weight of the exorbitant taxes imposed by the "Christian" General Feng, who was Chinese, sent a delegation to make a protest to that gentleman and he had all its members shot. The young Ga Ssu Ling, then a colonel, had been charged by one of the Ma of Sining* to take Hochow. It was a Moslem town but had fallen into the hands of the "Christian" General. Ma Chung-ying besieged it in vain for eight months. Then he raised the siege and became leader of a band of troops in the north of Kansu. By way of reprisal, the Governor of the province, who was a creature of Feng, executed Ma Chung-ying's father at Lanchow. Hatred of the Chinese was thus kindled in the young man's heart. Nevertheless he went to Nanking in 1930 and waited upon the uncontested chief

* Ma Chi, uncle of that General Ma Bu-fang who held the Koko Nor command when we were there.

of Northern China,* the Generalissimo, Chiang Kai-shek, who appointed him Military Governor of Lanchow. When he arrived at that great oasis in the south of the Gobi, Ma proceeded to enrol the population by force, and, with the help of a Turkish officer from Constantinople, named Kemal, raised an army of ten thousand men.

It was then, in the summer of 1931, that the Turkis of the north appealed to Ma for aid. In spite of the difficulties represented by the Desert of Gobi, he arrived before Hami with five hundred Tungans and laid siege to it for six months. But it was in vain. A message was got through by Petro, the engineer of the Citroën Expedition, and reinforcements were sent from Urumchi to the relief of the besieged Chinese of Hami. After making forty-three attacks on the town, Ma abandoned the struggle and returned to Kansu. The Tungans continued fighting side by side with the Turkis. First Barköl and then Turfan were taken and in January, 1933, they laid siege to Urumchi itself. But the capital was well defended by some thousand white Russians who knew they would have nothing to gain under a Moslem government. These Russians were so maltreated by the Governor, Chin Shu-jen, that they rose in revolt and drove him out—over the wall of his yamen and in nothing but his shirt, it is said—on the 11th of April, 1933.†

The Chinese officer, Sheng Shih-tsai, who took over the command, had studied in Japan and fought in the Manchurian war. He was deeply impressed by the growing power of Russia and made a commercial treaty with the Soviets. He also, it is said, raised a loan of five million gold roubles from them to be expended in the development of the province. Only 500,000 roubles were paid in money, the rest

* Feng, an independent General, was beaten in 1929 by Chiang Kai-shek's government troops.

† He is now in prison in China serving a sentence of four years for having concluded a treaty with a foreign power.

being represented by machines and aeroplanes, not to speak of Soviet advisers who came to direct policy. The loan was to be repaid by degrees with caracal and broadtail skins from the province.

Soon after this a delegate of the Nanking Government was so ill-advised as to come to Urumchi to try and restore peace. It appears that he only regained his liberty by promising that Sheng should be officially recognized as Military Governor or *tupan* of Sinkiang.

But the Moslems were now masters of the chief Sinkiang road to some distance south of Urumchi, and a second time they appealed to Ma Chung-ying for aid. Leaving the north of Kansu to be guarded by Ma Bu-fang, a distant cousin of his, he set out. And being very ambitious he decided to rally all the Moslems of the Turfan area to his flag. His strength of will and his courage were only equalled by his cruelty, and the triumphs of Jenghiz Khan and, more recently, of Tso Tsung-Tang inspired him to emulation. He had no difficulty in beating the White Russians in front of Urumchi. And then, suddenly, seven thousand Chinese troops appeared; they had escaped in the course of the Manchurian war, been interned in Siberia, and only just now arrived in Sinkiang.

They repulsed Ma Chung-ying and he retreated to Turfan to raise recruits among the natives. The Turki chief, Hodja Nyaz, deserted Ma and on receiving a promise that he would be given the south of the province, went over to Sheng Shih-tsai. The latter was simply an opportunist who enlisted the enemy generals to his cause whenever he could. In January, 1934, though the cold was terrible, Ma suddenly appeared in the plain before Urumchi and began preparations for a new siege. Sheng, who was tupan, took fright, and in February telegraphed to his Muscovite friends for assistance. Such troops as were near the frontier were soon on the scene and, to the number of about a thousand, Red Russians and White Russians fought side by side. Ma should have beaten them, only he reckoned without the decisive element in modern war. At the battles of Dawan-cheng and Tutung, the Tungans were terror-stricken by Soviet aeroplanes and bombs. Ma, himself, was obliged to fly and took the road to the south-west in the direction of Kashgar.

Events in Kashgar.

Meanwhile in the south of the province the three Emirs of Khotan had, in the beginning of 1933, provoked a fanatical Moslem rising. It was then that our friend Norin had fled by way of the Tsaidam. The Khotandis, with some of Hodja Nyaz's Tungans and Turkis, were badly armed but, led by Timor, they took Kashgar. It was defended only by the Chinese *taotaï*, Ma Chah-wu, and a few Kirghiz whom he had armed. Yarkand was besieged and fell also, every man of the two thousand Chinese survivors being exterminated in the desert by the Moslems, though they were under safe-conduct permitting them to go to Kashgar.

Then a dispute arose between the victorious Turkis and Tungans. These latter went off, and taking up their quarters in the New Town of Kashgar, some miles from the Old Town, stayed there six months. In November, 1933, Kashgar became the capital of a "Republic of Eastern Turkestan," with a president named Sabit, who had the support of the Emirs of Khotan. The republic lasted only two months,* for Hodja Nyaz, the Turki commander, got control of it on the 13th of January, 1934, and, as he had taken service with the Chinese Government at Urumchi, it was impossible for him to recognize the rebel republic.

And then, in February, the Turkis had to surrender the town to Ma Chung-ying's Tungans on their arrival after

* I only mention it because *Le Temps* has referred to it several times.

their great defeat. Reunited with those Tungans who were still in occupation of the New Town, they forced the Turkis and Kirghiz to flee to the mountains.

It was one of these men in flight who in some inexplicable way managed to wound the wife of the English Consul-General at her own door. Hodja Nyaz escaped and fled to Urumchi, where he became civil vice-governor. Two of the three Emirs of Khotan were killed. On the 13th of April, Ma Chung-ying himself arrived at Kashgar. He had been utterly crushed. His dream of supremacy over Sinkiang was shattered. But he did not seem despondent. The entire chain of oases to the south, where he had his partisans, was only waiting for him to declare his will. He would doubtless go there to take stock and build up his army again. And, sure enough, when the summer came, just as the Urumchi Government troops were advancing, he had proclamations posted up in Kashgar: the Tungans would take up their quarters at Khotan, leaving the rest of the country to Sheng Shih-tsai.

But, to everybody's surprise, Ma appointed his cavalry commander, Ma Ho-san, to be Commander-in-Chief and himself took the road to Tashkent and Russian Turkestan, thus going over, of his own free will, to the enemy of the day before. He was accompanied by Comrade Constantinoff, the secretary of the Soviet consulate at Kashgar.

A New Lawrence.

Since then, up to the time I write, nothing is known for certain about Ma Chung-ying and the most contradictory rumours circulate as to what has become of him. Ma arrived at Moscow—dead! Ma went to India to look for help! Ma was in Peking when we were leaving it in February, 1935—or so we read. The German Consul at Novo-Sibirsk announced in April, 1935, that Ma had just arrived at Alma

Ata in Kazakstan.* In 1936 Ma was reported to have arrived at Shensi, in China, to engage in Communist propaganda. As in the case of Colonel Lawrence, a legend had already grown up around him.

According to the Japanese and their newspaper, *Osaka Asahi*, the Tungans really revolted at the instigation of the Soviets, whose plan is to seize Chinese Turkestan. In support of this theory there is the rumour that Kashgar functionaries have declared Ma to be an agent of the Third International, receiving his orders from Moscow through Outer Mongolia.

Soviet newspapers commented very diversely on the news of the rising. According to some of them it was the Japanese who stirred up Ma to revolt against the Chinese, as part of the preparations for their own Manchu-Mongol empire which must be created at the expense of China. And the *Izvestia* observed that the headquarters of the Pan-Islamic League—which wants to turn Central Asia into a fortress of anti-Soviet politics—were in Japan.

But the Communist Party's Tashkent newspaper, the *Pravda Vostoka*, took a quite different point of view. It represented Ma as a leader of the peasants in a revolt against the militarist feudal system of Sinkiang. (This opinion is not ill-founded, only it has to be suggested that Ma may be out for himself, not for the peasants.) The paper added that the White Guards at Urumchi, a rabble of 2,000 *émigrés*, mobilized by the Chinese against Ma's rebels, went to battle crying: "Let us go and fight the Bolsheviks." This article is of peculiar interest when it is realized that two years later, in February, 1934, Red troops helped those same Russian *émigrés* to stamp out Ma's Turki and so-called Peasant revolt, in the interests of Chinese imperialism.

* See the *Revue des Etudes Islamiques,* Cahier II, 1935, article on Sinkiang by Joseph Castagné.

Finally as to England. She is assuredly implicated in these incessant struggles. According to the *Pravda* (15th of August, 1933), she was considering the creation of a great Tibetan empire with Sinkiang and Szechwan as dependencies. And I remember that when I was in Peking, a German who claimed to be well informed said to me that Lawrence of Arabia supported the Emir of Khotan, as it would be to Great Britain's interest to have a Moslem republic under its protection to the north of Tibet.

But it would scarcely be possible for London effectively to aid military operations in a country separated from India by six hundred miles of trails that wind over the Himalayas at crazy altitudes—some forty-five days' march, that is to say—through a country where no supplies are obtainable. Besides, there was the Tibetan question and because of it England wanted at all costs to maintain her existing friendly relations with China. And even if Moscow were all-powerful at Kashgar, how should India be affected? The barrier of the Himalayas would prevent even the idea of an invasion of India being entertained, and so far as propagandists were concerned, it was easy enough to discover them, since they would have to use one of the two or three tracks which are the only ways by which they could reach Kashmir.

It is, of course, true that there have always been Indian traders in Sinkiang, and through the Consul-General at Kashgar England tries, to the best of her ability, to protect the rights of these five or six hundred of her subjects. Their private trade must now inevitably decline, since Russian enterprises are organized by the State and facilitated by the proximity of the Turksib railway. Yet there is still a demand in the markets for English muslins and for the beautiful woollen goods of England, though they are very expensive. Indeed, the expenses of transport are already a difficult problem and, in addition, the authorities impose ever heavier taxes and endless delays on Indian caravans, by way of obstruction. In the autumn of 1935, England, having made up its mind to protest energetically against these vexations, succeeded in bringing off the remarkable feat of despatching a mission from Peking and getting it through by lorry to Urumchi—the two-faced capital, as one might call it. Sir Eric Teichmann and the Consul-General from Kashgar met there. They were both warmly received by smiling Chinese and assured that the terms of the trade agreements would, from then on, be faithfully observed. . . .

But there has been no change. As before, Soviet advisers and specialists run things in accordance with Soviet interests. The Soviets may well feel satisfied with the results, since, with their agents established everywhere, they control the entire trade of the province. It is not only furs and the output of some mines in the north that are taken by Russia. Most important of all, she takes—what she lacks herself—wool, all the wool in Sinkiang. I saw the endless caravans passing through Frunze with it in 1932. One may ask, however, whether at the end of the year the trade returns show the Soviets as the benefited party, for the organization of the traffic was costly and it is scarcely yet firmly established. But the point is not of much importance. State enterprises are always undertaken with distant objects in view. No doubt it is also as a result of the activity of Soviet agents that the White Russians, who in the past gave their assistance to the governors, found themselves obliged, as a matter of prudence, to "go Red."

It is whispered, even printed, that some day or other Sinkiang will secede from China and demand admission into the Union of Soviet Socialist Republics.* The natives have suffered so much in the last four years of civil war that, no

* When I returned to Paris my friends even met me with the question whether I had had difficulties at Kashgar as a result of the change of government that had just taken place there!

matter what proposal may be made, they are ready to believe it will be better than what has been. That such a move will be made is extremely probable. It would be a world-wide advertisement for Moscow, though an advertisement that might work both ways, for the Soviets are far from desirous of drawing the world's attention to their activities in Central Asia. At the moment they want to be friends with everybody and, above all, to develop their trade free from interference or competition, even the trade with remote Khotan, which town their agents have already reached. I cannot help thinking that if Sven Hedin, as leader of his "Chinese Expedition" charged by Nanking with the creation of a motor-road in Sinkiang, was "detained" at Urumchi, it was because the authorities feared his mission might have opened up a direct route to Nanking. But gradually realizing that the famous Swede was bringing about no change whatever in existing communications, they let him go in 1935.

What is going to happen? No peace treaty has been signed between Urumchi and Khotan, for Khotan wishes to be dependent only on Nanking. The rebellious town is still the capital of a Tungan republic armed to the teeth, but claims to be much more genuinely subject to Nanking than its enemy, the provincial government, which is in reality under Moscow's orders.

The enigmatic Ma Chung-ying is the only unknown quantity capable of upsetting the existing state of things. Is he going to emerge and put himself once more at the head of his men? It is insinuated that he is. He would have ten thousand rifles and three or four times as many men armed with swords. But it does not seem as if this could enable him to defeat Sheng Shih-tsai, who has twenty thousand rifles and, what is more, ten Russian aeroplanes.

Did the Soviets encourage Ma to take Kashgar three years ago, for fear England might get the upper hand in a

Moslem republic in Turkestan? And are the Soviets preparing to give Ma support? It is certain that the Soviet consulate at Kashgar had no trouble in seducing Ma. Perhaps it was with a promise to help him. Or did Ma, who set off as a powerful chief going to Moscow to discuss the terms of a possible alliance, fall into a trap in which he remains restive? Or has he simply abandoned his dreams of conquest to devote himself to the liberation of the oppressed classes in Asia? Heaven knows.

As long as Ma is away from Sinkiang things may remain relatively peaceful, and for the moment this is undoubtedly what the Soviets want, so that the country may rise from its ruins. Ma is like a pawn held in reserve for the Asiatic chess-board. Having the leader of the Tungans in their hands, the Russians control the south of Sinkiang. If Sheng Shih-tsai grew less docile, they could unloose the Tungans on him, with Ma at their head. If Japan definitively annexes Inner Mongolia, Ma Chung-ying and Ma Bu-fang together could lay down a Moslem barrage all the way from Kansu to Outer Mongolia.

The Tungans constitute a force that might be utilized. But on their own and without aeroplanes they could undertake nothing but desperate ventures. . . .

CHAPTER X

KHOTAN, CAPITAL OF TUNGANIA

WE were due to arrive in two days at the great oasis of Khotan, where, though for no good reason, we were hopeful of meeting some European, a missionary perhaps. Peter even wondered whether he might by lucky chance find a bottle of whisky there. . . . I remember one utterly exhausting ride during that trek. It was the day Peter decided that we should only stop when we reached Lop. At seven o'clock in the evening the three stage-houses at Baishtoghrak, in the midst of a desert-like region, proffered their mute invitation in vain. Without even getting off my horse, I drank out of a gourd brought from the well by a Turki, and we went on.

The desolation of dunes followed after a land of tamarisks. Tired out and craving to get off and lie down on the ground, I managed to keep awake by taking the lead and, in the almost absolute darkness, applying myself to keeping on the vague tracks marked in the sand. We went on, but the dark broken line of an oasis never came between me and the stars low down on the horizon. Had we lost the trail? Suddenly a cavalcade emerged out of the obscurity, the rays from pocket lamps making, as it were, luminous fasces at its head. It was soldiers out on reconnaissance. . . . What luck for them! Foreigners to arrest without any display of zeal on their part. Astonished at the sight of Peter they missed me and I quietly went on a little way. But we got off with nothing more than a fright. They accepted Tuzun's explanations and we continued our hesitating march.

Suddenly there was a tree and a sheet of water. Lop was still a long way off, but here was a solitary inn, and by shouting loudly we succeeded in having the heavy, barricaded door opened. There was nothing to eat, either for us or the animals, and the only thing to do was to get to sleep as quickly as possible.

As soon as we reached Lop the next day we sent out for food for the animals, but the men came back saying there was nothing to be had in the market and Peter went to the local commandant to make representations. Tuzun Ahun was of no use to us; he even alarmed us with his talk of the great river we should have to cross before reaching Khotan. "The water is dangerous for donkeys," he said, and added that we should have to wait till the next morning and then cross before the river was swollen by the melting of the snows.

But when we reached the river bank we found beasts and men crossing, for the most part fording, the three arms of the Yurungkash—the River of White Jade. Merchandise was being taken across on a ferry, women also. We did not want to wait and decided to ride across. But our timid horses had scarcely set foot in the swiftly-flowing stream before warning cries arose all round us and, willy-nilly, we had to go through the yellow water with sturdy men immersed to the waist leading our horses by the bridle. I gathered from them that there were dangerous holes in the river bed.

We were received on the left bank by the secretary of the aksakal of Khotan and a servant called Saduk, the latter oddly turned out with frayed puttees beneath an old gaberdine waterproof, the sleeves of which were too long. Saduk, who had glittering eyes in a parchment face, was very intelligent—he immediately understood Peter's Chinese. Some natives, wearing Union Jacks on their shoulders, acted as an entourage while we drank tea at a police shelter on the river bank.

Then, in blinding sunlight, we entered Khotan. It is a big town, but for some inexplicable reason I had expected it to be a place of obvious archæological interest like Samarkand, and I was disappointed in it. Stagnant water stank in muddy alleys, the booths were black with flies and I noticed that most of the inhabitants, even the young girls, were afflicted with enormous goitres. When, later, I went sightseeing, I found not the slightest vestige of the past, only some big modern mosques.

About half-way up the main street the English flag was hung above a wooden door. We entered a narrow, covered courtyard, stacked as high as the roof with bales of merchandise. The aksakal's house was used as a store by the caravans coming and going over the Karakoram passes. I was much impressed by some Indian merchants, close-shaven, moustached gentry in Turkish trousers and heel-less slippers turned up at the toe. Seeing them I suddenly began to feel that Hindustan was no myth. Only the Himalayas separated us from it. We who were not encumbered with Citroën caterpillars that would have to be taken to pieces for the road, should have no difficulty in getting across.

The Indian gentry broke off their game of cards to greet us. They did not speak English, but they knew odd words like *Times* and "tooth-paste." One of them who had just come in was carrying a syringe and some English and German disinfectants in his hand. And Peter, suddenly deciding to return to the ways of respectability, promptly borrowed a razor-blade.

We were led to a little kiosk in the middle of a luxurious orchard. It was open all round but had rugs on the floor. This was to be our lodging. And there, from morning to night, we were to hear the recruits drilling incessantly to the sound of trumpets, while their comrades rent the heavens with Turki songs. The aksakal was away, but his Afghan secretary saw to it that we wanted for nothing and Saduk acted as our servant. He slept in the garden in a worn-out cart and, no matter what the hour, if I woke up at night, the light of his little opium lamp was burning. When we needed him in the morning Saduk would appear, haggard and pale, like a ghost. It was he who helped us to understand something the secretary, with an air of great pride, was trying to tell us—that when he was in Kabul he had read a story translated from the French about a Hindu prince who was a man of genius and who, revolting against a usurper, spent his life in a submarine. The prince was, of course, Captain Nemo and the book, *Twenty Thousand Leagues Under the Sea*. Thus recalled at Khotan, so far from the nearest point of the ocean, the story seemed more fabulous than ever.

The aksakal's family lived in an old dark house in the shadow of a huge trellis on the other side of the orchard wall. It was there that I went to prepare enough apricot jam for the next stage of our journey; for apricot jam was almost the only thing we found pleasure in eating while marching in the broiling weather. On top of a trunk there were jars of rose jam surrounded by noisy wasps. Earthenware teapots ornamented recesses in the walls of the rooms. I noticed also an old Koran wrapped in a piece of precious embroidery. The women showed me silks they had woven from their own cocoons; and old coins found in the desert; and a manuscript similar to those Aurel Stein brought home.

On the morning after we arrived a donkey with a Union Jack at his ear passed before our kiosk. The donkey-man wore a leather belt with a glittering metal plate and on this we read the astonishing words, BRITISH INDIAN POST-MAN. We were forty-five days' journey from India and this was the monthly, consular post. Peter grew very excited, but when the big red leather bag was emptied and he saw several numbers of the weekly edition of *The Times*, his excitement reached a climax. They were not, however, addressed to the aksakal. He knew no English. They were for a certain Mr. Moldovack. We learned that he was an Armenian living in Khotan and we hastened off to his house.

Our First "European."

In a well-kept room where the walls were covered with books, we found a very old gentleman who, in his student days at Constantinople, had learned French and English. He was charming but he suffered dreadfully with elephantiasis and could scarcely walk. The doctor at Kashgar had pronounced him incurable. Originally a dealer in silks and carpets, it was twenty-six years since he first started business in Khotan. Later, at the time of the Bolshevik revolution he lost all his money, which he had been keeping at a bank in Russian Turkestan. So he set to work again, this time directing the workers who wove carpets, trying to perpetuate the traditions that, long ago, made Khotan carpets famous. He showed me a book with an inscription by Aurel Stein: "To the benefactor of the Khotan carpet-weaving industry." But now the State monopolized everything and he could do nothing to stop the output of inferior goods.

He confirmed the view that the general political situation was bad. All those, he said, who could find reason for claiming some connection with the British aksakal, and many who could not, hung out the English flag as a protection against the confiscations ordered by the dictator Ma Ho-san. And then, drinking our coffee, we listened to talk of different Europeans who had, at one time or another, come to Khotan. Mr. Moldovack was uneasy as to the fate of a Czech who came *via* Afghanistan and got arrested at Khotan after he had been for some time printing bank-notes at Kashgar for the short-lived Moslem republic. This was the same young man of whom we had heard at Cherchen.

Mr. Moldovack asked very precise questions about the European situation. Then he expressed astonishment at a speech made by the Japanese Prime Minister to the effect that it was of paramount importance for Japan to prevent the U.S.S.R. from getting control in Sinkiang.

It seemed curious listening to the echoes awakened by world politics in that exile's room behind the triple barrier of the Himalayas, the Karakorams and the Kuen Lun.

Back at our airy kiosk in the garden, Peter devoured the three-months-old *Times* which had been lent him. He found news of friends and he was rather pleased to see an article of his own on Manchukuo figuring in the central page. Also I found a photograph of the author taken with my little Leica in the illustrated page. Alas, there was no fear of any copies of my *Petit Parisien* turning up in Khotan. Heaven only knew what the latest financial scandal to occupy the French public might be. So far as Frenchmen were concerned, the continental policy of Japan was still in the nebulous stage, and no doubt my articles, though crammed with news of the existing situation, would be left lying in a drawer until they became stale. I grew gloomy at the thought,* but Peter in the meantime was discovering that in his own land a jubilee had been touchingly celebrated. I looked on as he showed everybody a photograph of George V in *The Times*, telling them that that was his king, and this the very paper which had sent him amongst them.

The Two Pillars of Power.

Those two pillars were the arsenal and the mint. The latter looked ordinary enough. It was a Chinese house, like any other in the main street except that there was an orderly on

* Justifiably, as I discovered later.

guard. On the flags of the courtyard thousands of coloured squares were drying in the sun. They were the bank-notes of the Tungan Republic. Squatting youths were arranging them in bundles of a hundred. Inside, behind the paper windows, in rooms where the atmosphere was alcoholic with the exhalations from the colours, men went on indefatigably printing notes on mulberry-bark paper with blue, black, red and green stamps. The director told us they had been turning out some thirty thousand a day for a year past, but he added that it was not enough; they needed as many more again. These were the notes we had received in bundles in exchange for a few dollars—one would need a suitcase to carry all there were—and we were never to discover their value, for it changed unceasingly. In the heart of Asia, even, inflation had appeared and its whole train of consequences as well.

The arsenal was housed in several miserable buildings. A pale, sympathetic young man saw us passing along the street and invited us in. There was less activity than at the mint. A dozen Chinese cannon painted green and blue, with some shell-cases similarly painted, were displayed in line in an exhibition hall. Further along, gun carriages were being made. Moulds used in making grenades were ranged along a courtyard and girls were busy taking rifles to pieces. Over a bowl of tea, the charming young man told us that there was no shortage of munitions. He seemed glad to have a talk with strangers who had come from distant Kansu. It was his native province. And we had the greatest difficulty in preventing him from ordering soup for us. I loved his innate ease and graciousness of manner, truly Chinese qualities which one is always coming upon and which add so much to the charm of travel in China.

Dictator Ma Ho-san.

Like most cities in Turkestan, Khotan has a Turkish town and a Chinese town. The oppressors of the moment resided in the latter. The Chinese name for Khotan is Yu-t'ien—the Town of Jade.

The tiny booths, with their rows of shelves, were similar in the two towns. But the populations were different. The conqueror's quarter had fewer Turkis in long robes and fewer women with squares of muslin on their heads. There were Chinamen with little short jackets and trousers gathered in at the ankles; and bareheaded Chinese women in brilliant satin trousers. Women from Kansu kept to the curious black turbans which made them look like dowagers.

Hundreds of horses went to drink along a slippery street, sprinkled with water drawn from a neighbouring canal. But the most astonishing thing was the ceaseless marching. Regiment upon regiment went up and down and down and up. The terrible Tungans were dressed in white pyjamas and wore piqué hats with brims that undulated like flounces on a dress, and over and over again they sang the same marching songs. Groups of conscripts, young and old, did the goose-step, accompanying it with wide arm movements. Their round, shaven craniums were often marked by the skin trouble that is so frequent in the country, and they certainly had not the air of men who were enjoying themselves.

We watched them one afternoon while our visiting cards were being taken in to General Ma Ho-san, who was expecting us. A Chinese custom dating back to pre-Christian times ordains that one must present one's *name-card* immediately on being introduced to a person, and when setting out on a journey one has to provide oneself with hundreds of cards.

After a time we were led into the courtyard of an immense yamen, and, turning off from the buildings, to a small low house with trees round it. There we were shown into a room that had glass in the windows and gauze curtains over the doorways to keep out the flies, and we were given seats at a council-table to wait for the General. A fragrant incense-stick was burning in a corner. We went over the questions to which we hoped to obtain answers. Ma Ho-san came in wearing white cotton garments like those of his soldiers. He was a well-set-up long-legged man with a very un-Chinese round head, regular features and impassive expression. Only the high and rather prominent cheek-bones combined with the small nose and short forehead might suggest that he was not a European.

He had calm and decision. In answer to his questions we droned out the same responses we had droned out a hundred times before, like a litany. "We have come from Peking. We set out five months ago. We did not pass through Hami or Tunghwang. They are closed to foreigners. We came by the mountains to the south. We hope that, in view of the long journey we are making, which does not allow of our bringing much luggage, we shall be excused for calling on so exalted a personage in such simple clothes. I am English . . . I am Swiss. . . . We are travelling for great newspapers. We speak no Turki and very little Chinese. We are going to Kashgar. We shall be in Europe this autumn . . ."

But what General Ma wanted most to know was Nanking's view of the Tungans. Far from accepting the idea of himself as a rebel, the idea propagated by the Government, he claimed to be a faithful subject anxious to rescue Urumchi from foreign domination. He wanted to know, too, what they thought in China of Sheng Shih-tsai, the tupan who nominated himself governor, and whether, when we came through Sining, General Ma Bu-fang had not forbidden us to undertake the dangerous journey to Khotan. (We had taken good care to give no information about our plans to Ma Bu-fang.)

We talked in rather sketchy English through a Tungan

interpreter who, wrapped in a great-coat, was trembling all over with fever.

The young dictator confirmed the rumour that a delegation from Ma Bu-fang had arrived from Sining and was at the moment in Khotan. He himself had sent a man to Nanking to lay the Tungan point of view before the authorities and ask for assistance. Ma Ho-san explained the problems he had to solve. His greatest difficulties arose from the fact that all the oases were not connected by telegraph. But the small supplies of money available constituted a grave difficulty too. All the fortunes that were lodged in the bank at Urumchi had fallen into the hands of the Chinese Government. If any of the Khotan merchants had gold in their possession they knew how to hide it. And then Ma was very much handicapped by the lack of aeroplanes. He had approached the English on this subject but without any success. I remembered that the aksakals we had met deplored Great Britain's refusal to lend aeroplanes to the Tungans in their anti-Bolshevist struggle. Ma said the bombs dropped by the aeroplanes had released terrible gases. It was clear that at the Battle of Tutung those bombs had put everyone to flight. He was trying to have masks made and wondered whether we knew the chemical mixtures with which they had to be impregnated. . . . As for munitions, he had enough. There were still plenty of the rifles captured in battle. Ma asked us to pay his compliments to the English Consul at Kashgar and also to the Swedish missionaries who had nursed him in their hospital. At the beginning of the war he had had a compound fracture of the thigh-bone and it was Doctor Hummel, of the Sven Hedin expedition, then (1934) interned at Turfan, who saved his leg.

At last, with the most innocent air in the world, we managed to ask the General whether he had good news of Ma Chung-ying—who, we were given to understand, was his cousin.

"Ga Ssu Ling has been away on an expedition this last year," we were told. "According to his last letter he will be returning shortly."

"We have heard of his bravery everywhere," said Peter, "and we regret that we are not to have the honour of meeting such a great commander. Perhaps we may be permitted to see his portrait—or even take a likeness of him to Europe."

"Of course," said the flattered Ma Ho-san. "Nothing is easier." And he went to look for a photograph in the next room. Through the doorway I could see a big standing mirror. . . .

Peter gave me a triumphant look. The photograph of Ma Chung-ying in Soviet cavalry uniform was under our eyes. He was a tall, well-built man and, contrary to Tungan custom, wore his hair long.

Though the sun had set, we went out into the courtyard to take photographs of the dictator. He had gone off and changed into a uniform of khaki drill with tight breeches which became him extremely well. He posed standing amidst his bodyguard, they armed with automatic rifles.

At last we took leave of him. He is an energetic man and may well be heard of again in connection with events in Central Asia. He seemed to have decided that he must, some day or other, set off for the north again and fight out the war. It would not be necessary for him to follow the principal trail and go round by Kashgar; Ma Ho-san would follow the Khotan river and cross the desert directly to Aksu.

CHAPTER XI

UNDER THE SIGN OF THE POTAI

THE night before we left Khotan the aksakal Badruddin Khan returned. He was an elderly Afghan who in thirty years had seen a good many English consuls succeed each other at Kashgar. His untidy robes were caught in about his corpulent body and kept in place by a pocketed belt. But he knew how to get things done. His servants were naturally a lazy lot, but how they busied themselves when he appeared! Teapots were refilled, the fans to keep away the flies were set in motion, great rugs were hung round our kiosk to protect us from the sandy wind that made Khotan dark with its dense masses of yellow dust.

We heard all about Kashgar, about the Russians who lived there, about its marvellous hospital. The British Consulate, we were told, was a great house covered with flowers, with water flowing when a sort of screw was turned, with enormous armchairs in the rooms. (We felt we had been sitting down Turkish fashion for years.) But the Consul himself had gone away to the mountains for the very hot weather. . . . At that piece of news all our dreams of a Kashgarian paradise collapsed.

In ten days' march from Khotan we should reach Yarkand, the first town on our route subject to the Provincial Government at Urumchi. We wondered whether the authorities there would be more difficult than those of the Tungans. But we were going to have all the time we wanted to wonder about that during the ten days' trek.

We set off accompanied by Saduk, who, in spite of his name,

which means "frank," did not inspire confidence. He said that the aksakal had ordered him to come with us. It was, of course, untrue, and, in spite of his linguistic talent, we determined to rid ourselves of him. He moved like a man suffering from hallucinations who could yet be reasonable. Once again I saw his opium lamp burning all night in the courtyard of the inn at Karakash. We started off early the next morning, leaving him behind us half-dead with fatigue. I knew what he had been up to, because I myself had scarcely slept at all. Those personal enemies of mine, the fleas, had once again treated me as if I were a parade ground. With the help of a torch I had engaged in mortal combat with them all night. It was the most exasperating thing about the journey for me. But how was I to escape from them? All round the covered courtyards of the inns there are little earthen platforms on which the clients sleep. When you arrive, the proprietor hastens to put down a felt rug for you. In spite of all my protests nobody would believe that I preferred the hard earth to those rugs with their hidden parasites.

We were able to do without Saduk because the aksakal had provided us with a servant such as was considered indispensable for travellers like Peter and myself. This one was called Nyaz. He was a timid lad, awkward, flat-footed, barefooted. Simple-minded, too. He was an orphan and we might, we were told, take him as far as London if we liked. He wore some British emblem on his smock. His mouth was enormous, his nose went up in the air and he claimed to be able to speak Chinese because he could interpolate a few words of that language into his Turki, the only result being that his speech became altogether incomprehensible. Each day when he came to report that the donkeys were starting, he began by pointing his chin at the four points of the compass. That done he said: "*Dzo la!*" ("Let us go".)

We were now in a rich land, and the oases were near to

each other. Wherever there was a mayor we had to change horses, donkeys and donkeymen. The fee was small but the obligation was most tiresome, for Peter had to go and palaver with the *shang yi* (mayor) every time. Nyaz would go round carrying our visiting cards, but he only rarely succeeded in obtaining new animals. So as not to be left, we made it a practice to insist on retaining the old donkeymen till the new ones appeared. Usually we were given horses that nobody had any use for and we had to use the whip unceasingly. That took a great deal from the pleasure of the journey.

Between the oases of Zawa and Pialma, a hovel stood beside a venerated tomb in the middle of the desert. There an old man eked out an existence on charitable offerings. Hundreds of pigeons nested around and it was the custom to buy a dish of maize and give it to them. They fought amongst themselves for the grains we threw, swooping down, darkening the day and making us feel as if we were smothering in the rustling clouds of them.

At Moji, where we arrived towards noon on the fourth day, I gave in to a temptation and bathed in a channel of cold, swiftly-flowing water in a field. We had passed many such streams in the country these last few days! When I got back to the inn I found Peter, reclining like a Pasha, listening to the confidences of some young Tungans who, a couple of years earlier, had been led away from their homes to serve with Ma. They were pining for their native village, but it was far away.

Peter's Disappearance.

That evening we arrived at Guma, a rich oasis where we saw corn threshed by setting the cattle to march round and round on it. The peasants were singing at the pitch of their voices and my mount, for once a lively mare, took fright again and again at the noise they made. But she had given me a perfect day.

The aksakal was away, but we were led into an entrance court from which I could see a blackboard in a room. While we were looking round us, a doctor arrived, accompanied by two little boys with great dark eyes. He was an Indian who had been settled at Guma for some two years, and, in the room where the blackboard was, he acted as teacher to the children of British subjects. He was doing well, for he was the only person in the place capable of treating the venereal diseases with which most of the population were afflicted. But he did not know what to do to guard his savings, as the value of the local currency was declining day by day.

Later a Russian Tungan from Tashkent paid us a visit. He had left his village in 1934 because there was no longer any flour. Delighted at the chance of talking, we bombarded him with questions. After all, asking questions was our business. He said that Soviet influence was becoming more and more perceptible at Kashgar. Amongst other things a school and a theatre had been opened, as at Tashkent.

The next morning, when we were expecting the animals we had ordered, the mayor and his secretary arrived instead and interrogated us. They made notes, demanded our passports and carried Peter off with them. The morning passed but there was no Peter and no message from him. Midday. . . . Two o'clock. . . . I grew uneasy. Perhaps the Tungan of the previous evening had made a report about the kind of questions we asked? Perhaps our enquiries had caused displeasure somewhere? But if Peter were arrested it was up to me not to let myself be caught too.

"Nyaz," I said, "we'll go. . . . Yesterday's donkeys? . . . It can't be helped."

But Peter came in, as phlegmatic as usual. He had reversed a situation which seemed more than dubious for us. The brigadier-general, before whom he had to go, asserted roughly that we had no authority to come wandering through Sinkiang. Peter played at being "surprised," and said his passport, like mine, *must* have the word "Sinkiang" in some corner or other. Then he hastened to ask whether the British Consul who was coming to meet us had yet left Yarkand. . . . And finally he engaged in a general conversation on the Manchurian wars, acting as if he found the General's company extremely agreeable. The scene ended with the General succumbing to Peter's flatteries and ordering that the donkeys we wanted be placed at our disposal.

And off we went again, I wondering how I should have extricated myself from such a pass had I been alone. Probably the General would have considered it beneath his dignity to concern himself with a woman like me. But once more I was in admiration of Peter. . . . To be frank, I, who find everything difficult, felt as much envy as admiration of the easy, even the casual, manner in which Peter surmounted every obstacle that life put in his way.

We were in the desert again, with sandhills and gravel as far as the eye could see. Every couple of miles or so since we left Khotan, the route was marked with truncated pyramids of brick put up by the Chinese. They were *potai**watch-towers. We could check our progress by them, for hour after hour they appeared with regularity on the edge of the trail. Thanks to these landmarks the desert now gave the impression of having been tamed.

Night was coming on and no misty line rose up on the horizon to indicate the vegetation of an oasis. It was only later, when it was quite dark, that we passed a tree and ascended the eminence which was crowned by the important fortress of Chulak.

The first court was a caravanseria. The second was

* *Potai* means a terrace of guns. These ones were constructed during the last Chinese conquest of the country, in the eighteenth century.

reserved for soldiers, but we were offered a cell there, a cell which had a fireplace let into its thick wall.

The sixth day we marched for five hours through a desert region strewn with carcasses. Then we came to the oasis of Khargalik, which is the terminus of the Karakoram route that leads from India via Leh. The Tungan we saw at Guma said that the English would never let Khargalik fall into the hands of the Soviet-controlled Provincial Government.

It was market-day and we met many people who were on their way home, laden with cloth or carrying spindles of white cotton like huge spinning-tops. Muleteers were dipping squares of bread into the river to make them less hard. . . . They had no doubt brought them across Tibet in their packs. I remember noticing the willows which had their roots in the water.

Nyaz led us to the house of the aksakal, an obsequious Afghan, young and thin, who was smoking a water-pipe with a few of his neighbours. I heard Nyaz announcing in the kitchen that we liked eggs and rice and chicken the same as other people! It was a long time since we had had a proper meal. Two old women, noticing that I found it difficult to rise owing to the stiffness in my back, set themselves to massage me, energetically and not without a certain competence. . . .

Frontiers.

On the 16th of July we had for some hours been following a shady road when we were stopped by Tungan soldiers and asked for our papers. What could this mean? We offered to take photographs of them—it always flattered their vanity. There was laughter over the posing and we finished by drinking tea with their lieutenant. As is the fashion in Asia, they had fitted forked props to their rifles, using a piece of tin marked "Cherry"—which showed how the boxes of the

Japanese cigarettes imported from India met their end. No objections were raised to our going on from this, the last Tungan post before the demilitarized zone which stretches to Yarkand.

We were now in rich country with running water everywhere. The little flooded ricefields were like so many clear mirrors, though here and there the surface was pierced by green shoots. Every time we came to an irrigation canal running across the track I hung on to my horse's neck and managed to get some water into my little wool-covered waterbottle. The contents grew cool in about ten minutes owing to the process of evaporation.

We spent the night in an inn at Posgam, a friendly village with a mayor, who proceeded to commandeer beds for us. We had the greatest difficulty in convincing him that we preferred our flea-bags.

We were anxious to learn how we should be received by the Sinkiang Government and next day crossed the wide Yarkand Darya or Tarim by ferry. Nyaz was unhappy. He was fearful of not being able to get back to Khotan, having heard tales of smugglers and closed frontiers.

At the first military post on the road we were stopped by a soldier. The Kuomintang emblem was displayed above the door, as it had been amongst the rebels. So as to have a better look at us, the military invited us to drink tea, to eat eggs cooked in the ashes, and to taste ripe apricots. Contrary to what one saw amongst the Tungans, there were men camped untidily in the shade of a tree. We asked why the road was barred to some natives who had no passports and laughed at the classic answer: "They are *tu-fei*"—bandits!

Yarkand.

An armed horseman who was acting as our escort wanted to take us straight to the mayor. Explaining that we could not pay visits until we had got into clean clothes, we succeeded in getting rid of him. Actually we were afraid of being treated as suspects, and hurried on, passed inside the crenellated walls of Yarkand and through tortuous streets, till we came to the aksakal's residence. It was a house that kept itself to itself, calm and cool; there was a basin on a table in a water-closet. I wanted to take a rest of two or three days at Yarkand and get back some strength. What with the heat, which prevented us from eating properly, and the magnesian water, which did not suit us, not to speak of the fact that at night I had been devoured by parasites, I felt at the end of my reserves and little inclined to hurry off sight-seeing in the town or to call on the Swedish missionaries. And I made no bones about telling Peter what I thought of people who travelled too fast and took no time to learn anything about anything. But Peter was crazy to get on as quickly as possible.

The aksakal was a tall, serious man with an intelligent face. He was of Tibetan origin and had been to Lhasa. The Indian Government had conferred a decoration on him for saving the lives of Europeans during the recent civil wars. The Europeans included the missionaries, whom, incidentally, we were not to see, as they were away in the mountains for the summer. He addressed me, Indian fashion, as Mem Sahib. A robust Turki with a blond beard was presented to us as Aurel Stein's interpreter. His name was Musa Ahun and he showed us a "West-End watch," with an inscription expressing Stein's appreciation of his services. (Unfortunately for us he had no English. He was an interpreter in Turki, Chinese and Persian.)

At the aksakal's we took the liberty of tampering with the Khotan post and reading Mr. Moldovack's *Times*. We learned from it that England was in mourning for Lawrence of Arabia. I find that I entered another piece of information gleaned from *The Times* in my notebook: "Mademoiselle Assia's dresses in *La Prisonnière* are by Lanvin!!!" But why I put three exclamation marks after it—I am usually chary of them—I am unable, after the passage of twelve months, to imagine.

We made our round of official visits next day. At several places a photograph of General Sheng, the Governor of the Province, hung on the walls. We found our knowledge of Russian useful in the course of our interviews. Ma Chung-ying, we learned, was anxious for peace, for he knew that he could not fight alone. He was supposed to have admitted, or to have pretended to admit, that there were as many Tungans against him as for him, and supposed also to be engaged in settling the terms of an agreement between Moscow and Urumchi.

But like the rebel mayor of Keriya, the government mayor of Yarkand, a dear old Chinaman from Yunnan, was unable to obtain the passport he had applied for, or permission to leave Sinkiang. What a number of countries there are in which people have no freedom!

Between Chinatown and Turki-town there was a vague stretch with ruined houses to remind one of the last war. There, a public story-teller was gesticulating in the centre of an attentive circle of people. In the streets were soldiers in grey uniforms, less robust-looking than the Tungans. The militia, on the other hand, were dressed in bright yellow. There was a crowd, for it was a bazaar day. We bought souvenirs of Yarkand in the shape of two pairs of soft leather knee-boots and some embroidered caps which we took from poles that stood in front of the stalls.

The next morning we were photographed, for the first time during the journey, in the court of the aksakal's house. It was just before we started off. The photographer was the slight Colonel Liu. He had a German camera which he had bought from the Soviet Consul at Kashgar. (The last occasion on which we had faced the camera was on the platform at Peking station.) These evidences of European influence reappearing gave us a better idea of our progress across Asia than we got from counting the number of miles we had covered.

CHAPTER XII

KASHGARIA

SOME hours after starting we stopped for tea at a village and found ourselves sitting beside a blue-eyed Turki who, Peter discovered, spoke Russian. We were soon engaged in a discussion on public affairs. Our neighbour, who came originally from Ferghana, was a cynical trader and claimed to be able to do business no matter who was in power. He had laid in no stock of political opinions and his observations seemed to me to be quite objective.

The natives, he said, had a hard life. A new tax had just been imposed, on top of those that existed already. This one amounted to no less than a tenth of everybody's harvest and was destined for the creation of modern schools throughout the country. In the matter of religious customs, it appeared that scarcely anyone now learned the Koran. The influence of the mullahs was diminishing every day to such a point that to get married it was now sufficient, as in Russian Turkestan, to register a declaration in the presence of four witnesses. But influential Moslems were protesting against these innovations.

Our Turki invited us to come and meet his wife. Though he was obviously over fifty, she was not more than eighteen. Noticing my surprise, he explained that his real wife and children lived at Kashgar, but as he had work in this region for two months, he had hastened to follow the local custom, according to which a man who is far away from his own place remarries in order to have a home. When he leaves, the young woman, who may perhaps be described as a provisional wife, returns to her own family. "Besides," said the man, "why should I hesitate? A woman like this isn't worth more than a hundred *piaodze*—about the same as a half-sack of flour." I tried to work out how much that might be in Europe and he began to talk in terms of *sar*. A sar is worth a Chinese tael. Fifty-two pounds of flour which, two years before, cost a sar now cost sixty sar.*

Because of the inflation the peasants keep their flour and there is none to be had in the market. The rich change their money for wool, which they send to India, where they have bank accounts. And anyhow it is prudent to hide one's wealth. Five of the more comfortably-off, propertied men of Kashgar had just disappeared—it was given out that while travelling they were attacked by bandits, and the authorities, accusing them of having been enemies of the State, confiscated their property. It was true that in the mountains there was a brigade of "Russians," Kirghiz from the west, who were regarded as insubordinate, but they seemed to be obedient enough to any precise orders given them. They had a song of their own in which they referred to themselves as Tortinjis, which means "men of the 'Fourth'."

We asked the man before us whether he thought the Soviet influence was good for the country. He knew more about it than we should ever have found out by ourselves.

"One has to face the fact that Sinkiang is a mediæval country," he answered. "The inhabitants are savages" (*dikii* was the word he used), "and everything that is done to help them is good. If Soviet influence makes it possible to recruit fifty or a hundred schoolboys and send them to Tashkent for a few months, it is good. But where it is

---

* We had crossed a new frontier and now there was a different currency, that of the Bank of Urumchi. There were also crude bank-notes, the ceaselessly changing value of which was to remain a mystery to us. The old sar was worth three Mexican dollars, that is about four English shillings.

done in opposition to the wishes of parents it is bad. In the name of goodness why not let those who still believe in the Koran go their own way?" "The Russians," he went on, "are most active in the north of the province, at Urumchi, where there is a Soviet military school. At Urumchi, also, the police system is so organized that everybody has to mind what he is saying, even in his own house. It reached the point that all White Russians who held to their own ideas had to leave the province. There are no real Russians here yet," he wound up, "only *Sart** advisers, who 'understudy' every village mayor."

Still Another Revolt.

We passed ten potai before we came to Kizil on the second day. The heat was torrid. Throughout the journey I never saw Peter's nose without being sunburnt, and when I think of him during the journey I see him lying down, resting on one elbow—he tired quickly of sitting Turkish fashion—and impatiently scratching the shrivelled-up skin of his nose with his nail. Not to have to suffer in the same way I wore an eye-shade. I had had it for months, and it was, with my knife, among my most cherished possessions. It was broken in three places, but with the help of some sticking-plaster I had prolonged its life by weeks. Only the adhesive material of the sticking-plaster melted in the sun and in the end the thing was unusable.

The next day Nyaz announced that it was eleven potai to Yangi Hissar. That was the day I first saw the very high snowy mountains which abut on the Pamirs. Away to the south they were glittering like rare silk and I scarcely took my eyes off them till the veil of dust that usually hangs over Sinkiang hid them once more. As in the Tsaidam, I was

---

* The name given to the settled natives of Russian Turkestan. The word is Indian and originally meant caravan-leader. About the thirteenth century it came to mean 'Moslem.'

pining to reach the summits. We were anxious to get to the end of the stage before the heat of the late afternoon, so trotted out our horses. Their two bearded owners followed at the same speed, singing delightfully. In spite of all they had to put up with, those men were bubbling over with gaiety, and that ride is one of my perfect memories.

Suddenly, when we thought we were coming to a mill because of the noise we heard, two mastodons appeared—lorries full of soldiers. My horse took fright. And certainly it was a surprise. So they had motor vehicles here! Since leaving Lanchow we had discovered that Central Asia was not exactly the place for motor vehicles.

When we got to the aksakal's house at Yangi Hissar, a native who knew Russian told us that the soldiers at Kashgar had revolted against General Liu Pin and set fire to his yamen because they had not had their pay for several months. Fifty of them were supposed to have fled to the mountains with arms and munitions. Well, we had seen their pursuers.

I said to myself that governing seemed to be a very difficult business. To pay the troops who kept the dictatorship in power the people were heavily taxed and rendered discontented. This was the position at Khotan. On the other hand, when a government tried to conciliate the taxpayers and to be reasonable about levies, it ran short of money and the soldiers revolted, leaving the town open to the depredations of mountain bands—Kashgar's plight! Which was better? Peter was not interested when I raised the point. He was considering an altogether different problem, which was this: Who would win an English law case in which a man, suddenly raised to the peerage with the title of Lord Bognor, brings an action against a poet for writing a tragedy with a hero bearing the hitherto unused name, it being essential for the balance of the poet's lines to retain the name?

Then Peter went off and had a bathe in public in one of those deep greenish ponds which serve all oases as reservoirs. Afterwards we spent an hour sitting on a rug beneath shady branches in an orchard, eating figs with sour milk, while a string orchestra played native airs in a gallery overhead. I only needed a khalat to fancy myself the central figure in a Persian miniature.

Disasters.

It was the 22nd of July, a month since we left Cherchen. Now we were only two days from Kashgar and we sent a messenger on ahead to give warning of our coming.

The green-and-white leaves of the little poplars on the side of the road were trembling against the deep blue background of the sky. I was ambling along, feeling happy. The donkeys had gone on before us and now, a little further along, not far on the other side of an irrigation channel, we overtook them. They had stopped, but at the time we had no suspicion that anything was wrong. Then we left the main road and took a short cut across some huge stretches of irrigated pasture land, the browsing cattle staring at us as we went by. My horse kept close on the heels of the mounted soldier who was acting as escort to us. Crossing a river, the soldier's horse stumbled, but recovered himself and got over. But before I had time to understand what was happening, my horse stuck, and, terrified, turned over on his side; and I was up to the waist in the river. However, with Nyaz's help I succeeded in dragging my horse out, swearing all the time at our incompetent guide and abusing him—in Russian, for lack of Turki words. My notebooks, passport, films and Leica were streaming with water. So was my sleeping-bag. Peter made the soldier come back and lend me his saddle, for, thinking my horse was in danger, the idiot had rushed off to get help from some shepherds.

247

There was no flour in the market at Yapchan, where we arrived that evening. It was only by addressing ourselves to the shang yi that we were able to secure some. While we were at supper, a Turki with clear-cut features and obviously used to giving orders—a surprising thing in a native—came and asked coldly to see our papers. He knew Russian, came from Andijan, and informed us that we should find no donkeys at Yapchan. But it is not on his account that I was long to remember my night at Yapchan. For anybody who did not mind being turned into a jumping ground by the most charming little toads it would have been a good night. . . .

On the morrow, the 23rd of July, the memorable day of our arrival at Kashgar, Peter opened his suitcase to get out his razor—only to find it full of water. And that was not all. The "canteen" box which hung opposite the suitcase had also been under water. A donkey had been nearly drowned in the irrigation channel where we passed them on the previous day. The donkey-boy was frightened and had not dared tell us.

So Peter the Impatient had perforce to postpone our departure. To prevent the damage from becoming serious we must get the things at least partially dry. The medicine chest was pulp, inside which pills, tablets and powder were dissolving. But the greatest misfortune was that several of Peter's films, some of which had already been exposed, were dripping wet and probably ruined. The typewriters, our only luxury articles—which we had very nearly had to abandon at Toruksai when our caravan was melting like butter in the sun—were already being eaten up with rust in their layers of mud. They were stuck, and it took an hour of drying and oiling—with gun oil—before my *Erika's* members came to life again. Peter's clothes were dripping on a rope, amongst them a now miserable-looking suit of light summer material, all streaked with the dye that had run out of a green scarf he got in Khotan. Every time he opened the case during these months past I had noticed the beautiful material and the impeccable crease of the trousers. I foresaw that in my pleated skirt (rolled up in a bundle ever since our departure) I could hardly expect to be taken for much more than Peter's cook when the time came for him, in his elegance, to take me out in Kashgar high society. Of course it was vexatious that his suit should have been ruined, especially on the main road, far from perilous trails, and with all Tartary behind him. But I wonder whether I felt as sorry as I ought to have done.

No new donkeys were available at Yapchan, so, by not paying him, we compelled the guilty donkey-boy to come on with us. The poor lad could not, as it was, pay for his night's lodging, and offered to leave his dagger with the innkeeper till he should be able to pay.

High Life.

This time Nyaz was to stay behind to see to the donkeys, and we set off at a trot to cover the last eleven potai between us and Ha-shih, as the natives call Kashgar. We soon reached the oases and the fortifications of the New Town. There our escort left us to return to his barracks. The walls showed many bullet-marks from the recent civil wars.

It was another six miles to that Old Town which, for such a long time, had haunted our dreams. There was coming and going on the road and we trotted along, all by ourselves and very proud, like children out without a governess. . . . A victoria was drawn up at the side of the road. As if by magic we found ourselves seated in it. And leaving our horses to a horseman dressed in red we went forward at a gallop.

We were carried into the cool shadow of great trees. A few telegraph poles, the vestiges of a line that had been broken,

rushed past us. I had the impression that we were driving
recklessly. And the sense of superiority it gives one to be in
the only carriage on a road! A rare feeling of joy possessed
me. It has always seemed natural to me to be wherever I
happen to find myself, but I knew that though we had often
speculated as to what it would feel like to arrive at Kashgar,
at Peking it had seemed crazy even to think of such a thing
as possible. The success of our expedition will remain an
unrivalled experience so far as I am concerned. Asia is
unique, and I, who care most for old primitive countries, find
none of the other continents comparable to it.

Happiness is the intoxication produced by the moment of
poise between a satisfactory past and an immediate future
rich with promise.

There was going to be a perfect welcome in a friendly
house, a long month's holiday to be spent in the Himalayas—
and no worries just yet. Incapable of expressing the joy that
rose within me in any other fashion, I broke into the uncon-
trolled laughter of a high-spirited girl, and gave Peter a few
digs in the ribs with my elbow.

Below the massive walls of the Old Town where there were
little kitchen gardens, a handsome cavalier in raw tussore
clothes and a topee was coming forward to meet us. He
introduced himself and bade us welcome. His name was
Arthur Barlow and he was the Vice-Consul. We followed him
to a gateway crowned with the coat of arms that has *Dieu
et mon droit* inscribed on it. We were at the British Consulate-
General. Himalayan mountaineers of the Hunza Company
stood on guard beside the laurels. I noticed that they had
ibex-heads as ornaments in their white caps.

The garden was a riot of flowers. Young ducks waddled
about on the English lawn. And then, the house! It was a
long house with a verandah, a cool hall, and well-polished
furniture; armchairs covered with chintz, books and

newspapers everywhere. . . . There was a youngish man, the English doctor at the Consulate, and a slight old lady who seemed to emerge out of a lace collar. "May I introduce . . . Miss Engwall of the Swedish Mission." And last of all, there was a table piled high with sandwiches and hot scones swimming in melting butter . . .

Behold me, obliged to try and keep my cup of tea straight on a slippery saucer, and saying with my very best "fashionable society" smile:

"Two lumps, please . . . Yes, thanks, we had an excellent journey."

CHAPTER XIII

THE TOWN OF OUR DREAMS

Joys of a House.

BEFORE my stay at Kashgar I had never had such intense delight in the numerous pleasures that a house can provide—sleep without having to fight fleas, hot water in the bath up to one's neck, the clink of bottles when one said "Yes" in answer to the query: "Have a drink?"

But for the semi-wild beasts that we had become, the pleasures of the table were, at first, the most absorbing. I could not have enough of the vegetables and salads I had gone without for five months, and I can still recall the gleam of crystal and silver and flowers on the mahogany table. The sight distracted my mind from the strain of sitting on a chair. There was the luxurious sense of black coffee perfuming the somnolence inherent in the partaking of a good repast. But more than anything I enjoyed my morning slices of bread drowned under butter and honey.

Towards the end of the afternoon, when it was time to take a little exercise, there was tennis. But neither my companion nor I knew how to play. On the other hand, Peter was as quick as lightning at squash, which he played with Barlow. I realized with surprise that his apparent stiffness hid great elasticity. Near-by, a dozen Hunza Scouts of the Consulate Guard enjoyed themselves like children, in a game of volley-ball. Twice a week we played football with them. They were great, strong, moustachioed men, as black as Sicilians. The football ground was below the fortifications by the side of the road followed by the slow wool caravans bound for

Russia. Afraid of being jostled, I took refuge on the outside right. But in fact, under Barlow's direction, everybody played scientifically, not roughly, the Hunza mountaineers included, and also some Indian business men who would join us after their day's work was done. When a goal was scored everyone shouted *"Shabash!"* The fact that I played football for all I was worth did not altogether discredit the rumour spread in the bazaar that a White Russian disguised as a woman had arrived in Kashgar with an Englishman.

In the evening we talked, and—it had occurred rarely since our departure—in a language familiar to the entire company. Or I took my ease, with one of the books out of the library on my knees. There was a day on which I was the proud discoverer of a paragraph in *The Times* to the effect that my Genevese comrade, Loulou Boulaz, had made a first-class sensation by climbing the Grandes Jorasses from the northern side. For once, Peter was not the only person to find news of his friends in the venerable journal.

During the greater part of the time I was a prey to a kind of chronic torpor through which occasionally consciousness of some exterior manifestation penetrated. England had grown uneasy when Peter's silence became prolonged and through the Secretary of State had asked Kashgar to try to obtain some information about him. That was why our arrival had surprised nobody at Chini Bagh, as the Consulate was called. Mr. Barlow now sent a reassuring message and added a word about me for our minister in London—I felt sorry I had never called on him. In Europe there seemed to be uneasiness on the subject of Italy's claims regarding Abyssinia.

But all that was very far away. I was more interested in the plans being drawn up between the Consulate and the Legation at Peking for the sending of a mission to Urumchi. That would be a difficult project to realize. I also learned the history of Miss Engwall, the lady we met the day of our arrival. She had lived in Sinkiang for thirty years and during the last civil war she was the only person in Kucha—where she had been settled thirteen years—whose belongings were left intact by the pillaging soldiery. One day, however, an officer tried to take her horse from her, and she boxed his ears to such effect that he went away utterly dazed. And when the Tungans offered to pay for the medicines she sold them with their depreciated bank-notes, she merely pointed to her walls, which were papered with newspapers, and said: "I have already got paper, thank you, and better printed than yours. I want money with which I can buy bread."

Miss Engwall wanted to go home and end her days in Sweden. Her heart was weak and she could not have stood the Himalaya passes. Consequently she had been trying, for quite a long time, to get a visa from Urumchi permitting her to use the new route by Tashkent, on which the highest pass is only about 13,000 feet. The day we were leaving the permit arrived. But her curious destiny was not to include a last sight of her own land. I learned long afterwards that the journey was too much for her and that she died in the train before it reached Moscow.

*The Round of the "Taotaï."**

Before long the Consul-General, Colonel Thomson-Glover, returned from the mountains with his wife and he also did everything in his power to make our stay enjoyable. We had to make a round of formal calls. Both our hosts accompanied us when we went to see the former *taotaï* of Kashgar, Ma Shao-wu. He was an old mandarin who came originally from Yunnan. Recently he had spent several months in hospital, for an attempt was made on his life one evening when he was driving back from his country house. Rumour

* Intendant or prefect; in fact, regional governor.

whispered that the attack was the work of his political adversaries, who resented the fact of his greater devotion to Nanking than to Urumchi. But officially the assumption was that the culprits were Tortinjis. Whoever attacked him, nobody had so far been apprehended. This constituted a serious "loss of face" for Ma Shao-wu.

We found the old man in a house in the New Town. He had a beautiful ivory-coloured face, wore a robe of figured beige silk and used crutches. His manners in receiving us were the manners of old China. Before settling down definitely at Urumchi Ma was going to Moscow to complete his convalescence, his little boy, Cho-ya, accompanying him. They were taking the new Irkishtam route and the boy was rejoicing at the idea of travelling in a real train. He had never seen a "carriage of fire" except in pictures. I noticed that the father kept his hands inside his wide sleeves. Apparently, he had lost two fingers as a result of his accident, and as his beautiful "mandarin's" hands were his greatest pride, he was inconsolable at the injury done them. To every one of the indiscreet questions that the interpreter transmitted for us, a diplomatic answer was returned:

"I lost my post when, as a result of the troubles, China lost her authority in Kashgar."

That was the kind of thing. I did not dare suggest that since the Chinese Provincial Government was once more in authority at Kashgar he ought, as a matter of course, to be reinstated in his post as taotaï. Perhaps Ma, being a Moslem, was suspect. And who could say but that his sympathies might lie with the Tungans?

Kung, the taotaï who had succeeded Ma Shao-wu, was a very modern type, though he seldom rose before midday. He wore a European suit of clothes, and as he had been a journalist, treated us as colleagues. We bombarded him with questions which seemed to put him out considerably.

According to him, Ma Chung-ying was already ancient history. He kept on saying: "I don't know." As a matter of fact, he gave one an impression of not knowing, and it was probably justified. Though he was head of the entire Civil Service, his subordinates took action independently of him. For instance, he was unaware of the fact that Mr. Barlow's luggage had been forced open on a journey to Khotan a short time before. From the point of view of Mr. Kung's prestige, such ignorance was unpardonable.

And sure enough, the day before we left, he was deprived of his post and his successor, Mr. Hsu, from Urumchi, came to call on the English Consul-General. Mr. Hsu had studied in Japan. He was a great swimmer and declared himself a fervent devotee of sport. I have no idea what qualities he showed as an administrator afterwards, but I know that it would be hard to find a more obsequious face than his. He drove away in the historic bottle-green brougham that had for ages been used by the successive taotaï of Kashgar. The horse, like all the carriage horses of the country, had a *duga* hoop over him. The vehicle had long ago been imported from Russia, piece by piece.

The Two Consuls.

The Soviet and British representatives at Kashgar were far from being the best friends in the world, though officially the relations were excellent. Some Russians came frequently to play tennis at the Consulate-General. That was how we came to meet Bokanenko, a sympathetic little man of exceptional intelligence. He spoke English and Chinese and he knew Manchuria—where we had been a very short time before—so we found his conversation captivating. His athletic companion Igoroff had not such fine perception. He said to me that he had just been reading an account of my travels in the Caucasus in the Moscow papers.

He did not know that it was five years since I had been in the Caucasus.

We got out of the victoria in the courtyard of the Soviet Consulate. Commercial agencies and a co-operative shop (where we bought vodka and cheese before leaving for the Himalayas) were housed all round. But that day we were calling on the Consul. He received us in one of the big rooms in the central building.

Tierkuloff was calm and sympathetic. His dark eyes gleamed behind thick glasses. He was a Tatar from the Crimea and knew Turkish and Persian well. We talked in Russian, over Caucasian wines and sweetmeats. The latest papers in from Moscow lay on the table. They were only twenty days old. One had a picture of Romain Rolland at Maxim Gorki's home. An article announced that the legations at Peking had been judged worthy of promotion to the status of embassies—there was irony in the fact that this should have been at a moment when China was betraying her weakness by letting the Japanese in Inner Mongolia advance in the direction of Sinkiang.

In order to find out whether the Irkishtam route was open to everybody we enquired as to the possibility of returning to Europe that way.

"The route is closed for ten days," Comrade Tierkuloff said. "Thirty cases of plague have been reported in the mountain area close to the frontier. Besides, it would require a fortnight to get a reply from Moscow about your visa."

To tell the truth, we had no desire to go to Russian Turkestan. We knew it already and wanted to take advantage of the fact of being in Kashgar—a rare enough thing in any life—to cross the Himalayas.

Then I made enquiries as to the Consul's opinions on Sinkiang's future. Perhaps, like Manchuria, it would declare itself independent.

"No," he answered at once, "Sinkiang will remain as she is. It is not to anyone's interest that she should be independent. Neither we nor the English have any desire to play a role similar to that of Japan in Manchukuo."

The flower-beds in the garden were masses of sunflowers and a splendid swimming bath of running water glittered in a sunny corner. We were not long in taking advantage of the opportunity it provided and swam about delightedly in the cool mountain water. Peter had to bear with the laughter provoked by the brown band round his knees where he had been tanned by the sun.

Unlike Tierkuloff, Colonel Thomson-Glover, our host, was exuberant, had a high colour and when he galloped his pony in a polo match reminded me of a centaur. Although the teams were made up with the bold Hunza mountaineers— polo is their national game—Mrs. Thomson-Glover took an active part and played with ardour. Yet a year before she had been shot through the lung by one of the men who were in flight towards the mountains. Chini Bagh dominated the river and the man had fired at the people on the terrace. It was at the time of one of the innumerable sieges. But it was not only the men in flight who were dangerous; there had been snipers on the ramparts of the town. These had the inner courtyard of the Consulate under observation and they fired on anyone who ran across it. Who could have given them orders to do that?

The Colonel was very kind about answering the questions I had to put him. England, he said, could not, it was evident, have much influence in Turkestan. Neither could she do anything to prevent the U.S.S.R. gaining ever greater control over the trade of the province. With the opening of the Irkishtam route Kashgar was only five days from Tashkent, and it was only three hundred-odd miles from Kashgar to the railhead at Andijan.

"But we must insist," the Consul-General continued, "that the rights of our nationals be respected. They are Indian merchants. There were Indian merchants here long before Great Britain assumed control of Kashmir in 1811."

There were also certain equivocal points needing to be cleared up. On these the Consul-General proposed to dwell when the British mission went to Urumchi, which was to be in a little while. The problem of the White Russians and their status needed to be settled. There were some twelve hundred of them quartered at Maral-Bashi, near Kashgar, under the orders of General Bektieff. They had no rights, no papers, and it was to their interest to adapt their ideas to those of every new government. Nobody was responsible for what they did and what they did was disavowed by every-body. But since they had fought for the Urumchi Govern-ment, why should they not become Chinese subjects?

"Then," the Consul-General went on, "for our own security and the security of our caravans these Tortinji raids must be stopped. The Tortinjis commit highway robbery and then make for safety in Kirghiztan across the frontier."

Another point was the fact that the taotaï now had no authority whatever.

"This," said Colonel Thomson-Glover, "is inadmissible. To have even the smallest matter of local concern dealt with, I have to wait for months while it is being referred to Urumchi. And, finally, if my caravan people are provided with visas by the Kashgar authorities, they must not be searched and sent back when they reach Tashkurgan."

When I asked the Colonel what he thought about Soviet activity in Sinkiang, he observed that it was inevitable. But, contrary to law, Russia had concluded treaties simultaneously with Nanking and with Sheng Shih-tsai, as in the past she had treated simultaneously with Nanking and Chang Tso Lin in Manchuria. As for proofs of Soviet activities in the province, apart from the support lent by Red troops in 1934, they could only be observed indirectly, for the technical advisers were covered by the native authorities. Thus there were times when the local press embarked on a campaign of atheistical propaganda, using all the arguments employed at Tashkent. Whether the Soviets desired to help in the creation of an Uighur Socialist Republic in Sinkiang, only time would show.

I found by experience that it was not very easy to leave Sinkiang. Each one of the muleteers we engaged had to get a passport with a photograph, and a Chinese Customs officer came twice to make an inventory of our belongings before we were ourselves free to leave. Our passports were only returned to us bearing visas in Chinese after a fortnight.

"We wanted to be sure," said the new taotaï by way of excuse, "that Fu Lei-ming and his companion Ma Ya Na would not leave before the great banquet that is being given this evening in their honour."

And as every consulate went by whatever time happened to suit it, Mr. Hsu, who was inviting us to the banquet, was at pains to give us *his* time.

An Original Banquet.

The banquet took place in one of the properties recently confiscated by the State. The guests arrived towards nightfall and were received, each one, with a flourish of trumpets that set the walls trembling and our horses rearing. At the end of a large geometrically-laid-out orchard two long tables stood on a platform painted sky-blue. The first was covered with tea-glasses, fruit, sweetmeats and cigarettes. Earlier arrivals sat at it waiting till everyone was in.

The various guests were accompanied each by a numerous bodyguard. Kashgar was like Harbin in that the weirdest rumours were ceaselessly being hatched out and everybody lived from day to day in fear of being overthrown or carried off.

In all there were three hosts receiving: the strong-looking, bearded Mahmud Hsing Chang—he was the Turki General in command at Kashgar; General Liu Pin, at the head of the Chinese forces, and Mr. Hsu, the new taotaï. We were not the only guests of honour. Two doctors, a man and a woman, had arrived by aeroplane from Moscow with a serum to be used in fighting the plague. It was rather odd to be told by the taotaï, when I asked him, that the two aeroplanes had arrived from Urumchi, not from Moscow. According to Doctor Bichkoff, on the other hand, they had arrived from Tashkent. And then somebody, I have forgotten who, told me about a third aeroplane which had had to make a forced landing in the Celestial Mountains.

Before long everybody was in: all the Russians (their wives dressed in modest silk robes), all the Chinese, all the Turkis, all the English, all the Indians—and the one Swiss, who was suddenly surprised to hear Madame Osipoff saying a few words in French.

Then we sat down to table. With the soup, our glasses were filled with benedictine, cognac or vodka, the only drinks there were. One had to be continually emptying one's glass to honour some toast or other. It was "Kaan-pei" or "Za vache zdarovie" all the time and one had to drink. Peter and I managed to get and hold on to a bottle of vodka, fearing lest the servants should serve us with the sweetish Caucasian benedictine. Now, if ever, it was a question of keeping a clear head, for Igoroff and I were engaged in an implacable duel. The men had taken off their coats and the atmosphere generally was Saturday night-ish. Still, Peter was a little uneasy. He was remembering that it was one of the little ways of the country to polish off one's enemies in the course of a banquet, and asking himself exactly how desirable or undesirable a *Times* correspondent might be considered here.

Igoroff was afraid of microbes and gave me details showing how anti-hygienic food and life generally were in Kashgar. But after a little while I was unable to follow what he was saying, for Liu Pin and Hsu would keep on pestering me with pathetic messages for the League of Nations.

"The League of Nations must realize how much Sinkiang needs to be helped . . ."

"But helped how? Against whom?" I asked.

"Just helped . . ."

In raucous and martial Chinese Liu Pin began the speech-making. He stopped at the end of each sentence and one heard the English, Russian and Turki translations of what he had said being uttered simultaneously by the interpreters. Liu addressed the most superlative compliments to the Soviet aeroplanes—the symbols of human solidarity. Then it was Geneva's turn. Geneva was the greatest city in the world—because of the League of Nations. And then *The Times* got its word. It was the best of all newspapers. Liu Pin did not carry his drink very well and he knew it. He was very pleased with himself, laughed at his own jokes and ended by remarking that he was afraid he might be repeating himself, since he did not know what he was saying, and sat down.

The Consuls responded in turn. Colonel Thomson-Glover observed dryly that the Soviet aeroplanes, which no doubt had been delayed while the serum was being fabricated, had been so kind as to arrive only two days before the special couriers from Gilgit in order to show that Moscow would not be alone in saving Kashgaria against a possible epidemic.

In the passage a Turki orchestra was playing dance music. And suddenly there was Liu Pin, the most comical of Chinese generals, performing a solo dance, his revolver swinging against his military breeches. Peter played a trick on me by announcing that I danced extremely well in the Turkish style. The diners began calling on me and I finished by getting up and partnered the General by imitating his movements. I tried to turn the tables on Peter by telling the company he sang beautifully—which was the antipodes to the truth. But it was in vain that they tried to persuade the blushing correspondent of *The Times* to perform.

At last Mrs. Thomson-Glover gave the signal for our departure and I followed her—doing my best to walk steadily.

CHAPTER XIV

ON THE PAMIRS

THE next day—it was the 8th of August—I had such a frightful headache that I was scarcely able to touch the last meal we were privileged to eat at Mrs. Thomson-Glover's.

I took a last survey of the panorama of Kashgar from the roof of the house. Here were the terraced roofs and dense verdure of the oasis, there the desert dunes. Far away to the west lay the Celestial Mountains, where I had been stopped at an impassable frontier three years before. To the south were the Kongur and the thousand years old Pamir road which we had to take to reach Kashmir.

The members of the Citroën Expedition, coming north on their way to Urumchi, had been the last Europeans to travel that route. We had three great passes to climb. One of them, the Mintaka, in the Hindu Kush chain, was over 15,000 feet high and marked the Indo-Chinese frontier. The other great trans-Himalayan route passed over the Karakorams at over 18,000 feet, to the south of Khotan. It also led to Kashmir, but it is a tiring route and provides the caravans with nothing for the nourishment of man or beast.

If I was to trust the books I had glanced at in the library at the Consulate-General, there were many for whom Kashgar was a lost city, isolated behind its mountains. For us, on the contrary, Kashgar really represented our true return to civilization, the forty days that lay between us and Srinagar being no more than a final stage.

At three o'clock in the afternoon we dragged ourselves

away at last from the delights of Chini Bagh, and set out for Gilgit, in India, which we should reach in twenty-five days.

We had turned a piece of our slab of gold into money to pay for our caravan, and that day we wanted for nothing. I felt for the first time that we were travelling according to the traditions, not like vagabonds escaping from China to conquer a dubiously uncertain Kashgar. Our papers were in order. We had hired five excellent ponies for forty Mexican dollars per animal. An English flag waved over our cases, intended, I think, to impress those with whom we might have to deal. The cases themselves were none of your broken-down and battered affairs such as had accompanied us to Kashgar. They were constructed on classical lines and were called *yakdans*. All the good things to eat that came from Mrs. Thomson-Glover were stored in them and day after day the giver's praises were to be sung. I had a new sponge with which it was a pleasure to wash. Peter, who had neglected the matter at Peking, was now provided with a better dentrifice than the Chinese paste he had bought at Sining. I felt remorseful for having steadily refused to share my *Pepsodent* with him. I had maintained that he must take the consequences of his negligence. Yet Peter had not hesitated about handing his air pillow over to me when he learned that I had left mine in Peking . . . I fear my selfishness was unpardonable, even when I recall that Peter was one of those people who do not know how to squeeze a sponge and who ruin tubes of paste by squeezing them plumb in the middle.

We left one humble memento with Mrs. Thomson-Glover, a full box of saddle soap. It was a preparation that has been famous in England for centuries. The quality of our harness scarcely permitted of my using it, but I kept it as a mascot, for it was a present from the Lattimores, who in 1927 brought their trek across Asia to a successful conclusion.

Like a true sahib, Peter rode a magnificent stallion. Its name was Cloud and the beautiful brute was to be given as a present to the Mir of Nagar from the Colonel. To complete the description of our caravan—there were two Chinese soldiers, Liu and Wu, who had to escort us to the frontier. Liu was a dreamer with a big mouth. Peter was charmed with his disarming simplicity. He was discreet and thoughtful for us, and insisted firmly on paying for the *k'tak* we used to drink on the side of the road. Only he did not know a word of Turki, which was a drawback in dealing with the muleteers and the natives.

Everything would have been for the best in the best of all possible worlds if, after the third day at Yangi Hissar (as far as which we had to return on our earlier tracks), we had not begun to have a bad impression of our caravan men. In spite of the clearest warnings, they had not prevented Cloud from kicking the animals near him. They had lost two tent poles. And they went on asking to lie up for a day on the plea that the animals were ill. Then we discovered that they were transporting four bales of rugs which were much too heavy for their horses. Satar would have to commandeer some yaks at the first Kirghiz camp, and a native would have to come with those "groaning cattle" as far as the camp after that, so as to bring them back to their owner. And nobody would be paid. We were very displeased and not less so when later we gathered that Satar was passing off his bales as part of our belongings.

We had left the oases with their channels of muddy water, left the villages with their shaded main streets, where easy-going Turkis in white placed slabs of dough in the round insides of ovens, and cut up their sheep with the eternal dust pervading the air about them. The caravanserais were behind us, and the life one lived lying on their platforms while donkeys lost their breath braying raucously at the heavens.

266

We crossed a desert of gravel that stretched in a vast bank along the foot of the Kuen Lun range. Then we came to a mountain valley full of fresh, vivifying air. Wu, the second of our soldiers, let his rifle fall into the water when his horse stumbled in the passage of a rapidly-flowing river. He was distracted. What was he to do? Some natives who came along were mobilized, literally roped in, for they roped themselves together so as not to be knocked over by the current, and, up to their waists in water, proceeded to sound the rocky bottom of the river. Their search was successful. And that very evening, our two Chinese grew so excited at seeing whistling marmots for the first time that they fired at them. But they had no success, apparently because Liu shut his eyes when he pulled the trigger! The only structures in these deserted valleys, where the nomads camped but rarely, were those of the dead. From a distance, the stone Moslem mausoleums, rising very close to each other, looked like eggs in square egg-stands.

Towards evening on the fifth day Peter, still in his shorts, and now shivering in an unexpected mist, was an object of pity. He pretended to be surprised that there was no longer any sunshine and talked of plunging head first into his sleeping-bag as soon as he could lay hands on it. We waited for our slowly moving caravan in the shelter of a cave. Liu arrived first, bringing a strayed sheep for the pot and feeling very proud of himself. Clearly it is not only wolves that lost sheep have to fear in those parts of the world.

On the Mountain Top.

At the end of the next day's trek we set up the tent at Kashka Su, close to three Kirghiz yurts where the people gave us smoked yak cream.

According to the map our route that day passed close to the Mustagh Ata, an important mountain towards the north of

267

the Chinese Pamirs, but from the depths of our narrow valley we could see nothing. As it was still early afternoon, I set off to attack the nearest spur of the mountains. It was very steep and great tufts of grass made a series of ledges which I had to clamber up. At the end of an hour I passed some sheep on their way down. At the end of two hours the yurts looked no bigger than three little brown mushrooms. I was out of breath and stopped for a while, admiring the gentians, and the edelweiss—it had such long stalks here—and listening to the silence of the desert regions of the world, that silence which I miss so much when I am amongst human beings, a deep silence which fills the heart with a sense of immensity.

I went on to the rocky summit that towered over a slaty region where nothing grew. At the top the wind was strong. I was on a level with numerous bare crests, but to the south there was no trace of the famous Mustagh that should have been soaring above the clouds.

The strain of climbing was telling on my knees and I suddenly began to feel afraid of the descent. Going up, my feet were all right, the toes gripping well, but going down, I knew from experience, my heels were liable to fail me on the oblique and slippery slate. For a half-hour of the descent there was nothing to prevent me from falling over into the sheer drop below the rocky scree. Peter would be the only person to be directly affected if I disappeared. Unconsciously I grew introspective. During the last six months I had often had the impression of being on another planet. In fact, I was as though I had been shut off from the rest of the world. My family and my friends had learned to do without me. My remoteness and my isolation had at last taught me that I was useless to "the order of things."

Yes, that was quite certain. But what mattered was myself, I, who was living at the centre of the world—that "I" who did not want to disappear without accomplishing something worth while, something that would carry me on, that would save me from nothingness, and satisfy—however humbly—the craving for eternity that existed in me!

Yet I had adopted an odd method of satisfying it, marching fifteen miles a day for months on end. . . . Once more, as in the many empty hours of the journey, I asked myself what it was that drove me away towards the four corners of the world. I knew that I liked ever-changing sights. I could repeat with Baudelaire:

Mais les vrais voyageurs sont ceux-là seuls qui partent
Pour partir; cœurs légers, semblables aux ballons
De leur fatalité jamais ils ne s'écartent
Et sans savoir pourquoi, disent toujours: Allons! *

But that was only an effect. What was the cause of the curiosity that spurred me on, of that need to see, to understand? Perhaps I created difficulties for the pleasure of surmounting them? What was the origin of those calls to me which I followed blindly and which made up my mind for me?

There were so many things still to learn . . . No, I did not want to slip now. I must keep away from the dangerous scree. So I negotiated a ridge and, as my luck was in, I got safely back to the pasture grounds.

It was twilight when I reached the tent. Peter was starving and with the best intentions had just melted down some fat for a risotto. But it took fire and his eyebrows were all burnt.

Next day, the seventh out from Kashgar, the trail led over difficult ground and we crossed two low passes where, owing to the passage of innumerable caravans, the soil was deeply bitten into. Reddish marmots ran about in the green

* But the real travellers are those alone who set out
  For the sake of setting out; hearts that are light, like balloons
  They never turn aside *from* their destiny,
  And without knowing why, are always saying, "Let us go!"

pastures and the rising sun flooded the neighbouring summits with a new light.

When the ponies stopped for breath, Satar, armed with the hooked needle he used for sowing up his sack of corn in the mornings, went to each one and gave it a sharp stab on the nose. This produced bleeding and was the method of combating the congestion caused by the altitude. That evening we camped at Tohil Bulung, at the foot of the chief mountain chain between us and the Taghdumbash Pamir.

The Chichiklik Pass.

On the 15th of August we went up a deep valley, down which a tumultuous river flowed. The trail, or rather the absence of a trail, led us to cross the river eight or ten times. I detested having to do it. The muleteers took the animals over one by one and sometimes had to lean heavily against them from the down-stream side to help them keep their balance when they stumbled. I realized then why the Consular postbag was involuntarily given a bath sometimes.

The tiny cornfields, which were yellow at the bottom of the valley, were greener and greener as we ascended. In the evening we camped in idyllic pasture ground close to high mountains. We had been six months travelling that day and we opened a bottle of brandy to celebrate the occasion. Peter, a dilettante, like all good Etonians, remarked that it was the first time in his life he had stuck to anything for more than six months. He talked of some of the posts he had held: dramatic critic, then secretary to an international conference at Shanghai—not a very successful venture, that one. He had also worked for a while in a Wall Street bank, but though, with an influential grandfather at his back, he could count on a career all ready made for him, he would not stay on. It was at the time of the great crashes. "The air was black with investors jumping off sky-scrapers," he said.

There were three yurts at the other side of the torrent. The Elder, wishful to pay us a visit, hoisted himself on a yak and set it at the whirl of water. The yak slipped and the old man was thrown off and in spite of all his efforts flung from one rock to another. But it was not long before his son managed to catch hold of him and get him out. That was exactly what I always feared was going to happen to me when I had to cross these streams. The Kirghiz must have crossed that ford many, many times without any trouble. A well-marked path led to it. It was just that his strength had failed him that day. Perhaps it was the first time . . .

We had no great difficulty in getting over the Chichiklik Pass the next day. On the way up we passed some dead donkeys. Satar hastened to tear their shoes off them, while vultures that Peter called lammergeyers looked on with impatient eyes. Then, having climbed amongst black rocks, we came to a green glacial lake below mountain peaks covered with hardened snow. After that we went up a desolate moraine in the middle of which some of the animals lay down and had again to be stabbed with the hooked needle. The sky was grey and the low clouds blotted out the view of Mustagh Ata, "The Father of Ice Mountains."

That evening we arrived at the edge of an immense table-land swept by winds. There, at last, we camped. But everything went wrong. The Worcester Sauce had got spilt over a bag of raisins. Peter would set up the tent his way, the result being that I slept with my feet higher than my head. Tokta Ahun, the half-wit who was supposed to be looking after us, did not bring the tea we asked for. And next morning when we were starting he saddled my horse anyhow, could not find the bridle, and had got one of my stirrup-irons broken. This last disaster made me very angry, for in the mountains one was in one's stirrups for eight hours of the

FORBIDDEN JOURNEY

day. Then some natives appeared out of nowhere. They talked with Satar, the only one of us who knew their dialect. It was not unlike Tadjik or Old Persian. The men were not Kirghiz, and with their black beards and high bonnets, they seemed to have come out of a Babylonian fresco.*

---

* Those long-headed men of white race may be the descendants of autochthonous Aryans. They belong to the Pamir Iranian group. It is possible that it was in the course of very early migrations they reached Europe, where their passage was to have such a great influence on our languages. These white races of the mountains must be mixed, for I often noticed men of a very different type, stocky, with wide heads and fair or brown hair, the *homo alpinus* amongst them too.

CHAPTER XV

GOOD-BYE TO CHINA

TASHKURGAN, our next objective, was near. We scrambled down the Valley of Stones. It narrowed to a gorge where there was no room except for the torrent. The animals jumped from one mound to the next and if no bones got broken, withers were certainly wrung. Each one had his load placed on a carapace of straw covered with a strip of woollen stuff. In outline, this pack-saddle was like a longish head-wreath or a horizontal horseshoe, only rather narrow across. It might be thought that after so many centuries the caravaneers had found it the most practicable thing of the kind for the mountains. And yet I wondered. For day after day Satar had to groove out the front part. The animals' withers were all raw flesh. And for the twenty-five days we were on the road their sores, which were as big as plates, grew deeper and deeper and the air stank where they passed.

We reached the bottom of the valley and then, in another wider valley, called the Sarikol or Taghdumbash Pamir,* which was about 10,000 feet up, we came to the bank of a powerful river. This was an affluent of the Yarkand Darya.

Tashkurgan.

The region was dominated by the embattled walls of

---

* In the language of the country a "pamir" means a pasture-ground, an "alp" as they call it in Switzerland. The name came to be applied to the mountains just as we use the word "Alps" in Europe. It must not be imagined that there are real tablelands on the "Roof of the World", as the Pamir region is called.

Tashkurgan, "the stone hill," which, beneath threatening clouds pierced by snowy peaks, looked superb. A few houses crouched amidst some poplars at the foot of the hill. This was the last village in Chinese territory. Ptolemy mentions it in his description of the road that led from India through Afghanistan. And in the year 642, Hsuan Tsang, whose journeyings I had already followed in the Celestial Mountains, passed through Tashgurkan on his way back to China after he had accomplished his famous pilgrimage to India.

We stayed in the little house of the aksakal, an Indian who had been resident in Tashkurgan for thirty years. According to him, the Turki soldiers who garrisoned the region were robbers. The people preferred their Chinese predecessors. But everything was changing. The Chinese *amban*, who was a fair-minded man, had just been deprived of his post. (We had, ourselves, passed the dismissed district administrator at Kashka Su.)

Four countries almost touched each other at Tashkurgan, China, India, Afghanistan and Russia. The frontiers were marked out in 1905 by an international commission delegated to solve the problem of the "incidents" that frequently occurred. It was then that the narrow territory of Wakhan was given to Afghanistan, so that Russia and India should not adjoin.

In the main street of the village varied races and customs jostled each other. There were the beardless Chinese in their booths or behind their cauldrons of soup. There were the Turkis of the garrison and there were dark-skinned Indians in imposing turbans and sometimes in coarse woollen cloaks for wear in the mountains. At the little inn they baked their corn pancakes in the covers of saucepans turned upside down over the fire. One of them had a monkey which I thought charming until it began to amuse itself by pulling my hair . . . And of course there were native Sarikolis who looked like my

274

mountain people at home. They are usually thought to be Galchas, Tadjiks from the mountains, and it is said that their Pamir dialect retains traces of the old Saka language. At the little school in Tashkurgan I found some twenty children tracing Arab characters on their wooden "slates."

Taking a walk out past the ruined citadel, I saw some curious tombs amongst the classical Moslem mausoleums. They were surmounted by tripods of earth glittering with whitewash. It seemed to me that they were intended to allow fires to be lighted on top. The fact is of interest if it be remembered that the Bactrian term "tadjik" originally meant "fire-worshipper," and that even to-day the Sarikolis are careful never to allow a lamp to be blown out by a tainted breath.

On the Roof of the World.

We had our passports viséd by the Chinese authorities before continuing on our way south. They took no interest in our luggage. Then we had a stormy scene with Satar. In spite of our objections he wanted to bring on his suffering animals. At last, on the 18th of August, we left, following Nadir, a handsome bearded man, who knew the river well. The crossing was said to be very difficult.

When the mountains disappeared in the low clouds one might quite easily imagine oneself in Holland. Fat cattle browsed in flat stretches of thick grass, separated by canals which, in fact, were so many branches of the river. We advanced over a green sea that came to an end at the foot of great cliffs of gravel. The passage of the river was effected without difficulty, but I was made giddy by the noise and rapidity of the water underneath me. My horse could not keep straight on, and I got my boots wet.

We spent the night at the house of some Sarikolis. Built of stone, it was a most asymetrical structure with a corridor shaped like an elbow which seemed to be intended to minimize draughts. There were two smaller houses in the yard. These were used as kitchens. They had no doorways and the women, who were constantly in and out of them, entered by the windows. The women themselves, tall, shapely, with bony faces and grey or brown eyes, wore ravishing embroidered caps over their long hair. One of them was pasting cakes of sheep's droppings up against the wall of the yard. Our relations with the people became a little strained when Talib (one of the two Turkis who had replaced our Chinese escort), for no apparent reason, proceeded to beat up the man of the house with his gun.

For three days after that, we ascended a monotonous valley, towards the frontier. On a grey morning our somnolence was suddenly dissipated by the sight of three people on horseback who had nothing in common with the caravaneers we had met so far. They were wearing topees and proved to be two ladies and one man missionary. A long pony caravan came on behind them. On suspicion of carrying arms they had been held up for a day at Mintaka Karaul, while a messenger galloped off to Kizil Robat, the first Russian post, for instructions. They also told us they were asked at Gilgit whether the gentleman of the party was Mr. Fleming, as there was a telegram for someone of that name.

That evening we went on in front of the caravan and slept in the shelter of the mayor's yurt at Dafdar. We were on territory which, though Chinese, paid an annual tribute of wool and felt to the Mir of Hunza, the ruler of the valley to the south of the frontier. This practice has existed since the Mir was appealed to and, coming up, exterminated the brigands who were ravaging the countryside. The Mir also has grazing rights in Sarikol. Nevertheless, in order to be on good terms with his neighbours, he sends every year a present of some gold to the authorities at Kashgar, so that the Chinese can affirm, without lifting an eyebrow, that Hunza belongs to them.

At Paik, the next evening, an officer with a blond beard tried to pick a quarrel with us and confiscated Peter's rook rifle on the plea that the Peking permit for it was not sufficient. He maintained that another one should have been obtained at Tashkurgan to cover the frontier region. As the superior officer for the area was at the Mintaka Karaul post, which was situated on our trail at a height of 13,000 feet, we all galloped off there (through a snowstorm) the next day. A great many horses were tied up around an immense yurt, and horsemen were riding in every direction over the beautiful wet grass.

We took shelter in the yurt, where there was also a Kirghiz woman wearing an embroidered bonnet with streamers, who gave us bowls of salted tea; a Turki family—its men folk wearing the fez—on the way home from India, and two snoring soldiers who had, no doubt, been on night duty.

Zamir, the officer in charge of the area, held the rank of *Lan Fu*. He was a small, bearded, grey-eyed man, dressed in black serge, with a belt of fine new leather. He made himself very agreeable and told us in excellent Russian that he was a Tadjik but had been stationed at Tashkurgan, "in Czar Nicholas's time," with thirty Cossacks and learned the language there. He had been all kinds of things—peasant, courier, etc.—before his linguistic abilities suggested the army as a career, for he knew Turki, Russian, Wakha and the Farsi of the Tadjiks. To roll a cigarette, he took a packet of "Makhorka," such as is distributed to Soviet troops, out of his pocket, and I asked whether the Russian Pamirs close by were more densely inhabited than the Pamirs here on the Chinese side.

He did not know. Then he asserted with unnecessary

emphasis that he had never set foot west of the frontier. Of course his father actually came from there . . . Zamir had already said that in the old days there was no frontier and that it was only quite recently that a post had been established in order to find out what was happening. He diverted the conversation into ethnographical channels. There were two thousand Sarakolis living in the valley where we were, and thirty mountaineers who were Indian subjects; and there had been two hundred Kirghiz. But the Kirghiz, always unfortunate and always pillaged, could never do anything right and in the end were chased into Afghanistan, where they were vegetating miserably. The Tadjiks lived in peace everywhere. They had better head-pieces than the Kirghiz and knew a great many things. Zamir finished his discourse by saying to me: "It is no use learning unless one has a heart to help one to understand!"

There was a yurt, reserved for the use of the British post, about a mile away, and Zamir, the Tadjik servant of the Sinkiang Government, escorted us to it. He maintained that the regulations with regard to the rifle were unalterable, though Peter was ready to pay a fine or bakshish. In short, Peter felt that the only alternative was to send the rifle back to the Consul-General at Kashgar.

The fire in the yurt made the snow on the roof melt and, melting, it came in through the holes in the felt and dripped on our heads. We had hidden our notes in the sleeping-bags for fear of any possible trouble, but they were still safely there. The men shared the shelter with us and they made it impossible to sleep. They were cooking rice and making tea for hours, and all the time asphyxiating us with the smoke from the argols fire which they did not know how to keep going. We remonstrated with them, but they felt no need of sleep and argued the whole night long.

GOOD-BYE TO CHINA

The Mintaka.

We were due to enter India the next day, having marched over three hundred miles from Kashgar. It transpired before we left that Talib, the head man of our escort, had gone off with one of my warm ski-ing gloves and the whip with handle of antelope horn for which Peter had given two boxes of matches at Bash Malghun. This was the first occasion on which we had been robbed since setting out from Peking. Then, Zamir acting as interpreter for us, we made Satar understand how unsatisfactory we had found him.

Our men went on ahead and I pointed out to Zamir that he had allowed Satar's carpets through, though officially they should not have come beyond Tashkurgan, and that he might therefore allow the rifle to go through also. Zamir was rather upset and ended by acquiescing. He said first, however, that if he had not sent the Turkis back it was out of consideration for us, so that we should not be left without pony-men.

Zamir was playing a very complicated game, but, unlike Peter, I saw no evidence that he was a Soviet agent.

And so we departed from the last inhabited place on Chinese soil.

Leaving the wide valley that led over the Wakhjir Pass to Afghanistan, we turned into a smaller one where before long we met two Hunza men, one carrying the weekly postbag and the other an umbrella. Their clothes of the white wool of the country were cut European fashion.

It was cloudy weather and the peak at the end of our grassy valley was soon hidden. No pass worthy of the name could be discerned through the mist, so we attacked the flank of the mountain. Peter was soon out of sight on his sturdy Badakshani, Cloud. But the steep trail was a calvary for the ponies, its zigzags running contrary to all common sense. The animals stopped every hundred yards to get their breath

279

or simply to collapse under their loads. Then Satar would pierce their noses, they would leap up terrified, jostle each other on the narrow path, and race onward with their loads slipping over. The men ran, swearing, and brought the ponies back on to the path by firing stones, well aimed, at their feet. Then mist and snow added themselves to our troubles. Down below we could see, as from an aeroplane, the thin white line of the river, but nothing else.

At last we came to three heaps of stones. They marked the summit of the Mintaka, 15,600 feet above sea-level, an enormous maze of black shining rocks. We had climbed nearly 3,000 feet in two hours.

I felt it was going to clear, for now the fine blue snow seemed to be falling from a transparent mist, and I waited, letting the others go on. To the east, on my left, I could just make out the summit we saw in the early afternoon. When I got to a point higher up I should be able to see the Himalayas, the "Dwelling-place of the Snows." And at last, straight in front of me, beyond the black curve of the rocky pass, appeared one of the faces of the Mintaka, a triangular wall of snow, glittering in the last rays of the sun. A proud mountain, with its head turbaned in cloud, its lower slopes were deep in shadows through which wound a river of ice. So far, I liked India.

CHAPTER XVI

INDIA

THE sun disappeared. I could make out nothing but boulders and glaciers . . . Where, in such cold, were we going to camp? The animals were exhausted and could only get on with difficulty. One of them had just fallen amongst the rocks, and—a rare occurrence—Peter swore at the men. "Come on, you bloody fools!" Once again, because of Satar's bales, the caravan was being held up. By the time the kitchen-box was in that evening we had already slept without having had anything to eat. The advantage of travelling with a sleeping-bag is that you can carry it yourself and, even without luggage, be sure, at least, of a warm bed. A Hunza man named Assa suddenly joined us and led us through blinding snow to the stone hut that was Gulkoja. It was somewhere near the glacier. Peter had given away his matches—I have forgotten to whom—and we had to wait till the men came in before we could make tea—there were dried tufts of wild camomile to make it with.

Except Tokta Ahun the men were utterly worn out and no sooner had they got in than they fell, one after another, in a heap and went fast asleep. Tokta had done practically nothing, as he suffered from mountain sickness.

In the morning the world continued to look different from anything we had so far seen. There were no more pasture lands at the foot of eroded mountains. There was nothing anywhere but walls of rock that rose at a single spring to finish in innumerable jagged edges, and through that enchanted region our valley wound in and out between the magnificent mountain chains of the Hindu Kush to the north-west and the Karakorams to the south. In little ravines there were curious dark red flowers, bell-like little things, and huge marguerites.

The torrent struggled to get between great detached boulders, and—the wonder of it!—close by was a clump of eglantines covered with opening flowers. There were also shrubs like cypress trees, giving forth a perfume that reminded one of Mongol temples. Our path showed evidence of being carefully kept. It was in striking contrast to the Chinese mountain paths and Peter was proud of his country—he was beginning to have the feeling that he had arrived somewhere. Yes, it was the beginning of the end. We should find letters before us in Kashmir to disunite our thoughts and turn our minds in different directions. There would be no telegrams for me at Gilgit and Peter, realizing that I was sad at the thought, said: "I'll lend you mine." And once again we discussed what we should have for dinner when we celebrated our arrival at Srinagar, the capital of Kashmir and the Venice of India.

Below us the valley flattened out where our river joined the Kilik. And there, plumb against a clump of willows, rose a solitary little house. This was Murkushi, our first "rest-house," with two rows of white stones innocently marking an imaginary road to it. It was not a very solid habitation. Cloud walked off with one of the wooden pillars of the gallery to which he had been tied, and when I sat on a chair it collapsed under me. But we were in out of the rain. There was a fireplace and as this was our first meal in India we cooked sausages and bacon on a wood fire. And, at last, we had a partition wall dividing us from the Turkis and their disputes.

The next day, the 24th of August, we descended the romantic valley of the Hunza River. Its two steeply sloping sides were formed of scree. We got through by spacing ourselves out, as one does when crossing an avalanche slope. I know nothing more disagreeable than finding a bed of stones slipping half a yard or more under your feet at every step you take. At the bottom of the arid valley we came now and again on enchanting oases of willows where the dead arms of the river were the colour of diluted absinthe.

The Consul-General at Kashgar had sent word of our coming to Gilgit and now we were met by a courier with messages of welcome from the Mir of Hunza and George Kirkbride, the Political Agent for these frontier valleys. They said they would meet us at Baltit, where they were going to be before long.

The First Post Office.

At last, the slope on the left side of the valley became less steep and a little barley showed in fields covered with slates. A well-constructed house offered itself to our view and against it leaned the first telegraph pole, the leading file in an army that covers the entire world.

This was Misgar, about 11,000 feet above sea-level. It was here, according to Peking rumour, that ten thousand Sikhs were waiting under Lawrence's command to invade Sinkiang. The telegraph line, laid down some eighteen years before, made it possible for Peter to collect the numerous congratulations waiting for him at Gilgit. Apart from rare messages for caravaneers the telegraph clerk had not much to do. He made notes of Reuter's daily telegrams and sent them on to Kashgar.

In the middle of that poor hamlet, where we could obtain neither eggs nor hay, the raging torrent was crossed by a picturesque bridge of stone slabs. The ponies got in each other's way on it. One of them went over and once more, furious with the muleteers, we had to dry our precious notes and our Leicas. But a grand palaver was held. Peter announced that he was now at home, in his own land, and that contracts would have to be kept. We would leave next day with our five ponies and were not going to concern ourselves with the animals carrying the bales. The telegraph clerk translated our English words into *Burushaski* and one of the natives then passed them on in Turki to the men.

The rest-house was delightful, small, with white walls which owed their imitation frescoes to the Citroën Expedition. I admired the profiles of Iacovleff and Hackin which neighboured gastronomic mottoes in old French and still-life studies of all the vegetables unknown at Misgar. The combination of those three elements was a surprise and a greater stir for me than for Peter. He did not like vegetables, French was not his mother tongue, and he had not met the members of *La Croisière Jaune*.

Baltit, the Hunza capital, was only four days' march away. In our closed-in valley, the cliffs, against which the dark waters lashed furiously, opened out here and there. Then cones of alluvium pressed their way through and out of them some few tenacious natives had, by means of irrigation, created oases. At Gircha the roofs of the houses were of a brilliant orange, for they were covered with drying apricots. The angles of the roofs were adorned with ibex horns. I like to think that in those mountains the men become peerless climbers.

Our path itself, the Gilgit "road," was the roughest imaginable. Happily, the river was crossed by a cantilever bridge, but for most of the way the road corkscrewed upwards, or hung like a balcony on the face of a cliff, or tumbled down amongst the boulders to one of the rare stretches of river-bank. We got on only very slowly through that deep fissure.

On the second day we had a local guide who came armed

with an ice axe, and towards the middle of the march we struggled painfully across the Batura glacier. This is a huge affluent, on the right bank, of the Hunza river. It is black, covered with rocks and stones and its bed is filled with what looked like frozen waves. Our poor animals stumbled, tore their feet, and often slipped, before finally getting safely on to solid ground at the other side.

That evening I saw, away to the west in the Hindu Kush, some soaring peaks of ice that stirred me to enthusiasm. They were so high (over 25,000 feet) that they looked at us over all the black buttresses that stood up in between. I shall always remember the twilight in the village of Hasani with a little girl beside me driving a quadriga of calves round and round on a threshing floor, their feet winnowing the corn.* The wise-looking child went round, with a stick in one hand and a brass plate in the other to catch the dung before it could soil the corn stalks.

The next day we slept at Sarat, and the day after that we reached Baltit in time for the official arrival of the distinguished personages who were expected: the Mir of Hunza, returning home; the Political Agent, and the English Resident in Kashmir.

The landscape had completely changed. The mountains were as high as ever, but the valley had opened out into an immense circus, with, for decorations, cultivated fields in terraces, and for background the magnificent mass of Rakaposhi on the opposite bank of the river.

Himalayan Capital.

Baltit, 8,000 feet above sea-level, is hidden in verdure, with, alone on a hill above it, the white fortress of the Mirs of Hunza, itself dominated, weighed down, by soaring

---

* In Turkestan the animals drag a heavy beam which has a surface bristling with roughnesses.

mountains. We were led to the Mir's summer villa, which had a terrace ornamented with stuffed ibex. In a shady orchard where ripe apples were falling with a plop, two tents had been prepared for us. The visitors' book lay on a table and amongst many famous British names I found also "Henri Montagnier, Valais." He was an American of Swiss origin.

At noon, a salute of guns announced the arrival of Colonel Lang, the British Resident in Kashmir. He visited this out-of-the-way valley only every four years. Now he was accompanied by the Political Agent from Gilgit and with them was the Mir. The latter had his beard dyed with henna. He wore gold-rimmed spectacles and on his head the national woollen cap. They passed under a streamer that said: "A Thousand Welcomes," the drums rolled and some natives executed a sabre-and-buckler dance while others waved banners.

Peter and I had been afraid that these distinguished persons would be in uniform and disapproving of our so very worn expedition kit. But nothing of the kind! Everything was done with charming simplicity, and a few days later we all together were laughing over our fears, for they and we had become the best of friends. George Kirkbride even made a confession. When he learned that the correspondent of *The Times* was due to arrive in company with a woman, he made up his mind that I would prove to be fat and forty and that Peter, representing the austere *Times*, would have an "inquisitive stoop" and be wearing spectacles.

From the time of our arrival in Baltit, we lived, thanks to our new friends, like people in story-books. At nightfall the mountain shone with a thousand fires. The natives, having done a three or four hours' climb from the village, lighted hundreds of oil lamps on the rocky ridges. The effect was prodigious. Beneath a sky in which the stars shone with an icy gleam, there was something infernal about all those reddish fires stuck in the black walls of our valley, which, far away, was closed in by the pale and unreal Rakaposhi.

By day we assisted at games of all sorts. Horsemen set off at a gallop and leaning out over their horses' shoulders, drew their bows and took aim at heart-shaped targets. Then other men, only armed with rifles instead of bows and arrows, did the same thing. These exercises took place on the polo-ground, the only flat part of the valley. It was a narrow strip of ground between two walls. As for polo, it was the national game of these mountain people and was a wild struggle, with players who looked like brigands and brandished primitive clubs, bound down by no rules and checked by no umpire.

From the terrace of the fort one looked out over the valley, while high above rose the mighty mass of Rakaposhi. The majestic summit, 24,000 feet high, marked the western extremity of the Karakoram range. It rather recalled Mont Blanc as seen from Brévent, and I thought it would make a marvellous objective for a first French expedition to the Himalayas. The natives call the mountain *Dumani* and think that nobody could ever climb it. They say that for three thousand years a dragon has been imprisoned in the ice. Every spring he tries to break his chains and, to make him stay where he is, they try to terrorize him by lighting great fires.

Every pillar on the terrace of the castle had ibex horns attached to it, and the arms of the Mir, a bow and arrow on a white ground, floated on a standard from the highest point of the roof. On the wall of a room I saw the genealogy of the Agha Khan, who is a descendant of Ali, Mahomet's son-in-law, and the quasi-divine head of the sect of the Mawla or Ismaïli Moslems.* The Mir's three-years-old son, Shah Khan, had an enamel brooch reproducing the portrait of the Agha Khan, fixed, amongst triangular amulets, in his

* See note, p. 301.

cap. Every two years caravans still go as far as Bombay bearing tributes of gold for the Agha from the faithful. The lands of Hunza and Sarikol, with the adjacent valleys, alone send him a regular contribution of thirty thousand rupees. Those who are poor will go so far as to borrow in order to be able to send the rupee that should assure them eternity. The representative of their religious head recently visited the country and gave orders for the renovation of the little mosques, which, incidentally, have charmingly sculptured woodwork.

The Mawla Moslems are allowed to drink alcohol, and there were some good vintages on our table each evening. We all met together for dinner, which was eaten by candlelight. The Mir was magnificently dressed in a khalat of wool given to his father by Yakub Beg, the conqueror of Sinkiang, and a superb otter cap. His eldest son, Major Sahib, whose reddish face and moustache gave him the look of an Anglo-Saxon farmer, wore a black frock-coat. Djemal, a grandson, was a Scout officer and though he was usually in his khaki uniform, he wore a jacket completely covered with gold braid the evening of the state dinner. He knew a little English, but was timid and slow to engage in conversation.

On the chimney-piece opposite me there were signed photographs of Lords Curzon and Kitchener, and chromo-lithographs of the Sacred Heart and the Agha Khan. The dinner was served in the English style and finished with liqueurs. In our honour the Mir opened a "jeroboam" bottle of Audoin 1865 champagne brandy which had been given him by the third group of the *Croisière Jaune* four years earlier. So, that evening, we felt particularly appreciative of the enterprising spirit of André Citroën and dedicated our most grateful thoughts to him.

After dinner the Mir and Colonel Lang exchanged presents. The latter was given soft skins of lynx and mountain leopard, an embroidered *choga*—the local cloak—and two horses. The Colonel asked that the horses should be kept for him at Baltit.

Then there were dances for our entertainment and in a small room four little boys in khalats moved gracefully in measured time with those movements of the neck peculiar to Turkish dances. They had long black wigs, which, it appeared, had belonged long ago to Kashgar women. I recognized the biggest boy. He was "nursemaid" to the little boy who had the Agha Khan's likeness in his hat.

Directed Economics.

Our Mir, Mohammed Nazim Khan, had been to Bombay and Calcutta, but now he lived far away from the rest of the world, reigning as absolute monarch over his fourteen thousand subjects. Illiterate, he was nevertheless quite aware of what was going on in the world, and was no longer wholly dependent on the Political Agent at Gilgit. That year, as a matter of fact, an agreement had been concluded according to which the Maharajah of Kashmir renounced all claim to interfere in the affairs of the little principality and withdrew his vizier and his troops. The Political Agency was therefore independent and its defence forces consisted entirely of native Scouts.

Now that the valleys were no longer divided by mortal enmities, it would seem that life ought to be perfect in a place so far from the political troubles of the world. But no. A keen struggle was being waged against Nature. As soon as the rise in population becomes appreciable there has to be emigration, for the valleys cannot support more than a given number of people. Nothing suitable for export is produced and the natives are too poor to be able to afford to buy grain from India. The economic situation is so arranged that they may not increase their flocks for lack of pasture and that the wool produced may be only just sufficient to clothe them. In winter they live on dried apricots. The cultivation of apricots is one of the chief industries of the valley, and Hunza women have a saying to the effect that their men must not emigrate to regions where apricots do not grow. Thanks to an amazing irrigation system there are also corn fields, often in the most unlikely places.

I saw water-courses like the Valais *bisses* dug through miles of cliff from the glaciers to slopes where, with irrigation, cultivation became possible. There was a time, not very long past, when the Mir of Hunza used to inflict terrible varieties of torture on those of his subjects whom he wished to punish. They were condemned to be compulsorily bathed in the icy water of those *kuls*. It depended on the period of immersion ordered whether the condemned person was to survive or not.

The other side of the valley, with its fifteen thousand mountaineers, is ruled over by the Mir of Nagar. For long ages the two princes lived in bitter rivalry. The Nagars, austere Shi'a Moslems, are said to be dark and of melancholy temperament, for their mountains are in shadow the whole winter through. The rivalry between the princes, which would have inspired a Shakespeare, may now disappear, for the two reigning families have just been doubly united.

I went to the women's quarters and in a court bright with flowers met Djemal's wife. She was a young Nagar with a long face and the large nose of her family—I was to meet other members of it some days later. When I spoke to her she grew timid and drew her veil about her. The Mir's wife, the Ranee, was a charming woman dressed in a grey robe of panne velvet and with a necklace of pearls and turquoises. In spite of a goitre—so many of the inhabitants of those mountains were disfigured by goitre!—she was very beautiful, with a distinguished carriage and an air of ease and good breeding. It was I who felt timid when she looked at me with her bright eyes. Through Djemal she made enquiries about my family and my country. We compared our ages and I learned that she was twenty-eight. She had five children. One of them, a son, had splendid green eyes encircled with mascara, and was as beautiful . . . as a prince. The mother made me a present of a piece of Khotan silk and a cap she had embroidered herself. In return, I could only take off the last of my red necklaces and give it to Bulbul, her delightful small daughter. My request to be allowed to photograph the Ranee was not, however, granted.

One beautiful morning, before leaving Baltit for good, we rode over, between little stone walls, to Aliabad, a village a few miles away, directly facing the unforgettable Rakaposhi. The rest-house there had been occupied during the preceding thirteen months by a studious couple named Lorimer. They had come here for no other purpose than to compile a grammar of the Burushaski language spoken in the Hunza region. Unrelated to any known idiom, it is a question whether it was the language of the country some two thousand years ago, before the diffusion of Sanskrit throughout India. Patiently, day after day, Colonel Lorimer works with the natives. Burushaski or *Kadjuna* is of unheard-of difficulty. Apparently it has no less than four genders and twenty-eight plural forms.*

The Mir of Nagar.

We crossed the river over a swinging bridge of interlaced branches of trees and were met by a native orchestra. Then we were received by the princes of Nagar. Each seemed more charming than the other, slender and beautifully turned out in impeccable khaki uniforms. The eldest had a

* See note, p. 301.

little black moustache and wore a silk turban, the fold of which streamed out when he galloped his horse. The second was fair, and his grey eyes, rimmed with mascara, were so engaging that we called him Rudolph Valentino. He played polo in a close-fitting sweater and white riding breeches, and when he set his pony at the ball he was as beautiful as a god . . . and he knew it. The third son, who wore sports stockings with red lozenges, really had too long a nose to be considered as attractive as his brothers, but he was perhaps the nicest of them all. The father, who stooped slightly, had some heart trouble. During dinner, which was served in the English way and at which we drank only water, I was able to study him not only in life but in art, for an admirably successful portrait of him by Iacovleff hung on the wall opposite me.

The Mir seemed genuinely to be friendly to the English, for he offered a thousand of his men to fight the unruly tribes in the Chilas to the south. When I expressed my admiration for this proof of friendship, George Kirkbride answered:

"They are sincerely glad of our presence in these mountains and they have more than one reason for being loyal. We have given them two precious things: money and—by putting an end to their guerilla wars—peace. As a matter of fact, in Kashmir we do all the work in the name of other people and we get nothing for it."

Another day we went on a further excursion, eastward to the edge of a glacier attached to the great Hispar, over seventy miles long. There we came on an unexpected sight. For the great ones of this world some folding chairs had been brought up and were arranged in a line along the cliff overlooking the glacier. It was there we picnicked—in rain that hid the panorama!

At Nagar, as at Baltit, a polo match was arranged for our

entertainment, and a tournament, and fireworks at night; also in the courtyard of the Prince's house, there was a kind of theatrical entertainment which was full of humour. The players disguised themselves as hunters, or as dogs with movable tails, or as eagles; or put on ibex skins with turned-back horns, or skins of markhors with flat horns growing backwards, or of orials with horns descending in spirals; and each one mimed the adventures of the most improbable hunting expeditions amidst shouts of laughter from everyone.

Like Princes . . .

During the three days on the road to Gilgit we had no work to do. The meals appeared of themselves, the tents and camp beds were already set up when we arrived, tubs of hot water were ready for our baths and at the end of the stage the horses were let out to rest themselves. The servants were called bearers or *chuprassis*. Everything was perfect, and I sighed after the primitive life we had been living.

On the 3rd of September, at the end of a day's march of nearly forty miles, we came out into the valley of Gilgit. At the confluence of two rivers, with desolation all round, an aerodrome had been established, and with it Gilgit's only contact with the rest of the world during the eight months of winter, for then the snows block the road to Burzil, which we were going to follow. Further on we passed some abandoned barracks and crossed the river by the longest suspension bridge in India.

I lost no time in paying a visit to a deserted fort at the centre of the oasis, where one victim of a modern triumph lay derelict. It was the *Croissant d'Argent*, the poor little motor-caterpillar which, after crawling from the Mediterranean to the heart of Asia where it was found to be unusable, was left here, exposed to every wind that blew and with its nose to the wall.

CHAPTER XVII

The Last Week

COMPARED with the bazaar at Cherchen, the lively bazaar at Gilgit gave an impression of wealth. There were numerous caravan people examining Russian, Indian and Japanese materials. They were choosing boots. . . . Tailors' sewing machines were whirring everywhere. . . . I myself was admiring a pair of brightly-coloured native stockings. . . . Suddenly I noticed an elegant white woman passing along the pavement. She wore close-fitting red beach pyjamas. I could scarcely believe my eyes, any more than the Indian stall-holders could conceal their surprise. Was I at Wengen or Crans instead of in the Himalayas? The lady was at dinner at George Kirkbride's that night, wearing, this time, a flowered voile evening dress. She explained that she and her soldier husband had just returned from Leh with a caravan of twenty-four ponies. She considered it quite inadequate. She disliked riding on horseback and was unable to tell me what itinerary they had followed, but, on the other hand, she gave a detailed description of an Austrian couple they had met on the road. A droll pair, these! They had only two ponies, wore no hats, drank water without having it boiled and actually succeeded in eating flour mixed in tea, like natives. . . . I did not realize the uneasy stare I was letting myself in for and said:

"But that was exactly what we did."

Duly vaccinated—vaccination is compulsory before entering India—washed and rested, we set out from Gilgit.

Our presents to our friend Kirkbride included the tent, which was of no further use to us, my big winter coat, the complete works of Shakespeare (still soaking wet from their bath at Misgar), two little rugs given us by the taotaï at Kashgar and three turnips from the garden of Chini Bagh. . . .

It became disagreeably hot as soon as we got clear of the oasis, for we were now only five thousand feet up. That same day we came to the Indus—flowing from Tibet—and crossed it by an impressive suspension bridge in an arid valley like a canyon.

Near the oasis of Bunji the clouds cleared away and, due south, the splendour of Nanga Parbat appeared at the end of what seemed to be a closed valley. Some twenty-two thousand feet above our desert, the summit glittered in the setting sun. I have never seen anything so majestic as that mass of ice. This "Naked Mountain," the most westerly peak of the Himalayas, had tempted more than one climber since the famous Mummery met his death on it in 1895. I thought with emotion of Merkl and his German companions who set out to clamber up its sides the previous year but never came down again.* Looking back, I could still see the face of that other giant, Rakaposhi.

On the 6th of September we turned our backs on the Indus and engaged in the jagged and torrid gorge hollowed out by the Astor river. We had to climb the Burzil Pass, 14,000 feet above sea-level, in order to get across the chain of the Himalayas, properly so called. We found better and better furnished rest-houses each evening, and Wahab, our servant, did the cooking.

In a smiling landscape near Astor we passed an odd-looking caravan with women dressed in shrouds. They were pilgrims returning from Mecca to Kashgar. The way by

* Those who want to tackle Nanga Parbat can now save time by taking the Kagan valley route, which is open, instead of going round by Srinagar.

India and the sea is long, but the service is so well organized that, in spite of Soviet propaganda, the pilgrims still preferred it to the railway service across Russia. The same day we exchanged a few words with some lady missionaries who, with numerous ponies and wearing topees and floss-silk gloves, were making their way to Kashgar. I could not but reflect upon the difference in those two religious caravans. And as two of the lady missionaries were Nordics with complexions like roses and lilies, I could tease Peter, for he had often deplored the absence of platinum blondes in Central Asia.

As we came nearer to the Burzil, the valley, with only a few pine-trees now, grew barer and barer. Untidy children in dirty woollen ponchos sat on the roofs of log cabins looking like so many birds fixed on a spit. The women were fair-complexioned but of savage expression. They wore great black hoods on their heads.

In that cold, lonely place I saw two groups of horsemen meet in a field and line up along two parallel rows of stones. They were natives who had had the bright idea of arranging a game of polo. And I admired the dash with which they played. To persuade their little horses into a gallop they gave a curious guttural cry which still echoes in my ears. It was in these isolated valleys that polo originated.

The Burzil region, so dangerous in winter with snow piling up to fantastic heights in the incessant hurricane, becomes a flowering pasture-land in summer; but to cross the pass is to penetrate into an entirely new world where the abundant rains produce orgies of greenery. The sides of the mountain are covered with forests of birch and pine and on every side one hears the murmur of water.

One might be in the Jura, only that here the natives have coal-black eyes and raven-black hair, and beg for matches as soon as they see you. Little girls in tangled black scarves were gathering berries. Their chests were covered with

necklaces and they wore a little silver star stuck in their
nostrils. The sky was of an extraordinary blueness, the
butterflies were enormous. And the waters of the limpid
river in which I bathed were destined to reach the Bay of
Bengal by the Jhelum and the Ganges.

We were not far from Srinagar now and we sent a telegram
to a garage for a car to be sent to meet us at Bandipur, where
the real road began. At the post office in Gurez we met an
English colonel who was worrying over the fact that he had,
that morning, somehow managed to get a fishing-hook
caught in his dachshund's ear. He asked us to lunch at a rest-
house close by where he was spending a trout-fishing holiday
with a delightful couple.

One more pass, the Tragbal, still separated us from
Srinagar. Our last night "in the wilds" was spent at
Koraghbal, at the foot of it. My thoughts ran to the accom-
paniment of a roaring torrent near-by. I felt very melancholy
to be at the end of the easy life that had for such a long time
been mine under the great skies of Asia.

Kashmir.

From the height of the Tragbal's 12,000 feet, we suddenly,
on the 12th of September, looked out at the luminous
ring of Kashmir. A vast lake gleamed in exquisite tones of
blue. There were hills of pine-trees. The sky was soft, and
involuntarily I recalled another blue ring far away in
Europe, Lake Leman as first seen from St. Cergues as one
comes out of the Jura.

But 6,000 feet lower, it was the heat of summer, it
was the fertility of gilded ricefields, high farmhouses of
brick with pointed thatched roofs . . . and the car waiting
for us under a tree. There I gave away things that had
been my dearest possessions: my comfortable Chinese saddle,
our saucepan, my sheepskin sleeping-bag, all hardened now

since its immersion in the water. My return to modern methods of locomotion was not very glorious, however, for in the car I somehow felt my heart groggy.

Before long we were making our way, with horn sounding, through the swarming streets of Srinagar, which was streaming with electric light.

In the dining-room at the hotel we amused ourselves like true savages, when prim couples, bare-backed and massive-chested, manifested open disapproval of our shabby clothes, untidy hair and buccaneer-black faces which no topee had ever shaded.

But our amusement soon wore thin. It was depressing to be so near that world, all dressed up as though it was going to act in a comedy. After our months and months of anticipation it was almost without pleasure that we clinked our champagne glasses.

From Fifteen Miles a Day to Fifteen Hundred.

Good-bye to the careless life of the trail! Shadows of war were hovering over Europe. Italy was attacking Abyssinia and there was talk of closing the Suez Canal. We must get back at once.

For the return to Europe, Peter wished to confide himself to the care of Imperial Airways. I would join the Air-France line at Karachi. That return by aeroplane remains mainly a memory of bewilderment.

We flew over deserted, lunar-looking mountains in the south of Persia, and it seemed to me that we had scarcely started when, with ear-pieces on, "the-man-who-talks-to-the world" was announcing our arrival at the next airport. The Persian Gulf . . . Mesopotamia . . . a few hours' sleep at Baghdad . . . and then it was Damascus and the Tricolour floating on the breeze.

We crossed Lebanon by car to Beirut. And there at last

was the radiant Mediterranean, a sea on which I felt at home, where the colours, the atmosphere and the sailing ships themselves all looked familiar.

And now it was Greece, the islands like beads in the midst of the intensely blue sea. Then in one hop we reached France. A bare ten years before, on the *Bonita*, we had sailed from France to Greece in a month—at about caravan speed, in fact.

It is an astounding contrast to be going at fifteen miles a day one day and at fifteen hundred the next. I had so got into the habit of moving at the same rate as people did a thousand years ago, with the camels, that now I found it difficult to realize I was every day flying over new countries inhabited by different races. Centuries of history! Cradles of religions! They seemed to be huddled into a little space, whereas, from Peking to India, Asia had seemed endless. But though Europe was so small, misunderstanding was more rife than ever amongst its occupants. Yet they all have fresh water and grass growing on their lands. . . .

And then, after so many strange places—Japanese, Chinese, Tibetan and Mongol—I had scarcely set foot on French soil before the aeroplane gave itself, as it were, a shake and was off again. The smart woman sitting in front of me had just time to make up before we reached Lyons. There was a short rest at the airport, where a crowd of people ate and drank and smoked *gros bleu* tobacco. Noisy children were running about in all directions and everybody seemed to be shaking hands with everybody else.

Night was falling when the vast swarm of lights that was Paris appeared in the north. . . .

Suddenly I understood something. I felt now, with all the strength of my senses and intelligence, that Paris,

France, Europe, the White Race, were nothing. . . .
The something that counted in and against all parti-
cularisms was the magnificent scheme of things that we call
the world.

Lebanon, September, 1936.

NOTES

1. Page 49.

Like the Mongol and Ming dynasties, the Manchus reconquered the Tibet that adjoins the frontiers of China and re-established their suzerainty at Lhasa. But after the revolution of 1911 the Chinese garrisons were expelled and English influence became predominant.

A conference was held at Simla in 1913 and it was decided that Inner Tibet should be controlled by China, while Outer Tibet should be an autonomous state but under Chinese suzerainty and British protection.

It was in order to be able to oppose Tibetan encroachments more successfully that in 1929 China organized Inner Tibet in two provinces, Hsi-kan and Koko Nor.

2. Page 68.

The Dalai Lama resides at Lhasa, the capital of Tibet, of which he is temporal head, whereas the Panchen or Tashi Lama, the spiritual head, lives at Shigatse. The last Dalai Lama died in 1933. By virtue of "infallible" signs, it is known in what child—perhaps born at the same time at Jye-kun-do—the spirit of the defunct has become reincarnate.

3. Page 109.

It appears that before the camels are turned out to fatten on the summer pastures they are put on a diet of plants containing certain salts intended to promote the fall of their winter coats.

4. Page 136.

The Tsaidam Mongols, who are descended from the Khochuts of Dzungaria, mixed gradually with the Panakas and Andowas, Tibetan tribes whose customs they have adopted. The influence of the Goloks, rebellious Tibetans, dominates in the east of the Tsaidam.

The Mongols conquered the region in the seventeenth century when the Oirat tribes—they were Dzungarian Mongols—were being divided up. Khochut Mongols got as far as Lhasa and turned out the last Tsang king.

The province of Koko Nor, which includes the Tsaidam, is divided into twenty-one Khochut "banners" forming five principalities: Barun, Dzun, Teijinar, Kuket and Kurluk. The language of the region is a ded-Mongol dialect which has not yet been studied. Ded means "living high-up."

Under the Manchu emperors, this area was administered by a Frontier Commissioner who resided at Sining. His authority was merely nominal. A tong-sheh, or interpreter, whose business it was to collect the taxes seldom went there. To-day the whole Koko Nor region is controlled by the Tungan General Ma Bu-fang. The word Tsaidam means "salt marsh."

5. Page 287.

Mawla is the name by which the Ismaïlis of Hunza are called. The Ismaïlis are a branch of the Shi'a Moslems. In Persia they are also called "The Assassin Sect". Marco Polo describes them as Mulehets (impious or irreligious men), grouped under a chief called The Old Man of the Mountain. In 1840 a gentleman from Khorassan fled to Bombay for political reasons. He was descended from The Old Man of the Mountain and was an ancestor of the Agha Khan.

6. Page 291.

I was not able to discover anything very precise about the origins of the inhabitants of the valley. The governing families declare that they came from Iran and trace their descent from Alexander of Macedonia. The majority of the Burushaskis are probably descended from the Tokarehs, Indo-Europeans who long ago were obliged to fly from their oases in Chinese Turkestan and reached the Indus Valley. They have been identified with the Yu-chihs. In the Indus Valley they founded an Indo-Scythian empire which flourished under Kanishka.

INDEX

ABD RAKHMAN, 178, 180
Absalom (stallion), 186, 187, 189, 196, 197
Abyssinia, 253, 298
Achik Kul Tagh, 166
Afghanistan, 4, 274, 278
Agha Khan, 287, 288, 289
Aghe, 191
Air-France line, 298
Akmolinsk (Siberia), 134
Akpan, 143, 145, 146, 155
Aksu, 232
Ali (Mahomet's son-in-law), 287
Aliabad, 291
Allah, 144
Alma Ata (Kakakstan), 217
Alps, 145
Altyn Tagh mountains, 150, 172–4, 180
Amban (Chinese official), 274
Amdo region (Tibet), 49, 59
Amnje-ma-tschin, 69
Amurh Sain, 123
Andijan, 248, 258
Andowas, 301
Annenkov, 10, 133, 134
"Arab, The," 100, 104
Arakshatu, 112, 124, 128, 132, 133, 143
Aryans, 272 (footnote)
Asia, 73, 82, 98, 114, 137, 139, 144, 147, 196, 206, 207, 221, 228, 238, 242, 265, 293, 297, 299
Asiatic Marathons, 166
Assa Khan, 151, 153, 155, 156, 157, 159, 160, 161, 163, 166, 167, 168, 170, 172
Assia, Mademoiselle, 241
Astor river, 295
Atalanta, 96
Austrian Mission, 54
Ayak Kum Kul, 156, 162
Aziz, 187, 188, 192, 195, 201

BABYLONIAN fresco, 272
Badakshan, 206
Badakshani ("Cloud"), 279
Badruddin Khan, 233
Baghdad, 298

Baishtoghrak, 222
Baltishan, 206
Baltit, 283, 284, 285, 286, 289, 291, 292
Bandipur, 297
Baptist Mission, 20, 23
Barga country, xii, 8
Barköl (Sinkiang), 182, 213
Barlow, Arthur (Vice-Consul), 250, 252, 253, 256
Barun, 101, 301
Barun, Prince of, 57
Barun, Princess of, 56
Bash Malghun, 169, 170, 171, 173, 279
Batura glacier, 285
Bayan Ho, 105
"Beautiful Mongol," 124
Beirut, 298
Bektieff, General, 259
"Belt marriage," 77
Bengal, Bay of, 297
Berne, 43, 165
Bichkoff, Doctor, 261
Bisson, T. A. (*The Dismemberment of China*), 210
"Black gobi," 110
Bognor, Lord, 246
Bokalik Tagh (Marco Polo mountains), 142 (footnote)
Bokanenko, 256
Bokhara, 51
Bökkenkamp, 28
Bombay, 139
Bonita, 299
Boro: *see* Borodishin
Borodishin, 112, 124, 127, 128, 131–9, 140, 142, 143, 145, 146, 147, 149, 150, 151, 153, 154, 155, 194
Boron Kol, 141, 142, 145
Boron Kol Valley, 142
Bosshard, 15
"Bo'sun, the," 82, 87
Boulaz, Loulou, 253
Boxer Fund, 38
Brévent, 287
Buddha, 21, 52, 59, 62, 63, 108
Buddhas (terra-cotta), 144
Buddhism, 49, 91, 108, 114, 115, 206

303

INDEX

INDEX

INDEX

INDEX

INDEX

INDEX

INDEX

INDEX